NITASSINAN

The Innu Struggle to Reclaim Their Homeland

MARIE WADDEN

August, 2003

Dear Pauline, Ken, Madeline & Francine,

Many thanks for your warm, warm welcome to Chris, Nicholas, Naomi + I. This book is about a peoples' efforts to reclaim something vitally important to them. I feel I've reclaimed a friendship 💗

Much love,
Marie

Douglas & McIntyre

Vancouver/Toronto

Douglas & McIntyre Ltd.
1615 Venables Street
Vancouver, British Columbia
V5L 2H1

Canadian Cataloguing in Publication Data

Wadden, Marie, 1955–
    Nitassinan

    Includes bibliographical references and index.
    ISBN 1–55054–001–7

    1. Montagnais Indians—Land tenure. 2. Naskapi Indians—Land tenure. 3. Indians of North America—Newfoundland—Labrador—Land tenure. 4. Indians of North America—Quebec (Province)—Nouveau-Quebec—Land tenure. 5. Montagnais Indians—Claims. 6. Naskapi Indians—Claims. 7. Indians of North America—Newfoundland—Labrador—Claims. 8. Indians of North America—Quebec (Province)—Nouveau-Quebec—Claims. 9. Montagnais Indians—Government relations. 10. Naskapi Indians—Government relations. 11. Indians of North America—Canada—Government relations—1951–★ I. Title.

E99.M87W3 1991   346.71804'32'089973   C91-091651-9

Design and composition by Eric Ansley
Cover design by Robert MacDonald/MediaClones
Cover photograph of Mistamanian Selma and Maniaten by Robert Bartel; photograph of jet bomber preparing to land at Goose Bay by Marie Wadden
Photographs courtesy William Brooks Cabot Collection, National Anthropological Archives, Smithsonian Institution; Stephen Loring; Anthony Jenkinson; Louise Oligny; Robert Bartel; Jim Roche; Camille Fouillard; Nigel Markham, and Marie Wadden.
Map by Polaris Communications Ltd.

Printed and bound in Canada by D. W. Friesen & Sons Ltd.
Printed on acid-free paper

"What will you leave me, grandfather?"

"All of my territory with everything you find on it.
All kinds of animals, fish, trees, all the rivers,
that is the heritage I leave you.
Down through the generations
this is what you will need for survival.

Don't ever forget what I am going to tell you.
During your lifetime do as I do—respect all the animals,
don't ever make them suffer before you kill them,
don't ever waste anything by killing more than you need,
and don't ever try to keep an animal in captivity
because the animals are necessary for the survival
of future generations."

CONVERSATION BETWEEN
A DYING INNU MAN AND HIS GRANDSON
FROM
Qu'as-tu fait de mon pays?
BY AN ANTANE KAPESH

Contents

Acknowledgements

Funding was provided by the Canadian Studies Directorate of the Secretary of State and the Canada Council Explorations program. Tony Williamson, Marguerite MacKenzie and Dr. Ruth Pierson supported my grant applications. I would also like to thank the Atlantic Bureau of the National Film Board of Canada.

I am indebted to many people for sharing their expertise on this subject, in particular: Nigel Markham, Selma Barkham, Stephen Loring, Anthony and Janet Jenkinson, Camille Fouillard, Peter Armitage, Adrian Tanner, Michael Bryans, Louise and Rick Cober-Bauman, Richard Budgel, John Olthuis, Jim Roche, Audrey Shirmer, Martin Duckworth, and Bob and Dorothy Bartel. I am especially grateful to José Mailhot who, although busy writing her own book, was always available to answer my questions. I also owe a great deal to Boyce Richardson for his inspiration and help with the writing, and to his wife Shirley for her kind support.

I received a great deal of moral support and encouragement from my family, especially sister Jane and brother Bob, the Bellaar-Spruyt family, Sally and Charles Landon, Charlie and Nicolle-Feraud Lewis, John Goddard, Gordon Montador, Pauline Joly de Lobinière, Ken Bassett, Elizabeth Summers, John Lubar, Bev Brown, Rick Emerson, Anne Fouillard, John Duckworth, Oriana Barkham, Eduardo Alvarez, Patrick O'Flaherty, Paul Bowdring, Elizabeth Murphy and Jack Eastwood. The contribution of two very dear friends, Kelly Haggart and Chris Brown, is immeasurable. I would also like to thank my editor, Barbara Pulling.

Finally, my heartfelt thanks to the people who are the subject of this book—the Innu, in particular the people of Sheshatshit who trusted me with their story. My wish is that they will soon get justice and enjoy happier lives than they have known for most of this century. I dedicate this book to them.

Foreword

My people refer to Labrador and Eastern Quebec as Nitassinan, and it is our homeland. Many Innu people continue to hunt, trap and fish there. We believe that if we do not keep the door open to the hunting way of life we will be nothing as a people.

When we are living in the country we are healthy, happy and stronger—physically and spiritually. We escape the terrible problems of alcohol abuse, family violence and attempted suicides that are making our lives in the village utter and complete hell.

In the country we do things that are meaningful, that enrich us, that give us pride and enhance our self-esteem. Our children respect us there. We work hard in the country and are extremely productive. Life there contrasts greatly with the misery of life in our villages.

We are also able to practice our traditional religion in the country. This religion is based on a belief in animal masters and other forest spirits. When we hunt we must show respect for the animal masters. We place the bones of the caribou, bear, marten, mink and other creatures in tree platforms so the dogs do not eat them. We do not overhunt or overtrap areas where animals are scarce. If we do not show respect in this way, the animal masters get angry and punish us by not giving us any animals at a later date. Our elders communicate with the animal masters through dreams, drumming, steam tents and a form of divination called *Matnikashaueu*. A caribou or porcupine shoulder blade is placed in the fire until it is charred and cracked. We read the marks to discover the future location of game.

Our hunting culture thrives in the bush. We do things that very few non-Innu know anything about. Non-natives think they know us because they see us in their stores and at their hockey rinks, but they don't realize that there is another side to us, a side that they would have trouble understanding unless they spent time with us in the bush.

We go to the bush for the kind of spiritual tranquillity that many others associate with their churches. But now the noise of low-flying jet bombers has destroyed our peace of mind in the bush. The jets startle us, terrify our children, frighten our animals and pollute the waterways. These low-flying jets do not fly just anywhere in the skies of Nitassinan. They fly in river valleys, over lakes and marsh areas—places that are also best for hunting, trapping and fishing. Our harvesting areas overlap with the military low-flying routes to a great extent.

How can the Innu people survive increases in low-level flying, the sonic booms created when jets rehearse air-to-air combat, the loss of more land to bombing ranges, the military sports hunters, the sexual abuse of young Innu women who live near the base and so on? I think it will be very hard, if not impossible, for us to continue our hunting culture if military expansion continues.

The Canadian government tells us we should compromise. Chambers of commerce tell us we should compromise. We are accused of being selfish if we do not.

Well, we think we have made enough compromises. We compromised when some of our best hunting and trapping territory was flooded at Mishikamau Lake to make the Smallwood Reservoir. We compromised when the mines at Schefferville, Wabush and Labrador City were built. We compromised when non-Innu trappers moved up the Mishta-shipit, Mishikamau-shipu and other rivers, helping themselves to our hunting and trapping territory, then driving us away from land we had so generously shared with them when they first arrived. We compromised when exclusive harvesting rights to salmon rivers were given to the Hudson's Bay Company and later to private fishing clubs.

These compromises caused starvation and other serious hardships for my people. In fact, there are people alive today who remember what it was like to starve, what it was like to undergo tremendous hardships that resulted largely from contact with Europeans. They suffered new diseases and watched their land be swallowed up. We are tired of compromises. Our backs are up against the wall. We have nowhere else to go.

Forty years ago we were like someone standing in the middle of a field. You could push that person, he'd move a bit, but it wasn't the end of the world. Today we are like someone standing on the edge of a cliff. To push someone standing in the middle of a field is one thing, but to push someone standing on the edge of a cliff is another matter altogether.

We are, I fear, on the brink of collapse as a distinct people. Like indigenous peoples all over the world, our distinct culture and economy are being crushed by an incredibly greedy and environmentally irresponsible industrial order.

Unless the Canadian, Quebec and Newfoundland governments change their policies towards us, we will fall off the cliff. We will fall into a downward spiral of alcohol abuse, family violence, despair and all the other symptoms of cultural collapse.

This is a depressing forecast, and we try not to let it get us down. We know that it is very important to keep hoping for a better world, for a better relationship with the industrial society that so eagerly grasps at our lands and its resources.

As you know, we have not been sitting back passively and watching all this happen. We have been fighting back with everything we've got. We have made great sacrifices by going to jail far away from loved ones. It has been emotionally draining and very stressful for us, but it has also strengthened our resolve to keep fighting to protect our way of life and our rights in Nitassinan. We and other indigenous peoples around the world need to stand together in opposing militarization and all the other devastating changes that industrial countries are imposing on us. But we will need the support of others, particularly of the newcomers who came to our lands and may not have been aware of the harm their governments have caused us.

Recently we entered into land rights negotiations with Canadian governments, but many of my people have a deep mistrust of the whole land claims process. They feel it is a real estate deal where they lose their land and rights for money. I sincerely hope they are wrong. We are not at all interested in this type of settlement. We want a fair settlement for the Innu Nation as a whole.

This is where other people can make a difference, too. I hope after reading this book many people will come to know us better and understand the plight we face. We have fought with dignity and ingenuity, but our struggle isn't over yet.

Daniel Ashini
Chief land rights negotiator
Innu Nation

July 1991

A Note on the Spelling of Innu Words

The plural of Innu is "Innut," but to avoid confusion with the word "Inuit" I follow common usage and employ the word "Innu" throughout.

I am also following common usage in the spelling of Sheshatshit. Place names in the Innu language end in "it" or "u" depending on where you are when you speak of the place.

In conversation, most Sheshatshit Innu call outsiders "akaneshau," which means "English speakers." The Innu do not normally refer to people by their colour, as in "white people," although some have adopted the practice when speaking English. I use the terms "non-Innu," "non-native" or "Euro-Canadian" except where "white people" are referred to in direct quotes.

The Innu you will meet in this book have several names—Christian names given them by missionaries, Innu names (Innu pronunciations of European names or old names passed down through families), and nicknames. I refer to individuals by the names that I am most familiar with using in their presence.

Linguists are now working with the Innu to standardize the spelling of their language, Innu-aimun. For the spellings in this book, I have relied for help on two prominent ethnolinguists involved in this process: José Mailhot in Montreal and Marguerite MacKenzie in St. John's.

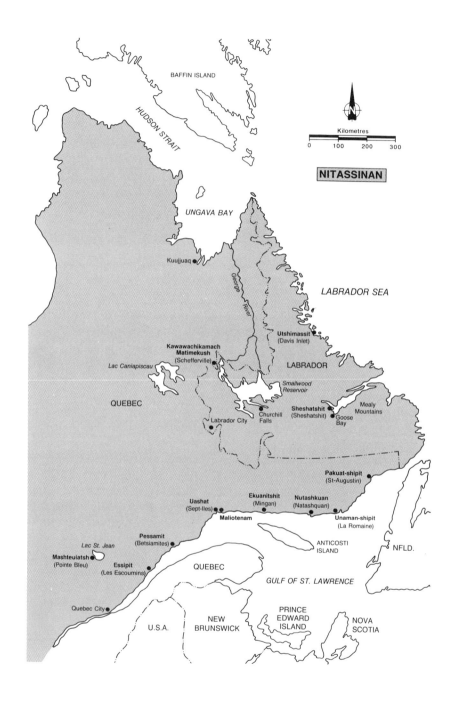

BAFFIN ISLAND

HUDSON STRAIT

UNGAVA BAY

LABRADOR SEA

Kilometres

0   100   200   300

NITASSINAN

Kuujjuaq

George River

Utshimassit
(Davis Inlet)

Kawawachikamach
Matimekush
(Schefferville)

Lac Caniapiscau

LABRADOR

Smallwood
Reservoir

QUEBEC

Churchill
Falls

Sheshatshit
(Sheshatshit)

Mealy
Mountains

Goose
Bay

Labrador City

Pakuat-shipit
(St-Augustin)

Uashat
(Sept-Iles)

Ekuanitshit
(Mingan)

Nutashkuan
(Natashquan)

Maliotenam

Unaman-shipit
(La Romaine)

Pessamit
(Betsiamites)

ANTICOSTI
ISLAND

NFLD.

Lac St. Jean

Mashteuiatsh
(Pointe Bleu)

Essipit
(Les Escoumins)

QUEBEC

GULF OF ST. LAWRENCE

Quebec City

U.S.A.

NEW
BRUNSWICK

PRINCE
EDWARD
ISLAND

NOVA
SCOTIA

Introduction

A small boy stands on a dusty unpaved road, clad in a T-shirt and droopy jogging pants. He has a finger in his mouth and looks shyly at the camera. There is a canvas tent in the trees behind him, a form of shelter that the Innu—nomads until fifty years ago—still cherish. Off to one side are a couple of dilapidated wooden buildings. "The Innu don't know how to live in houses," I used to hear people say in Labrador.

I took this photograph of Jean Paul Penashue in the spring of 1988 at an Innu village called Sheshatshit, forty kilometres north of Goose Bay. Jean Paul's father, Peter Penashue, is an old friend of mine. Seven years earlier Peter and another student from Sheshatshit, Edward Nuna, had boarded at my house while attending high school in St. John's.

Peter and Edward suffered profoundly from homesickness that year and might not have stayed had it not been for the frequent Innu visitors who came to the city for meetings or medical care. Marguerite MacKenzie, a non-Innu linguist at Memorial University, hired the boys after school to help her compile a dictionary of the Innu language. They also translated for Innu patients in hospital and assisted Innu newcomers to town. One day an Innu woman came to St. John's to attend a conference. When she tried to check into the hotel where the other delegates were staying, the desk clerk insisted she pay for her room in advance, something none of the others had had to do. Stung by this discrimination, she left the hotel and came home with the boys.

The two boys saw other evidence of racism in St. John's. They made few friends their own age, and hardly anyone they met had heard of the Innu before.

I had never heard of the Innu myself until my first trip to Labrador in 1978. I was amazed to discover another culture there—other cultures, in fact, because farther north live Inuit people whose history was not taught to Newfoundlanders of my generation either. Prior to the 1970s the Innu and the Inuit rarely figured in political or public life. Their existence was hardly acknowledged by schools or the media. Today more is known, although people often confuse the Innu with the Inuit. Both are northern peoples, but the two groups have different histories, languages and customs. The word "Innu" means "human beings."

The Innu have inhabited the Quebec-Labrador peninsula for at least two thousand years. Their culture and their language, Innu-aimun, are similar to those of the Cree, the Micmac and the Beothuck, peoples classified by anthropologists as Algonkian. There are ten thousand Innu in Canada. The majority live in eleven villages along the north shore of the St. Lawrence River; the other two thousand live in the Labrador villages of Sheshatshit and Utshimassit. Because they hunt in the mountains (*les montagnes*), the Innu are called "Montagnais" in Quebec. Some Innu are called "Naskapi," an old Innu word meaning "those beyond the horizon."

The Innu once moved freely throughout the Quebec-Labrador peninsula, which they call Nitassinan, meaning simply "the land." It was their country, the place that gave birth to their culture. They named every lake, river and mountain. The oldest resident of Sheshatshit, Mani Asta, was born in 1905 near Caniapiscau Lake. Throughout her life she has travelled by canoe and on foot to practically every corner of Nitassinan—from Sept-Îles north to Kuujjuaq (formerly Fort Chimo), across to Utshimassit, south to Sheshatshit and along the north shore of the St. Lawrence River—covering an area greater than the whole of the British Isles.

A border drawn across Nitassinan by the British Privy Council in 1927 has resulted in serious damage to Innu unity and to the people's national identity. Today Innu hunters are frequently arrested for hunting on the "wrong" side of the border and their children are taught to speak different languages in school: French in Quebec, English in Labrador.

The Innu could have adopted a European style of life four hundred years ago had they wanted to. Early French missionaries taught the people to farm and encouraged them to settle down. But the Innu remained hunters and gatherers, a way of life they continued to follow until the middle of this century, when their land was taken for mines and hydroelectric projects and their forests reduced to pulp and paper. Even though they have never signed a treaty or land claims agreement with Canada, the Innu were not consulted about the seizure of their hunting territories. Houses were built and welfare provided, but they are little compensation for the damage that has been done to Innu society.

The Innu once faced enormous challenges in their struggle to find food, and they thrived on this. Today unemployment is high in their villages, and people are restricted from hunting. Many have tried to drown their boredom and despair with alcohol.

Father Edward O'Brien, a good friend of my grandfather's, went to the Labrador coast every summer from 1920 to 1946 to meet Innu families who customarily came out from the interior to fish and escape the murderous swarms of blackflies. He baptized babies, married young couples and preached about Jesus Christ. Under the watchful eyes of Catholic priests like O'Brien, Innu religion was forced underground. Hunters had to wait until they were back in the bush to drum themselves into trances or to summon animal spirits into the shaking tent. Like the other priests, O'Brien considered these practices heathen and barbaric and would not tolerate them in the village. He realized too late that the spiritual dispossession of the Innu, coupled with the loss of their land, had left them with little to hold onto. In 1939 he told the St. John's *Daily News* that "The privation and hardship of the Indians is largely a result of their restricted hunting grounds. . . . The wilds of Labrador, their birthright, have been divided among so many that in most years someone has to go short—usually the Indians."

Every year more evidence of the ancient presence of the Innu in Nitassinan is erased as newcomers impose their own imprint on the land. In the beginning, there was little the Innu could do since so few spoke English or French. However, an important turning point came in the mid-1980s, when a massive air base to train NATO bomber pilots was proposed for Goose Bay, Labrador. The Innu and neighbouring Inuit were horrified at the prospect of their homelands becoming a vast military playground. Their cries of protest were ignored until people in Sheshatshit, the only native community linked to Goose Bay by road, began a civil disobedience campaign. In the fall of 1988 hundreds of Innu were arrested and imprisoned. Some risked their lives by camping on a bombing range, while others trespassed on the runways of the Canadian Forces Base at Goose Bay.

During this time I worked on a film about the protests called *Hunters and Bombers*, a coproduction of the National Film Board of Canada and the English company Nexus Films. We heard grim testimonies of how Canadian laws, particularly those that restrict hunting, have destroyed Innu lives. Peter Penashue's mother, Tshaukuesh, wept when she explained how her marriage had been ruined by alcoholism, a problem her parents did not know in the bush. Now a grandmother, Tshaukuesh has been jailed several times for her role in the fight to preserve land that she considers her children's birthright.

The campaign to keep the bombers away from Nitassinan brought the Innu international attention, as people around the world heard of them for the first time. In the end NATO cancelled its plans, not because of Innu protests, but because the Cold War had ended. The Innu had received so much public support, however, that the Canadian government agreed to negotiate the people's land rights, a process that may take many years to resolve.

The borders of Nitassinan will have to be redrawn to accommodate the increasing number of non-Innu living there, but there are some things the Innu will not give up. They say they will not extinguish their rights to Nitassinan in return for the cash settlement and much smaller land base that Canada is offering. They want to maintain meaningful control over future developments to protect the land and the environment. The largest wild caribou herd in the world roams the Quebec-Labrador peninsula, and Innu hunters still speak with bitterness of the thousands of caribou that drowned one year because Hydro-Quebec carelessly opened one of its dams on the Caniapiscau River as the animals were migrating.

The Innu are off to a good start as they work to rebuild their society. The people are regaining their pride and confidence, and young Innu are helping out. Peter Penashue was recently elected President of the Innu Nation and Edward Nuna, a competent bureaucrat, works with him.

I keep the picture of Jean Paul near me as I write to remind me of what the Innu are up against. I took it the day we walked together to the Hudson's Bay store across the river from Sheshatshit. Measured in the short steps of a three-year-old it was a long and sometimes perilous trip. A strong wind blew hard against us as we crossed the bridge above the North West River. One gust sent him reeling back-wards. He laughed nervously but pressed on, pushing against the wind with his shoulder, then playfully punching it with his small fists. Along the way he spoke to me in his language, and he looked at me quizzically when I replied with words that meant nothing to him.

"*Mani. . . . Uapimin*"—these two words were said more frequently than others. *Mani* means "Mary" or "Marie," and not knowing what *uapimin* meant I assumed he was trying to pronounce my surname. I humoured him by nodding my head up and down, saying one of the few Innu words I did know, "*aheh*." Yes.

I selected the items I wanted and brought them to the counter. "*Uapimin . . . uapimin*," Jean Paul urged, grabbing at the leg of my pants as I handed money to the cashier, who reached over a box of apples on the counter to give me my change. She didn't speak Innu-aimun either. I took the boy by the hand and led him out of the store.

The first gust of wind defeated Jean Paul, and he had to be carried piggyback across the bridge. When I put him down on the other side, he refused to take my hand and showed little enthusiasm for the chocolate bar I offered. Once home he threw his jacket on the kitchen floor and went to the living room, saying something to his mother in a tone of disgust. I asked what was wrong. She told me he had gone to the store to get an apple. *Uapimin*, she explained, is the Innu word for "apple." I hadn't bought any.

Sometimes I tell this story to children and they cluck sympatheti-cally. A child understands how it feels to be misunderstood. Jean Paul was just learning to speak his own language. Now he must start all over again so he can communicate with non-Innu. He'll be disap-pointed again if it turns out to be a one-way process.

Nutshimit

*"The real beauty of this place is that, quite simply,
the land is just as God left it."*
ROYAL AIR FORCE NEWS, MARCH 1985

I arrived in the Innu village of Sheshatshit on 19 April 1988. There
was still snow on the ground hiding some of the garbage, beer cans
and sewage that make the village such a grim sight when the snow
melts. In winter it doesn't look so bad. The dilapidated houses on
the outskirts of town, thin trails of smoke rising from their chim-
neys, look quaint and cosy surrounded by huge banks of pure white
snow.

But the Innu do not live in their villages all the time. Many leave
whenever possible, to live as the Innu have always lived—in tents,
eating the animals they hunt, sleeping on boughs they gather, speaking their own language and telling ancient tales that are the bedrock
of their culture.

I too would soon leave the village, to visit a place I had heard my
Innu friends speak of with great affection, their home before moving into the ramshackle houses of Sheshatshit. I was going to *nutshimit*,
the interior of the Innu homeland. It is sometimes called "the bush"
or "the country" in English, but nutshimit means a lot more to the
Innu people. It is the place that gave birth to Innu culture, and it is
the only place where life returns to normal for many Innu families
today.

I found Daniel Ashini in the band council office. The thirty-year-
old chief greeted me with shy formality and acknowledged receiving
my letter. I had explained to him that I wanted to write a book about

the Innu, based on my long association with several families in
Sheshatshit. I knew that many Innu were alarmed by the increasing
presence of jet bombers in the bush, and they felt their concerns
were not being taken seriously by the media or government. I decided to see for myself what was going on and sample the way of life
the Innu treasure so highly.

Daniel and I pored over a large, well-worn map of the Quebec-
Labrador peninsula, formerly called the Ungava peninsula. Coloured
tacks pinpointed the location of spring hunting camps. I was eager
to go to the Mealy Mountains, which the Innu have crossed for generations to reach the north shore of the St. Lawrence River. On clear
days you can see the high peaks of the snow-covered mountains from
Sheshatshit. But Daniel cautioned me.

"You won't see many jets if you camp in the Mealy Mountains; it's
not on their flight path. The people complaining the most are there,"
he pointed, "near the Red Wine Mountains, because there's a military target there."

Daniel rhymed off the names of the families in each camp. I finally
chose Penipuapishku-nipi (Hope Lake on English maps), ninety kilometres northwest of Goose Bay, because several of the outspoken
young leaders I wanted to interview were camped there. Daniel promised to radio the camp and prepare the way for me. I then waited
impatiently in Sheshatshit for several days until I received Daniel's
call telling me to be at the airport for my flight to nutshimit.

Greg Baikie, a helicopter pilot from a well-known settler family
in Goose Bay, was busy fastening a canoe underneath the aircraft
when I arrived, and he looked surprised to see me.

"You're going into the bush?" he asked.

"Yes, I'm doing some research. I want to find out about the low-
flying jets."

"I see, well, that sure is controversial," Baikie said. "You'll get a
different opinion from the people around here, you know. Most people
in Goose Bay support the military. They think the Innu are complaining to spoil things for the rest of us."

Greg invited me to fly in the front of the helicopter. An Innu
couple and their two young children sat in the back. As we lifted off,
I had a good view of the former American air base in Goose Bay that
is now home to sleek state-of-the-art jet bombers with names like
Tornado, Phantom, Alpha Jet and Hornet. Each bomber costs approximately $30 million to build, and millions more are spent main-

taining them and training young pilots to fly them. The jets were lined up on the tarmac ready to take to the sky, where they fly up to 900 kilometres an hour and as low as thirty metres from the ground.

"It's been a bit hairy up here," Greg told me. "There wasn't much coordination. I was afraid there'd be a collision between their aircraft and ours, but we're ironing things out now, although I don't know what's going to happen when the number of flights increases like they say it will."

"How many flights a day are there now?"

"A couple of hundred, when the weather is good. There are about 6000 flights a year now. That's supposed to go up to 40,000 from what I hear."

"That's the Goose River," Greg told me, pointing to a broad river that moved for a great distance in spirals like a huge snake. "The jets like to follow it to a target site in the Red Wine Mountains. You won't be able to see the target from here, but you'll hear the jets going back and forth while you're in the camp."

Forty minutes after takeoff we circled a large lake surrounded by a dense canopy of tall black spruce trees. I wondered how we would ever find a few small tents. "Look, there's some orange tarpaulin below," Greg shouted above the noise of the rotors. "They've moved camp from where they were a couple of weeks ago. I'll land down there on the ice."

It was then I noticed how nervous I'd become. Even though it was mid-April and spring was on its way to southern Canada, temperatures here were still well below freezing, especially at night. Would I survive a couple of weeks in a cold tent? Would I be able to eat the wild meats? I calmed myself. One of my Innu friends in Montreal, Mary Selma, had been very matter-of-fact when I told her what I was doing and had helped me shop for supplies. José Mailhot, an ethnolinguist who has known and studied the Innu for more than a quarter of a century, had lent me her snowshoes. But I was still a bit apprehensive. It didn't help when Greg turned to me and said, "If the ice melts fast you may not get out until June, so I hope you're prepared for a long stay."

The helicopter dropped to the frozen lake. A crowd of Innu women and children gathered around us. They all looked surprised when I jumped down from the helicopter and started to unload my supplies. The other passengers were met and led up the hill by a convoy of relatives, but there was no one to meet me. Greg shouted the names written on the boxes that he tossed to the ground until shy teenagers or women came forward to claim what was theirs. No one seemed willing to claim me. As I stood among my bags a few children looked curiously at me.

"Who are you?" one of them asked in English, with the musical lilt of the Innu accent.

"Marie Wadden. I'm a reporter. Daniel said you were expecting me here. I'm supposed to see Sylvester Andrew. Can you show me where he is?"

"He's out hunting," a girl of about ten told me. "Come on, I'll show you where his tent is." She grabbed the largest of my bags and teetered away towards shore with it. The other children followed and soon I had my own convoy of helpers.

We clambered up a hill, sidestepping other children who were gaily careering towards the lake on toboggans and sheets of cardboard. The young girl in front put down my heavy bag and let out a big sigh. She smiled at me with an irresistible grin and said, "We'd better take a rest. You sure got a lot of stuff. How long you staying?"

When I told her I'd be there for a couple of weeks, she turned to the others and spoke in Innu-aimun. When she finished conferring with them, she said, "I don't know where we are going to put you; the tents are all pretty full now, unless you stay with the priest." At this the other children laughed, and we continued on our way. It was starting to get dark, and my presence was drawing only the mildest curiosity from the people we passed, who were busy chopping wood or gathering their children in for supper. My nervousness became mixed with excitement as I saw the collection of cosy-looking tents buried in the snow, each with a pipe sticking out in front, like a unicorn horn, from which smoke billowed. Outside the tents were little mats of spruce boughs, and the ground nearby was carpeted with wood chips. Snowshoes hung on the front tent posts, and alongside most tents were piles of supplies covered in tarpaulins. My guide, whom I later learned was Yvette Michel, dropped my bag with relief outside one tent and disappeared inside. I waited respectfully, figuring she was asking permission for me to enter. The other children set down the rest of my baggage and scattered. I waited and waited until I saw Yvette's little head poke outside the tent flap.

"What's wrong with you? You shy?" she asked.

She held open the flap and I threw in my duffel bag and knapsack, then gingerly stepped over three stacked logs that formed a threshold. The tent was lit by candles, and in the dimness I picked my way unsteadily, my feet sinking into the deep pile of spruce boughs that carpeted the tent floor. The boughs and the smell of wood smoke perfumed the air. My eyes were drawn to the flickering flames of a tiny wood stove that generously heated the tent. I took off my coat before settling down beside my bags. There was a feeling of luxury and comfort inside the tent, which surprised me. Once my eyes adjusted to the light I was able to study the other occupants.

I smiled at an old woman who sat in the far corner beneath a large print of the Last Supper. She wore a huge silver cross around her neck and was smoking a pipe. Yvette introduced us.

"That's Caroline, Sylvester's mother. She's deaf. Don't bother talking to her, she won't hear you."

I hadn't planned to speak anyway because I assumed the older woman would not speak English. A middle-aged woman I recognized from previous trips to Sheshatshit as Mary Adele Andrew, Sylvester's wife, leaned towards me to shake hands. I was relieved. Mary Adele was a great friend of José Mailhot's.

"Yvette, tell Mary Adele that José Mailhot says hello."

Yvette complied, and Mary Adele's eyes widened as she looked at me with renewed interest.

"Tell her I'm a friend of José's. She lives up the street from me in Montreal."

When Yvette had finished, Mary Adele shook her head up and down and said, "aheh, aheh," which I knew was Innu for "yes," or in this case, "yes, I see." Yvette reached behind me and passed Mary Adele the snowshoes I had brought. "She wants to know where you got these."

"They're José's, she loaned them to me. They're from . . .," and then I felt like a fool. I searched through my bags for the piece of paper on which José had written the name of the Innu village in Quebec where she had been given the snowshoes. José knew I would be asked where they came from. I had carefully learned to pronounce the place name in Innu-aimun, but just when I needed it, I forgot. I thought I remembered what it was called on maps, however.

"It's Pointe Rouge, or something like that, in English, I mean in French," I blathered.

"You mean Pointe Bleue," Yvette said, and she translated for Mary Adele, who was admiring the intricate woven design and the colourful fabric decorating the frame of the snowshoes. The Innu take great pride in the things they make by hand. Mary Adele then passed them on to her mother-in-law. The old woman said something and Yvette translated: "Caroline says they are spring snowshoes, they'll be good for you here because the snow is getting soft. But Caroline says they don't look like they've been used much."

Caroline was right. I think José regarded them more as a work of art than as practical footwear for Montreal sidewalks, and I confessed I had never worn snowshoes before. This seemed to lead us nowhere, for a long silence followed. Yvette slipped outside and I was left alone with the two women, unable to communicate any further except by smiling.

Mary Adele busied herself at the wood stove and before long laid a tea towel on the boughs in front of me. She placed a plate, knife and fork on the towel, followed by a tin mug of hot tea. She motioned for me to help myself from the pot on top of the small sheet-metal stove. I scooped out a generous portion of caribou stew and took some bread from the round loaf Mary Adele passed me. I poured canned condensed milk into my tea and sat back, happy to have something to do that didn't require talking. As I ate hungrily, Mary Adele worked at some sewing and Caroline continued to puff on her pipe, studying me contemplatively, meeting my smile with one of her own. Before long I started to feel tired and very uneasy. I still had no idea where I was going to sleep. Could I stay here? There was no sign of bedding, no invitation to stretch out; we all seemed to be waiting for somebody, something, to resolve this. I decided to find Yvette, or someone else who spoke English, to learn what was going on.

I staggered about in the dark, walking from one tent to another, distracted by the wide band of northern lights that shone brilliantly in the sky overhead. I walked to the edge of the camp to look out over the lake, and there I saw a distinctly non-Innu person taking frozen clothes off a line outside her tent. It was Lyla Andrew. Easily recognizable because of her curly red hair, Lyla was a Torontonian who had moved to Sheshatshit years ago as a social worker and then married an Innu hunter.

"Lyla! Thank goodness, a familiar face. I didn't know you were here."

Lyla looked less surprised to see me. "Hi, Marie. I heard you got in today. I was going to come see you once Apetet got back and the kids were in bed. Come into our tent."

I followed her inside a tent like that of Mary Adele's but smaller and a little more cluttered because of the children's clothes strewn about. Lyla's daughter, the eldest child, was sitting on the spruce boughs playing cards with her brother. The baby was lying in a hammock, a traditional Innu crib. I had seen Innu mothers in the village use the same kind of hammock. The baby is swung back and forth as mothers sing a song that sounds like "Bough, bough, bough." It always seems to put even the most recalcitrant child to sleep almost immediately. Lyla began hanging the stiff clothes on a line near the stove.

"Where are you staying?" she asked.

"I don't know," I said nervously. "I took my stuff to Sylvester Andrew's tent, but neither his wife nor his mother speak English and I have no clue if they want me to stay there or not."

Lyla laughed. "I can imagine what they're saying. They probably have been teasing Father Jim, who's also living in that tent, threatening to invite a single woman to stay there as well."

Father Jim Roche was Sheshatshit's Catholic priest, an Oblate missionary who had been stationed in the village for the past five years. He was one of the community's most popular priests because he spent so much time in nutshimit.

"Well, where else can I stay?"

"You could stay with us, I guess, but you wouldn't really get as much out of it as you would if you stayed with an entirely Innu family. You won't learn much about 'being Innu,' except what I've managed to pick up over the years."

"So?" I asked.

She scratched her tousled red hair. "It's not going to be easy since all the tents are pretty full. Josie Pone just left to take her son to the hospital so there's room in her tent. But it's full of men, you can't stay there. I don't know," Lyla concluded. "You'll have to wait until the hunters get back. They'll probably have some sort of meeting about it. Don't worry, I bet you'll be comfortably housed—I mean tented—before the night is out."

Lyla started getting the children ready for bed, so I took my leave and walked a little despondently back to Sylvester's. I picked my way carefully in the dark, wondering how I'd find my way back when all the tents looked the same. I heard someone call my name, turned, and saw an Innu woman, her body halfway out of her tent, motion to me.

"Come and see my tent," she invited, and I happily accepted. The woman introduced herself as Janet Michel. She is the wife of Ben Michel, an outspoken young Innu leader and charismatic speaker. The Michel tent was well lit by a Coleman lamp. It was tidy and orderly, the small space efficiently organized.

Janet knelt on the boughs and invited me to join her. Then she smiled gently. Her English was halting and uncertain, but she asked so many questions I began to feel I was being interviewed. Finally we discovered common ground, our mutual friend Camille Fouillard.

"Camille, she stays with us whenever she comes to Sheshatshit. My kids, they like her; Ben and I like her too," Janet said.

I told her that Camille had lived for a time at my house in St. John's and that her sister Anne was also a good friend of mine. Janet began to relax. She then asked where I was staying.

"I don't know," I replied wearily.

Then I waited, feeling sure she would offer to let me stay in her tent. The much-longed-for invitation didn't come. She just said, "Okay, now I've got to go find my kids and make Ben's supper. He's over in Sylvester's tent, you'll see him there."

Crestfallen, I found my way back to Sylvester's tent. I climbed over the threshold and sat down next to my bags, which had not been moved. My presence seemed to go unnoticed. A group of men sat sprawled in a semicircle by the stove. They were leaning back on their elbows, straightening up only when a saucepan of tea was passed to each of them. They spoke in Innu-aimun, their conversation sprinkled with laughter. If this was a meeting, I thought, it certainly didn't have any tone of immediacy about it. But when the men rose to leave, Ben Michel looked over at me.

"You can stay with us if you want."

He grabbed a couple of my bags while his daughter Yvette, my first friend in the camp, hopped up and grinned. "Yaaay," she said. "I'm glad you're staying with us."

I started to feel foolish about all my anxiety. I should have known from experience that the Innu are very methodical about making decisions. There is a consultative process that must be followed until all the ins and outs are weighed and consensus is reached. Each person concerned has a say.

I didn't realize until much later that to accommodate me other people had to be shuffled around the camp. Janet and Ben had to find another tent to house Janet's cousin, Joachim Selma, and a mentally impaired foster child Joachim was looking after. The two young men ended up in the all-male tent, and when I learned this I understood the resentful looks Joachim had given me when he saw me around the camp over the next few days. An all-male tent is a cheerless affair, with no one to cook or keep the tent warm while the men are out hunting.

But that night I was unaware of the special arrangements made for me. I unrolled my sleeping bag before the rest of the family was in bed and happily began to snore.

■

It didn't take long to adjust to the routine of camp life. Every morning Janet and I hung the sleeping bags, quilts, blankets and sheets outside in the spring sunshine. While Janet finished feeding her children and supervising their dress, I took our water buckets down the hill to the lake. Sitting on one overturned bucket, I slowly dipped a saucepan through a hole in the ice and brought up the icy fresh water, marvelling that there was still someplace in the world where you could drink from a lake without getting sick. There was no local source of pollution here, at least not yet. By the time I got back to the tent the children had gone to play and Janet and I were left alone to discuss plans for the rest of the day.

Janet is a pretty woman, her heart-shaped face framed by long dark hair parted in the middle and tied in the back. Then twenty-eight, she had married Ben when she was just seventeen. She told me that her grandparents, who raised her, didn't approve of the marriage at first. Ben had been sent away to school and hadn't spent much time in nutshimit, so they were afraid Janet would never get to leave the village. She had been brought up in the country, and her grandparents wanted her to continue living in the traditional way.

It is a custom in Innu society for parents to give away one child to be raised by its grandparents. This gives the grandparents the pleasure of having a child around and provides them with someone who will be directly responsible for them when they are too old to look after themselves. But this tradition has another important purpose. People like Janet become skilled in nutshimit and are an important repository of Innu customs and values, while others her age, forced to attend school, know far less about life in the bush.

Early in their marriage Ben encouraged Janet to teach him how to live in nutshimit, and they are committed to passing the skills on to their children by taking them to the bush whenever possible. The Michels are often in trouble with Newfoundland school officials because their children miss so many classes.

Ben and Janet want their children to learn about Canadian society, but they think that can best be done in the summertime when the Innu are not hunting. Those who run the school in Sheshatshit say the children would find it uncomfortable being indoors in hot weather. Janet speculates that the real reason is that non-Innu teachers, who are the majority in the school, don't want to give up their summer vacations.

Janet is one of the busiest people I have ever met. She rarely sits still; once all the work was done in our tent she would go visiting, which usually meant helping someone else with a chore.

I didn't accompany the men on their hunting while I was at Penipuapishku-nipi. It would have been highly unusual for a woman to do this, and I also knew I would have trouble keeping up with them, as they often travel long distances on snowshoes in search of game. Instead, I happily spent my time close to camp, where I shared the women's routine.

Everyone works hard in nutshimit. Bread is made almost daily by the women. Some make yeast bread, but most bread is made with baking powder and cooked over the stove in an iron frying pan. The women wash their families' clothes the old-fashioned way, by heating water on the stove and scrubbing clothes on a washboard. They set rabbit and partridge snares, clean and prepare the trapped animals, chop wood, gather boughs for the tent floor, and pick berries and medicinal plants. When caribou are caught, the heavy carcasses are butchered by the men and carried to the camp. All this hard work is valued by the Innu because it keeps them in close contact with nature and with each other.

Life in nutshimit is communal. The responsibility of caring for children is eagerly shared, and mothers who want to leave camp to check their snares or gather boughs can always find a relative or friend willing to help out.

I used whatever free time I had in camp to read some of the books about the Innu I had brought with me, among them Jesuit priest Paul Le Jeune's accounts of Innu life in the seventeenth century. I was amazed at how little life has changed in nutshimit.

On the surface, many things are different. The Innu do not travel nomadically across their land as they once did. Their shaking tent ceremony, a religious rite that enables hunters to contact the animal spirits, is no more, and some other religious practices, long denounced by priests like Le Jeune, have ceased. Tents are no longer made from birch bark or caribou skin. For the most part, people wear modern dress, although mitts, shoes and some pieces of clothing are still made from caribou and trimmed with animal fur. Hunting jackets, now cotton, are still decoratively embroidered.

There are also many consumer goods from non-Innu society in camp. Boxes of Dainty Rice, Catelli macaroni and peanut butter are common among Innu supplies, not to mention an array of junk food treats. Like mothers anywhere, Janet dished out candies and potato chips to her children judiciously—*after* they'd eaten their caribou and partridge. Store-bought provisions have eliminated the risk of starvation that was a common feature of life in the past.

Battery-operated clocks seem incongruous out in the wilderness, as do radio newscasts, but I tuned in as eagerly as everyone else whenever the CBC news came on. It is even possible now to radio for an aircraft to take an ill person to hospital or back to the village. These are new features of life in the country, features the Innu have adopted because they find them useful.

But a great deal is happening in nutshimit to ensure that Innu culture remains vital and alive. One day, sixteen-year-old Makus Andrew invited me to see something he had built. We walked a short distance from his mother's tent, where he showed me a sweat lodge, a sort of sauna that the Innu have been using for thousands of years. The stones are heated in the fire, then carefully taken into a heavily insulated oval tent where cold water is thrown on them to create steam. The lodge is used for both physical and mental cleansing, and hunters believe that the steam carries their prayers to the animal masters. Makus had built the sweat lodge after hearing descriptions from the elders.

The daily routine in an Innu hunting camp today is much the same as it has been for centuries. The return of the hunters causes great excitement, and the catch is always shared. Young children at Penipuapishku-nipi went from tent to tent carrying plates, bowls or saucepans of food covered with tea towels. Those offerings might contain a piece of porcupine or beaver meat, the prized organs of a wild goose or some freshly killed caribou; no matter what, food is still passed around ceremoniously to elders, relatives and guests in respect of ancient customs that not only ensured survival but also demonstrated Innu civility.

There were about sixty people in our camp that spring. The eldest Michel child, Jamie, who was twelve, teased his sisters unmercifully, especially the youngest, Matshikuan—"fat cheeks"—who at eight was something of a crybaby. My favourite was ten-year-old Yvette. She had a mischievous smile and often lived up to her nickname, "the witch." I noticed, though, that whenever Yvette had to do something for her mother, she took her responsibilities as the eldest daughter seriously and could even be left on her own to tend something cooking on the stove. The Innu give their children great responsibilities at a young age. At fifteen an Innu teenager is expected to make the larger decisions about his or her life.

Innu parents admit that life for young people has become far more complicated than it was in the past. Today drugs and alcohol are common in the village where it is harder to supervise children, another reason families prefer to take them into the bush. In nutshimit, Innu parents can once again exercise meaningful influence over their offspring.

The Innu go to nutshimit for more than the taste of wild meat. Here, non-Innu society does not intrude. Family life is strengthened, and people are drawn closer together because they are more at ease. The pride of the hunter is restored, and everyone abides by codes of conduct and behaviour that have been passed on through Innu society for thousands of years. Many words in Innu-aimun refer to aspects of life in nutshimit. If this way of life is abandoned, more than the Innu language will be at risk.

An Independent People

*"I even think we were here when Christ was born. I am not sure,
I do not want to go back that far, but it seems we have always been on
this land. We have always lived the same way."*

ANTOINE MALEC, INNU ELDER

It is difficult to put together an accurate account of how the Innu lived before European contact because there are no written records. All that exist are the pieces of an incomplete jigsaw puzzle. The pieces provided by archaeologists, anthropologists and historians are valuable, but systematic archaeological research in the Innu homeland started only twenty years ago, and a great deal more work needs to be done. The earliest written records come from Europeans and are coloured by their prejudices. Slowly, however, a picture is emerging of a people who, despite centuries of contact with Europeans, clung to their nomadic hunting way of life until industrial developers came uninvited to their land fifty years ago and took control of large sections of it.

Who are the Innu? Historian Alan Cooke says that before the arrival of Europeans, Algonkian-speaking peoples, among them the Cree and the Innu, inhabited the whole Quebec-Labrador peninsula, which is bordered by James Bay and Hudson Bay to the north and west, the Atlantic coast to the east and the mouth of the Saguenay River to the south. Cooke believes there were no prehistoric differences between the Cree and the Innu, but thinks their paths diverged in the eighteenth and nineteenth centuries after contact with various segments of European society. The Cree were influenced by the

English-speaking Protestant traders of the Hudson's Bay Company, the Innu by French settlers and traders in Quebec.

The Cree and the Innu today regard themselves as separate nations. Their languages are similar (although not easily understood by one another), as are their customs and religious practices. In this they are somewhat like the Italians, Spanish and French in Europe, who share a common Latin heritage but have separate national identities and languages. The Innu living in territories claimed by Quebec today are called by their French name, Montagnais. The term "Naskapi" was used by priests and traders to refer to the Innu who remained the longest out of reach of European contact. These Innu call themselves Mushuau-Innu, which means "the barren ground people," because they traditionally hunted above the tree line.

Survival in one of the coldest climates on earth was the heroic task that occupied the Innu long before the arrival of Europeans. The climate of the Quebec-Labrador peninsula is totally unsuited to agriculture, so the Innu remained on the move all the time, pursuing nomadic caribou herds. They supplemented their diet with other meats and fish, and with berries and plants that were gathered for food and medicine.

Innu stories and legends, passed on orally from one generation to another, communicate the people's world view. Pishum—the moon and the sun—watch over the planet. Humanlike attributes are assigned to animals. Close observation of animals and their habits has brought with it an ideology that assigns no greater importance to humans than to animals. Humans are the "caretakers" of an environment shared with many other creatures, each relying upon the others for survival. The Innu believe that humans were put on earth not to dominate the animal kingdom but to coexist with it.

Through various rituals, the Innu communicate with the animal creators or "masters" whenever food is hard to find. Rituals also exist to show respect for these masters. The antlers of the *atik*, or caribou, are hung in trees; fish bones are thrown back in the water; a gift is left in the lair of the most humanlike of animals, the bear, and a feast is held whenever a bear is taken for food. Bear grease is applied to the hair of hunters invited to the feast, and some of the grease is saved for the next feast or *makushan*. The Innu practice of dressing up in ceremonial clothes for the hunt also shows their respect and deep connection to animals. Before they adopted Euro-

pean dress, hunters wore beautifully decorated caribou tunics and
pants. The hunt is still a special occasion; today hunters carry embroidered game bags across their shoulders and wear decorated jackets, snowshoes and moccasins.

When the hunt was poor, the Innu sought help from the animal
spirits by constructing a special tent called the shaking tent. Hunters
with special powers invited the animal spirits inside the tent to ad-
vise where game was available. The tent shook from the power of
the spirits that entered. The ceremony is described by an Innu hunter
named Mistanikashan in the superb film series *La Mémoire Battante*,
directed by Montrealer Arthur Lamothe:

> *When the Kakushapatak [one imbued with great power to contact ani-
> mal spirits] went into the tent, he wasn't completely inside when it
> started shaking . . . he didn't touch the ground. He was raised up
> about a foot off the ground, inside the tent. He was in the air. He
> danced inside. He danced. Through his song he invoked his spirit,
> Mishtapeu. He danced and we heard his steps. His steps resonated as
> though he was dancing on sand. We heard it like that. And when he
> came out, we did not see his tracks . . . nothing was broken . . . the
> branches were as though they had never been touched when the Kakusha-
> patak came out.*

Another Innu hunter, Pien Tapit, told Lamothe about his experience inside the shaking tent ceremony that he participated in in the
1950s:

> *I heard all sorts of voices. . . . I felt a wind blowing inside. . . . When
> he comes in, that which we call Papakassik, the spirit master, that's
> less pleasant. It's as though it suddenly gets very cold. . . . And then
> he starts talking. That's when the tent stops shaking, and if you look
> all around you see nothing . . . if you look above you, you will see the
> sky. Then if you look at your feet you will see a deep pit and you will
> get dizzy. It is better not to open your eyes at all. Sometimes you will
> become very dizzy while spinning around.*

Not everyone has the gift of communicating directly with the
animal masters. The power to do so comes only when certain trials
are undergone, trials not unlike those encountered by Gilgamesh on

his journeys or by Arthur in his quest for the Holy Grail. The strange journey begins for the hunter when, in his travels, he comes upon a stagnant pond, as hunter Jean Baptiste Ashini told Lamothe.

A bird swims around and around the pond causing the water to swirl and eddy creating a hole in the centre. . . . If one saw the creature Matsheshu one would have to pass underneath all of the beasts around him to touch the one in the centre. . . . The hunter must choose a colour that comes from this vision, each colour represents a certain animal. This is how one gets power. . . . The man comes back from this with a saddlebag . . . and this is where he keeps his power. One can never put this bag on the ground inside the tent. It must always be kept in a tree.

Other ceremonies that bring luck to the hunter are still practised today. Sweat tents are still in use, and some hunters enter a trancelike state when they sing and play their drums. As Mistanikashan explains in *La Mémoire Battante,* "While he [the hunter] sings at night, when there is no light, he sees a flame . . . the fire corresponds to where the caribou are. The fire is about as big as a match flame. He sees it by his imagination, and it says exactly the name of the lake where the caribou will be. . . . After having dreamed, one can say where the caribou are."

"The drum is sacred, one doesn't play with it," warns Kanatuakuet, a respected hunter in Sheshatshit. "Children don't play with it. You use it when you are in trouble. . . . Even just to tap on it, even just for fun, you must not do it."

And while some traditional practices may have ceased, the beliefs on which they are based shape Innu thought today and will continue to shape that of subsequent generations.

The Innu traded sporadically with their Micmac and Iroquois neighbours to the south. They also had contact with the Newfoundland Beothuk; both groups crossed the Strait of Belle Isle, which in one spot is just twenty kilometres wide, by canoe. Ramah chert, a stone found in northeastern Labrador, was widely used to make tools. Objects made from this stone have been found in ancient dwelling sites thousands of kilometres from where it was quarried, indicating that the Innu, or a culture that preceded them, may have conducted vigorous trading with other indigenous groups long before the arrival of Europeans.

Where did the Innu come from? The people themselves believe
that they have always been in North America. One of their most
popular legends tells the story of Tshakapesh, who slew the Mam-
moth, a prehistoric creature that became extinct 10,000 years ago.
Many indigenous North Americans dispute the popular theory that
they came across the Bering Strait from another continent, and archaeologists are finding evidence that dates human presence in North
America earlier than was first thought. In British Columbia, 10,000-
year-old burial sites have been discovered. It is certain, however, that
no one could have lived in the Innu homeland before the end of the
Ice Age. According to archaeologist William Fitzhugh, parts of northern Quebec and Labrador deglaciated as early as 13,000 years ago; he
suggests that "As the ice retreated . . . a corridor was created into
which tundra vegetation, animals and finally man migrated from the
south. Caribou will have been present within a few centuries following deglaciation, and sea mammals will have been present off-
shore."

Fitzhugh believes the first humans to arrive encountered a habitat
rapidly adjusting to the retreat of the glaciers. Parts of Nitassinan
were still covered with ice 3000 years ago, but by 5000 B.P. (before
the present) the land had taken on the physical form and the ecosys-
tems that exist in the region today. What is not clear is whether the
first inhabitants of northern Quebec and Labrador, a people archaeologists call the "maritime archaic," are direct forebears of the Innu.

Thousands of years separate the maritime archaic from modern-
day Innu culture, so it is difficult to know if the two are related.
Stephen Loring, an archaeologist now based at the Smithsonian Institution, has taken great interest in solving the riddle of Innu ori-
gins. He believes the Innu once lived year-round on the sea coast, as
did the maritime archaic people, eating seals, walrus and other sea
creatures, until the aggressive Thule/Labrador Inuit pushed the Innu
inland in A.D. 1400, forcing them to rely almost exclusively on the
more precarious caribou migration for survival. (Since their populations fluctuate wildly, caribou cannot be depended on as a primary
food source. The animals very nearly disappeared from northern Quebec and Labrador in the early 1900s, yet today there are half a million in the George River herd alone.) Loring says the Innu ability to
adapt to their new way of life at that time was heroic. "It is in the
tenacity of groups to define and hold on to their identity by adjusting to new conditions," he writes, "that we can find an explanation

for the successful adaption of the Naskapi/Innu and their prede-
cessors to the land which we call Labrador and which they call
Nitassinan."

Loring is prepared to say with certainty that Innu roots go back
2000 years in northern Quebec and Labrador. Whether the Innu
have been there even longer than that will not be known until a
great deal more archaeological work is done.

The first European visitors to the Innu homeland were probably
the Vikings a thousand years ago. The next recorded European visit
was that of John Cabot, who sailed off the coast of Newfoundland in
1496. In his journal, Cabot spoke of encountering people with "red
skins"—the Beothuk. (Even though the Beothuk were the only people
who traditionally applied red ochre to their skin, all indigenous peoples in North America thereafter became known as "redskins.")

In the early 1500s Basque whalers established themselves on the
southern coast of Labrador at Red Bay. When whaling operations
were at their peak, more than twenty ships supplied carcasses to as
many as 2000 workers who toiled onshore. There is some evidence
that the Basques and neighbouring Innu may have worked together
and exchanged fish for bread. According to scholar José Mailhot, it
was the Innu, in conversation with the Basques, who coined the
term *aiskimeu* to refer to their Inuit neighbours. She believes the
word meant "those who speak a strange language," not "eaters of raw
meat" as is popularly believed. The Innu word was eventually spelled
"esquimaux" by the French and "eskimo" by the English.

Portuguese, Norman, Breton and Basque fishermen soon became
regular visitors to the Atlantic coast in search of the riches Cabot
spoke of, eventually settling there year-round. The Innu were frightened of the newcomers and believed that the Europeans had ma-
levolent supernatural powers because of the deadly diseases they
spread. It is difficult to know how many people lived in North America
before Columbus's voyages, but Francis Jennings, in his book *The
Invasion of America*, estimates that 90 per cent of the population was
wiped out by 1650. Priests brought strange witchcraft in the form of
crucifixes, rosary beads and communion wafers.

Curiosity soon overcame fear, however, and somehow trust was
established. Trading between the Innu and European merchants was
going on even before Jacques Cartier sailed up the St. Lawrence River
in 1534. Cartier wrote that the Innu came on board his vessels fear-

lessly, and the people had probably already been trading with Basque and Breton fishermen.

The Innu were happy to exchange fur-bearing animals for the iron axes and copper kettles brought by Europeans. They were spending more and more time inland and had adjusted their economy accordingly. But the Beothuk were not so lucky. They continued to live mostly on the sea coast, and thus came into frequent contact and conflict with the European fishermen who came to Newfoundland in greater numbers each year. The Beothuk raided fishing installations that encroached on their land, and this led to a war they were poorly equipped to fight. The Europeans had guns, the Beothuk just bows and arrows. Before the mid–nineteenth century, the Beothuk people and their ancient culture, believed to be one of the oldest in North America, were wiped out.

The Innu were probably more numerous than the Beothuk at the time of European contact, and they were indispensable to Europeans during the fur trade. The people were accustomed to travelling long distances across their homeland in search of caribou. In his book *Newfoundland*, Harold Horwood says that the Innu travelled "a thousand miles north and south from the Gulf of St. Lawrence to the Hudson Strait, and there are still some Indians living who can draw rough maps of the entire peninsula from personal knowledge and observation."

The introduction of European-made goods made life easier for the Innu and brought prestige to those who could get their hands on the new items. In exchange, the traders received beaver, marten, mink and otter pelts. The furs taken by the Innu were highly prized; the long cold winters gave special qualities to the pelts, which brought higher prices than furs obtained farther south. By the end of the sixteenth century, Tadoussac had become the busiest fur-trading centre in North America. The new trade did not come, however, without conflict between the Innu and other native groups, and eventually with the French themselves. As anthropologist Bruce Trigger explains, "European traders clearly made huge profits from the fur trade. They charged native people high prices for goods that were often of poor quality. As native peoples became dependent on these goods, they depleted their environment and were drawn into destructive inter-tribal wars in an effort to obtain adequate supplies."

By the time Samuel de Champlain arrived in New France in the early 1600s, a group of Innu near Quebec City had become middle-men between the French and native traders from as far away as southern Ontario. The Iroquois, who were expanding their territory, frequently blocked the movement of trade goods up the St. Lawrence River, so Champlain encouraged the Innu to oppose them. Wanting to protect their advantage in the fur trade, the Iroquois fought back fiercely, and the competition touched off a series of bloody confrontations. The Innu, who were being supplied with arms by the French, won most of the skirmishes.

The Innu did try to maintain some distance from the French, however. They resented Champlain's efforts to meddle in their political affairs; he tried to appoint chiefs and convince the people to give up their nomadic way of life to become farmers. Champlain insisted that a subservient alcoholic named Chomina (which means "grape" in Innu-aimun) be named head of a council of distinguished Innu chiefs. Trigger writes, "Although the Indians must not have understood clearly what he [Champlain] was doing, his honouring of the despised Chomina clearly amazed them." Finally, fed up with French interference, the Innu helped the English seize Quebec in 1629.

The earliest written accounts of how the Innu lived at the time of European contact are contained in the *Jesuit Relations*, the diaries and letters of early Jesuit missionaries. Father Paul Le Jeune kept a detailed account of the winter he spent with three Innu families on the south shore of the St. Lawrence River in 1633–34. It is clear from what he wrote that the Innu had a well-developed, comfortable way of life.

Anthropologists Eleanor Leacock and Edward S. Rogers have carefully studied Le Jeune's diaries for information on how the Innu lived. According to them,

> *Robes were usually made of bear or moose hide in the St. Lawrence area, or from five or six beaver skins. . . . To the north, clothing approached the style of the Eskimo. . . . In this area, hide clothing continued to be worn long after European clothing had come into use in the rest of the peninsula.*
>
> *Bear skins were used as floor coverings. Infants, diapered with sphagnum moss, were wrapped with soft materials, such as the skin of a caribou embryo, or placed in a decorated moss-filled leather bag . . . mattresses were occasionally made from canvas filled with moose or caribou hair, and small pillows filled with duck feathers were used.*

Food was quite varied:

> *Moose, caribou, bear, beaver, porcupine, fox, hare, marten, woodchuck, badger, snow geese, brants, ducks, teals, loons, grouse, woodcocks, snipes and passenger pigeons. Eel were important and other fish taken were salmon, pike, walleye, sucker, sturgeon, whitefish, catfish, lamprey and smelt. Seals were hunted, and turtles caught and eaten. Raspberries, blueberries, strawberries, cherries, wild grapes, hazelnuts and wild apples were gathered, as well as red martagon bulbs (a plant with licorice-like roots) and what was probably the Indian potato. Maple trees were tapped for their sap.*

Le Jeune remarked on the egalitarian nature of Innu life. He found no class system in the bush camp, nor competition between the sexes. A hunter's prestige came not from the meat and goods he acquired for his family but from what he gave away and shared with others. It was inconceivable to a hunting people that food would be hoarded or that one family would eat well while others went hungry. Sharing ensured that everyone ate no matter whose luck was good on a particular day. The sharing ethic is part of both the religious and the cultural ideology of the Innu to this day.

Le Jeune's European prejudices are widely reflected in his writing; he consistently refers to the Innu as being "ignorant" and calls them "savages" and "barbarians." He was amazed that they did not share his view of European racial and cultural superiority. He wrote: "Often they told me that in the beginning we looked very ugly to them, with as much hair on the mouth as on the head, but little by little they grew accustomed to our look and we began to look less deformed to them." (According to Bruce Trigger, "Indians traditionally associated hairiness with a lack of intelligence and pointed to beards as material evidence of the stupidity of Europeans.")

In the seventeenth century, when Le Jeune lived with the Innu, ten to twenty people travelled together during the winter, comprising what Eleanor Leacock calls a lodge group. Often as many as thirty-five to seventy-five people stayed together but split up to hunt over a wide area, always keeping in close contact with each other so that no part of the group would go hungry. During the summer, large groups of Innu, often 1500 or more, came together at an interior lake, river mouth, trading post or mission station. Here people relaxed after the hard winter; marriages were arranged, groups were formed for the winter hunt and people enjoyed a social life. Once traders introduced alcohol, however, things changed dramatically, and these large summer gatherings deteriorated. Leacock notes: "Friction and conflict were particularly apparent around the French fort and settlement, in sharp contrast to the easy tenor of life reported by Le Jeune and others for the interior, even in cases where fairly large groups gathered together."

Father Le Jeune tried to encourage a group of Innu to settle and operate farms at his Sillery mission in 1637. Trigger says this was the first "Indian reserve" in Canada, and it failed. Even though houses, food and clothing were provided, the Innu preferred their own way of life and eventually moved away to continue hunting and gathering.

As the Innu gradually adapted to the growing European presence, they generously shared their land with the newcomers. They found that the trade goods they obtained from the Europeans made life in the bush a little easier. Yet the fur trade was a mixed blessing, for it began the process of undermining Innu independence.

Historian Alan Cooke, in his study of Hudson's Bay Company records from the eighteenth and nineteenth centuries, concludes that the traders deliberately set out to destroy the economic independence of the Innu by making them dependent on goods they could obtain only from trading posts. Two items were made particularly seductive: alcohol and gunpowder.

The Innu who proved the most difficult to lure with new trade goods were the Naskapi, the Mushuau-Innu, who lived farthest north and had the least contact with Europeans. They went about their lives without European-made products, remaining aloof from the fur trade, preferring to hunt caribou instead. Cooke writes that the Mushuau-Innu disliked the traders who tried to encourage them to hunt animals that were inedible. "To the Naskapis, roving hunters, . . . food was caribou," he states. "The traders seem never to have understood that simple point. Mere liberality of payment in trade goods was no comfort to crying children with empty stomachs in the face of a real threat of seasonal starvation."

Some remote trading posts, like the one at Fort Chimo, were notoriously unreliable as a source of supplies. Often Mushuau-Innu families travelled hundreds of kilometres with their furs only to find that the traders' shelves were empty. They wisely refused to make the fur trade a central feature of their lives.

John McLean of the Hudson's Bay Company was one trader who

was determined to create Innu dependence on trade. "As trading posts . . . are now established on their lands," he wrote, "I doubt not but 'artificial' wants will, in time, be created that may become as indispensable to their comfort as their present real wants. All the arts of the trader are exercised to produce such a result, and those arts never fail of ultimate success. Even during the last two years of my management [1841–42] the demand for certain articles of European manufacture had greatly increased."

Traders like McLean worked hard to make "firepower" an indispensable feature of Innu life. By the mid-1840s the Mushuau-Innu in the Fort Chimo area were killing caribou with guns and ammunition. Even after the Mushuau-Innu became dependent on guns, however, fur was not being brought to the trading post in quantities satisfactory to the Hudson's Bay Company. Some traders tried to stock their district with more "industrious Indians" by inviting Innu from the south to hunt and trap near Fort Chimo, a policy that had dire results. Many died because they were in strange territory and failed to find enough food.

No trader went as far as Donald Henderson to procure furs from the Innu. Henderson refused ammunition to Innu families at his post in 1846, hoping that they would learn a lesson and return the following fall with furs to exchange for gunpowder. Instead, thirty-six people starved. Henderson repeated his murderous policy the following year, and there was more starvation. A fellow trader, William Con-nolly, laid the blame for these deaths squarely at Henderson's door. "I would not be in [Henderson's] place for all the world, for he will assuredly have to answer one day for all this to that Divine Being whose creatures he has so harshly treated, in not supplying their wants in November last. They only ate two otter skins and all the deerskins and tentings." Connolly wrote in May 1849 that the widow of chief Paytabays was so weak she was obliged to crawl to the trading post where she reported more than a hundred deaths from starvation.

The traders' policies of creating "artificial wants" was ultimately successful; by the 1900s the formerly proud, independent Innu around the Fort Chimo area were fewer in number and severely demoralized. A sad postcript to the story of these people was noted by Jules D'Astous, regional supervisor of Indian Agencies in Quebec. He wrote in 1953 that those who were forced to settle in the mining town of Schefferville "were sick, totally destitute and now living almost solely on relief."

Innu in other parts of Nitassinan had also been having problems with European encroachment. In 1848 Innu from the upper Saguenay area presented a petition to the governor-general of Lower Canada stating that they were no longer able to supply their own food and clothing because they had lost so much land to settlers, and they requested that a large parcel of land be protected for Innu use along the Péribonca River and near Lac Saint-Jean. The Innu also asked to be paid the royalties collected from traders and logging operations and from the sale of Innu land, which went to the government. The only response to the petition was the establishment of the small reserve of Pointe Bleue nearly ten years later.

Small tracts of land were set aside near trading posts and Catholic missions in the hopes that Innu would settle on them year-round. A reserve created at Betsiamites became a popular mission and trading post for the Innu during the summer, but between 1863 and 1911, ten epidemics struck Betsiamites, killing many of the people who visited there. In the 1850s Innu hunting in that area was restricted, at the same time that the government granted fishing rights to non-Innu along the lower north shore of the St. Lawrence. In 1869, Charles Arnaud, a priest at Betsiamites, wrote, "The government is killing these poor Indians and reducing them to misery with its fishing regulations." Between 1896 and 1900 the Innu of Betsiamites were forbidden even to trap beaver, their major food source, forcing many to rely on government rations.

Fortunately, there were some Innu who continued to enjoy great freedom from European interference. William Brooks Cabot, a Boston engineer, spent eight summers, from 1903 to 1910, with the Mushuau-Innu of northeastern Labrador (many of whom now live at Utshimassit) and wrote a book called *Labrador* about his experience. In it he describes a particularly successful caribou hunt he witnessed in the fall of 1911. Fifteen hundred caribou were speared and then distributed to many families.

In such times of plenty the Indian life is peculiarly attractive, perhaps more so than the life of any other hunter race that survives on earth. The people are lords over their fine country, asking little favor save that the deer may come in their time. It was one of the notable privileges of my wilderness days to have the best of their country to myself for some years, unexplored as it was, and even more to me was the relation with the people themselves.

"Little the people are asking," Cabot wrote. "Their country is still theirs, and the deer, and long may they so remain."

Much of the Innu way of life remained intact long after Cabot's visits among them. In 1935 trader R. Hammond wrote, "They are still . . . a most ingenious people and doubtless could, if it became necessary, subsist quite independently of outside aid."

All of this changed after the Second World War, and Cabot's wish for the Innu was not fulfilled. The fur trade collapsed and the Innu homeland was soon in great demand by industrial developers who did not share Cabot's respect for the way of life of these nomadic hunters.

Mushuau-Innu hunters posing for a
photograph outside the Hudson's Bay
Company post at Utshimassit (Davis Inlet)
in 1903.

A hunter at his camp in Mishta-nipi, 1906.

Innu couple portaging supplies in 1921 past a fenced Innu grave site on the east site of the Mishikamau-shipit (Naskaupi River) that is now underwater.

Mushau-Innu woman making *niueikan* (dry powdered caribou meat) in preparation for winter travel.

Canoeing along the Kamikuakamiu-shipu
(Red Wine River) en route to Nipississ,
1921.

Equipment and meat scaffold at
Tshinutipish (near Indian House
Lake), August 1910.

Bear skulls and caribou antlers
placed in a tree to show respect for
the animals at Kanishutakushtasht,
August 1982.

Innu woman and daughter on
portage trail opposite the mouth
of the Kamikuakamiu-shipu, en
route to Atshiku-nipi, 1921.

Mushau-Innu women relaxing at
Kanekaut in northern Quebec
(east of Indian House Lake),
on their way to Utshimassit,
August 1910.

Tshaukuesh removing marrow from
caribou bones in preparation for a
makushan, an Innu feast, fall 1990.

NIGEL MARKHAM

Shuashim Selma after successfully trapping a beaver near a camp at Uashikanishteu-shipu, 1987.
ANTHONY JENKINSON

Tshani Rich and Ispastien Benuen at Amishku-shipiss in the Mealy Mountains, 1987.
ANTHONY JENKINSON

A proud hunter, Tshani Rich, pulls a butchered caribou (wrapped in its own skin) back to his camp at Kukumessat-kataht.

ANTHONY JENKINSON

Jets over Nitassinan

*"One can spend a one-hour mission at low-level and never see
another human being. The only humans present are
occasional Innu families who hunt and fish out of small camps
on a seasonal basis.
When occupied these camps are carefully avoided by
low-level flying aircraft."*

DEPARTMENT OF NATIONAL DEFENCE PROMOTIONAL BROCHURE

I settled into the routines of life at Penipuapishku-nipi during my
first few days in camp, enjoying the peace and quiet that make
nutshimit such a special place for the Innu. I got into the habit of
walking each day with the children to the edge of the lake, where a
river had burst free from its ice cover, a sure sign spring was on the
way. We sat on the rocks listening to the musical rhythm of the water.
On the way back we checked fish lures in the ice, while little Sylvester
Rich charged along beside us mimicking a snowmobile or a helicopter. Occasionally we heard jets in the distance travelling so fast that
they were just a short-lived interruption to the otherwise delicate
silence. I always carried my tape recorder and camera with me in
case a plane came near, and it became a game with the children to
run and warn me. "Get ready," they would yell. "Here they come!"

On the morning of 29 April 1988, I had been at Penipuapishku-
nipi for eight days. Once again there was glorious sunshine. The
temperature had dropped below freezing during the night, so a hard
crust on the snow made walking easier than it had been. Ben and the
other hunters were long gone by the time I got up.

There was mounting excitement in the camp since geese were expected to arrive any day from their winter sojourn in the south. I could sense competition among the hunters to see who would get the first goose of the season. Three of the Andrew brothers, Makus, Eric and Nikashan, had been teasing us for days with imitation goose calls that sometimes drove children outside their tents to look up into the sky.

"Today," Janet told me as she brushed Yvette's hair, "Ben is with Apetet. I hope they get geese, it's my favourite meat. We can roast it outdoors."

I went down to the lake for water, and the distant honking of geese penetrated the stillness of the wilderness. I thought one of the Andrews might be playing another practical joke. But the sound kept getting louder and finally I did look up. Overhead, half a dozen geese flew past in a neat straight line.

The morning chores done, I languished outside the tent on spruce boughs that made a warm, dry seat in the snow. I washed the break-fast dishes and drained them on the boughs while savouring the hot sun on my skin. I heard Jamie and Yvette laughing and talking as they ran alongside their father, who had returned holding a dead goose by the throat. Jamie carried his father's gun, which he care-fully, almost reverently, passed to his mother. He then turned to me.

"My father got the first goose," he said with pride. "He shot it with one bullet, just over there on the other side of the lake. Apetet got one too, but our father was the first."

Ben smiled indulgently, barely able to hide his own pleasure. I followed them inside the tent, where Ben laid the bird by the stove and sat near Janet, who began to roll him a cigarette.

"I could hear jets, and I was hoping they wouldn't scare the birds away," Ben reported. "I'm not sure if Sylvester and those who went closer to the mountains will be as lucky. They're too close to that target site. I think the geese were scared off."

The target in the Red Wine Mountains was widely used by jet bomber pilots from Goose Bay. The Innu consider the flights to be the most serious encroachment ever to take place on their land. In the past, developments had been confined to one area, but the low-flying jets, increasing in number every year, fly over many thousands of square kilometres.

Jamie looked earnestly at his father and asked him a question in Innu-aimun. Ben replied, then translated for me.

"Jamie wants to know when he can go hunting with me. I have had to explain to him that he is still too young, he will be ready in a few years. It is very hard on a child to sit still like we had to this morning. We were out there for four hours before any geese came by. We couldn't make noise, we had to stay hidden. Jamie is too young to do that without getting bored. Next year, maybe."

Jamie squirmed impatiently but did not contradict his father. Janet handed Ben a mug of tea and emptied from his hunting pack the lunch of bread and fried partridge that he wouldn't need now. Ben soon got to his feet and invited Jamie to help him get wood. The boy jumped up readily and ran outside to get the axe. Once they were gone Janet asked if I wanted to join her while she cleaned the goose in the woods behind the tent. I started to load film into my camera while she waited outside.

Suddenly I was hit by an abrupt, incredible blast of noise. The tent canvas shook. I fell back on the floor, my ears rang, and I felt my heart begin to pound painfully. Before I had time to recover I heard Janet scream my name. My tape recorder was on the ground beside me and I pressed the record button just in time. Another blast of noise struck, and the recorder's volume meter jumped crazily in the split second it took another jet to fly over us. I felt shaken and stood up unsteadily. My initial fear had changed to anger. I stepped outside the tent, cursing the jet, the unexpected intrusion.

I had read about the startle effect caused by low-flying jet bombers, and now I was experiencing it first-hand. According to experts, the startle effect is produced when noise increases dramatically in a short time. A low-flying bomber will cause normal ambient sound, usually measured at about 40 decibels, to increase to about 120 decibels in half a second.

The twenty-tonne jet bomber had swooped just thirty metres above our heads, flying at 900 kilometres an hour. Scientists say that jets travelling this quickly create noise measured at between 110 and 140 decibels. (A jackhammer, for purposes of comparison, is measured at 80 decibels.) One hundred and twenty decibels causes pain in humans. Janet had seen the jet pass overhead before any of us heard it.

Outside our tent I found Janet comforting Matshikuan, who was clinging to her mother and sobbing. Mary Martha Rich stood beside them.

"Matshikuan was playing underneath those trees over there," Mary Martha said. "I saw the trees bend when the jets flew past. She fell to the ground, she got such a fright."

We were soon joined by other women, all of them with their own stories of jet terror. Although it was five minutes since the jet had passed over, my heart was still pounding rapidly.

Until this day I had thought Innu reports of this problem were exaggerated. I knew the noisy bombers were a potential nuisance and I could see why children would be frightened, but I didn't expect people to suffer physically. Now I knew better.

Innu throughout Nitassinan have been complaining for years about the low-level flights. In 1986 an Environmental Assessment Review Panel (EARP), at the request of the federal government, travelled throughout the Innu homeland collecting testimonies from aboriginal hunters and their families who had been overflown by jet bombers.

"I cannot express what I felt the first time I heard such a tremendous noise," Mrs. Wapistan of Unaman-shipit told the panel. "I was so shaken up that I even forgot about my children and my husband who were around me. Some children asked me what was going on, what was happening, and I could not answer, I was so shaken up."

George Gabriel of Schefferville said that people were afraid to take their canoes on the water because low-flying jets might cause them to capsize.

"I can assure you that even if there is only one plane, the noise is tremendous, the noise is awful," Charles-Api Bellefleur testified. Another hunter, Ambroise Lalo, said some men from Nutashkuan had fled in terror when they were overflown. One man lost his false teeth in the rush to get away.

Inuit hunters also complained to the panel. George Koneak of Kuujjuaq asked how his people were expected to live if the animals in the largest wild caribou herd in the world, the George River herd, were frightened off by the jets. "Since we live off the land here, since we are very concerned about the animals that live off the land, since we do not have any agriculture up here and since we do not have any domestic animals to live off of—what are we to do for food?"

Willie Gordon, also of Kuujjuaq, asked this of the military official travelling with the panel: "If we have no more meat anywhere around these areas that you are disturbing—the [caribou] calving grounds—and if we have no more caribou migration, are you going to guarantee us that you will feed us for free?"

Janet took Matshikuan inside the tent. I followed. I wanted to find out what I had recorded. I listened first with headphones, fearful Matshikuan might be frightened once again by the noise, but

Janet asked to hear it. We listened to an indisputable record of what had happened. Janet's scream is heard, then the terrifying blast of noise, which lasts for a fraction of a second and sounds impressively shrill even through my small speakers. Then Matshikuan is heard crying.

"They never believe us when we say this happens, but maybe now they will, when you play that on the radio," Janet said. She added, "Matshikuan is afraid of all planes now. When the helicopter comes to take us back from the country she runs and hides and says she doesn't want to go. She won't go down to the lake with the other children when a plane or helicopter comes to the camp. The jets have made her afraid."

Yvette came to the door of the tent holding the goose Janet had dropped when the jets flew past. We set off to pluck it, still reeling from our fright but determined not to let it spoil the rest of the day.

Some distance behind the tent I knelt beside Janet on the ground, the goose between us. I plucked the feathers slowly and methodically, as Janet had showed me, but I was only a tenth as quick as she was. The work became more tedious when we reached the small feathers close to the skin, especially as I was being careful not to inhale them. I was relieved when at last Janet announced that the work was done. She lit a fire to singe the rest of the feathers off the bird. "It will taste nicer this way," she said.

After a few turns in the fire the bald, tanned goose was taken back to the tent, where Janet cleaned it. The intestines, an Innu delicacy, were braided and threaded on a stick to roast before the fire. Other valued parts of the bird were then extracted. The liver was set aside for one of the elderly women in the camp, the heart for Sylvester's mother, and so on, until much of our goose was apportioned to other households. "We give away much meat this time," Janet explained, "until everyone gets their own goose."

When I went outside the tent to get something from our cache of supplies I saw Ben and Jamie coming back with firewood. Matshikuan sat beside her father as he sharpened his axe and plaintively told him what had happened. Janet joined them and continued the tale. Ben shook his head from side to side, saying nothing, but picked up the axe and started to chop wood. I gathered up armloads to take inside for the stove.

Just as I was leaving with the last load, Ben, wiping sweat from his brow, said, "Jamie and I heard those jets while we were getting wood.

We didn't know they'd go right over the tent. Matshikuan isn't the only child traumatized by this. Many children now beg their parents to stay in the village because they are afraid of being overflown by jets in the country. My fear is that parents will start listening to the children and fewer families will go into the bush."

"Don't you think people will get used to it?" I asked.

"What do you think? You were overflown today. How did you like it?"

I thought about it. I figured that I could get used to hearing jets in the distance, even though this detracts from the pleasure of the normally tranquil wilderness, but there is no way to habituate yourself to the startle effect of an unseen jet. The chances of jets straying off course, and flying more frequently over humans and stress-sensitive caribou, are high. Approximately three thousand of these flights a year are permitted at night. And there are hazards other than noise associated with the practice.

As Ben and I were speaking, we noticed a commotion near Sylvester's tent.

"*Petute*," Sylvester called. "Come here." The senior hunter held a tiny partridge in his hand. Two young men were standing beside him.

After a discussion in Innu-aimun, Ben explained to me, "These boys found the dead partridge while they were out walking today. There's no sign of any external wound so Sylvester thinks the bird died of fright when the jets flew past."

Thinking back to my own quickened heartbeat, it did seem possible that this bird, with its far more fragile cardiovascular system, might indeed have died of fright. Some Innu fear that the shock of the loud noise could cause heart attacks in the elderly.

There was a sombre mood to our supper that night despite the feast of fresh goose. Afterwards, I read by the Coleman lamp while Janet and Ben sang and told stories to the children. When the children were asleep we began once more to talk about the jets.

"The military has a phone number you can call to tell them where you are camped. They say they can ensure jets won't fly over people. Have you used it?" I asked.

"It's a waste of time," Ben replied. "We used to let them know where we were, but it didn't work. Mistakes are made. The military knows where this camp is. They check with the private helicopter companies to see where they've been taking us. Hunters get overflown when they leave camp to travel by canoe and when they are looking for animals long distances away. The caribou can't call in to say where they are. What's the point of going to the country if our wildlife is destroyed?"

Ben sighed, and I thought our conversation was over. I put out the lamp. The only light in the tent came from the glowing embers in the stove. Ben spoke again.

"It saddens me that a people who have the best that the world can offer, which is our way of life out here, will have it taken away from them. There is no alcohol here, there are no problems as we have in the community. There is the togetherness of people here. In the community that is gone. There's many different problems that the Innu are being put into by this activity, and if it increases, where does that leave the Innu people in future?"

Before long, news that a reporter had been overflown reached the Goose Bay base commander, Col. John David, and he flew to our camp to apologize and assure the Innu publicly that it wouldn't happen again. But it did. The Penipuapishku-nipi camp was overflown several times afterwards, despite the commander's best efforts to prevent it.

■

I met with Colonel David when I returned to Goose Bay. He told me that life in nutshimit is a thing of the past for the Innu, and military expansion should not be held up because of it. "Sure, it's important for the old people to go back on the land and eat the animals they hunt," he said, "but it's not feasible economically for the younger generation."

As I listened to the familiar phrases that reduce the value of life in nutshimit to dollars and cents, I thought of the young people I had met at Penipuapishku-nipi. I could still see seventeen-year-old Joachim Selma carrying a freshly killed caribou across his shoulders. The handsome, tanned and healthy young man was doing what his father and grandfather have always done to feed their families. Back in Sheshatshit, Joachim joins other teenagers, drinking beer and trying to live up to the lifestyle shown in beer commercials. He and his friends listen to Def Leppard and dress like the young people in rock videos. Many Innu his age are confused about which way of life has more value, more legitimacy.

There is no official recognition of the life Joachim most enjoys, that of nutshimit. It is never seen on television, unless shown as something folkloric, and is rarely talked about in school or in the media.

When the Innu way of life is talked about by non-Innu it is devalued, denigrated. A young Innu who chooses to be a hunter, to live in the bush, makes a difficult decision that goes against the powerful voices that now control much of his or her life: the schoolteachers, the game wardens, the social workers and the media, who have never lived the Innu life in nutshimit yet make judgements about its viability.

Fifteen-year-old Kanani Penashue was one of the top students in grade 10 at Peenamin McKenzie School in Sheshatshit. Her teacher sternly disapproved of the teenager's decision one spring to accompany her family to the bush, saying she would miss an important part of the school year and risk failing. Kanani's mind was made up, however. Completing school was not as important to her as this trip to the bush with her family.

"You're throwing away your life," the teacher warned.

"How can I be throwing away my life by choosing to live the way of my culture?" Kanani retorted. Later Kanani told me, "Ever since I was in school, they gave me books and they taught me more English than Innu. They gave me books to read in English, they never gave me books to read in Innu. Being in the country is my life, following my parents' footsteps and my grandparents' footsteps, that's my life. The teacher said, 'Kanani, you're losing your culture now, the only thing you should look at is not losing your language.' And I told her, 'We go in the country to keep our culture because if there's no culture, there's no language.' I didn't really like what she said." Kanani returned to school, of her own accord, the following fall. She says she will get whatever formal education she feels is necessary, but in her own time, mixing both worlds as she sees fit.

One Sunday at Penipuapishku-nipi a little girl came into our tent carrying a plateful of cooked trout. Janet said it was a gift to me from the Ashini family. I accompanied the child back home to thank her family. The Ashini tent was set apart from the others, near the shore of the lake, and as we walked towards it I thought of my last encounter with Jean-Pierre Ashini.

Eight years earlier I had done news reports on the plight of Innu students who were living in St. John's for the first time. Jean-Pierre was among them. He was bright and articulate, and I felt he had a great future ahead of him. I was disappointed when he told me halfway through the term that he was leaving school to go back home. I tried to change his mind.

"You're throwing away a great opportunity," I warned.

"The more education you get, the more white you become," he replied. "The longer I live in your society, the harder it will be for me to return to my own."

"But you'll be able to help your family if you get a good job," I said, "and for that you need more education. You could become a teacher, or a lawyer, and fight for your people's rights."

"That would mean a long absence from my family and perhaps I wouldn't want to ever go back, but live comfortably instead in your society," he told me. "That's not what I want right now. I've made up my mind. I am going to the country with my grandfather. He needs me, my mother needs me, that's where I belong."

Jean-Pierre's father had died when his son was just ten years old in an accident related to alcohol. I later learned that if Jean-Pierre had not gone back to his family that year, his mother and grandfather would have been forced to stay in the village, idle and on welfare. Their diet in the village was far inferior to bush food, and Pien Joseph Selma, the grandfather, would have ached with boredom and loneliness for his land.

For a few years after returning home, Jean-Pierre worked as a court translator, but he grew tired of seeing a steady stream of Innu file through on charges of illegal hunting or crimes related to alcohol abuse. Jean-Pierre had begun to understand that the problems the Innu faced were political; they stemmed not from a lack of formal education but rather from his people's inability to choose how they wished to live.

These thoughts preoccupied me until I reached the Ashini tent. I pulled up the tent flap and sat on some logs near the doorway. Jean-Pierre greeted me informally. I said hello to his wife, Katie, who looked away shyly and began playing with their child. A middle-aged woman and an old man, Jean-Pierre's mother and grandfather, were repairing a fishing net.

I was used to the absence of conversation in Innu company and took advantage of the silence to look around me. I was impressed with how healthy everyone looked. There was none of the obesity that is common among those who live year-round in the village. The Ashinis were lean and strong, their teeth glowing white against their tanned skin. They looked totally at ease in their surroundings.

"You made the right decision, Jean-Pierre," I said, wondering if he would remember that long-ago conversation in St. John's.

"I know," he said, his face breaking into a grin. "We've only spent six weeks so far in Sheshatshit this year; we've been in the country the rest of the time."

That was quite a record: nowadays most Innu families spend an average of only six months in the bush, returning to the community during the harshest winter months and in summer when blackflies threaten to eat a person alive.

"I couldn't have done it without my grandfather," Jean-Pierre acknowledged, nodding his head in the direction of the old man, who didn't look up from his work. "He's a very good hunter, he knows all the places the animals live, he knows the animal masters, he respects the land."

Pien Joseph Selma was a revered, seasoned hunter. Though he was seventy-five when I met him that spring, he looked much younger. His death the following winter was a blow to the family and to people throughout Nitassinan. The loss of an elder is felt by everyone. It signals a severe break with the past, because the elders have an irreplaceable knowledge of the land and the animals. Their knowledge can only be passed on to children who spend time in nutshimit, the school of Innu culture.

When I heard the news of his grandfather's death, I wondered if twenty-three-year old Jean-Pierre, now head of the household, would be confident enough to travel and hunt on his own. I am told he continues to take his family to nutshimit but avoids some of the areas he used to frequent with his grandfather; the separation still brings pain.

Many non-native people think that because the Innu have adopted some of the ways of Euro-Canadian society they no longer have a distinct culture, and therefore no legitimate claim to their land. This is certainly the view of the former mayor of Goose Bay, Hank Shouse. Shouse claimed he couldn't understand why the Innu were opposed to military expansion. "The Indians of Sheshatshit shop in the Co-op, drive cars, watch colour television," he told the visiting Environmental Assessment Review Panel. "They are not that much different."

But there are other non-natives who show more understanding. Thomas Berger, the judge who spent a great deal of time visiting Inuit and Dene communities in the Northwest Territories as Commissioner of the Mackenzie Valley Pipeline Inquiry, wrote in his report: "It is native peoples' profound desire to be themselves that has led to the present confrontation. Far from deploring their failure to become what strangers want them to be, we should regard their determination to be themselves as a triumph of the human spirit."

The Innu have been resisting the efforts of others to change them ever since their first contact with Europeans. They have kept their language and their traditions, and they are determined to pass on the peace and joy of life in nutshimit to future generations. It is a tribute to the endurance of Innu culture, and something of a miracle, that so much has survived. Now the people are facing what could be the most lethal threat of all—the jet bombers.

Churchill Falls and Other "Improvements"

"The Churchill Falls project did not deprive a single person of his home or livelihood."
AUTHOR PHIL SMITH IN *BRINCO, THE STORY OF CHURCHILL FALLS*

The Innu people were not consulted in 1986 when Canada signed agreements with the U.S., British, Dutch and West German governments, permitting them to train their air forces over Nitassinan for a ten-year period. But this was not surprising. Canadian governments have always acted as though the Innu, and their land rights in Nitassinan, do not exist. Mines, hydroelectric projects and pulp and paper mills have sprouted up all over the Innu homeland during this century, enriching the coffers of provincial governments and multinational companies but wreaking havoc with Innu lives. This fact was most forcefully brought home to me when I accompanied two Innu women on a journey in 1989.

From the air, the subarctic tundra of the Quebec-Labrador peninsula looks marshy and impassable. Rivers snake along, then abruptly stop. Small lakes empty into larger ones or sit stoically on their own.

We had been flying for a little over an hour, en route to Churchill Falls from Sheshatshit. As I surveyed the land below, I found it hard to imagine that anyone could make this trip on foot and by canoe, yet generations of Innu families did just that, and travelled much farther in the same way. Churchill Falls was not even the halfway point on many of their journeys. When families left Sheshatshit in the fall, some spent Christmas at the Catholic mission in Uashat (the

Innu name for Sept-Îles), 580 kilometres away. They returned to the bush after the holiday and in the same fashion headed towards the mission or trading post where they planned to spend the summer.

The trips made across this terrain each year were long and arduous. They involved manoeuvring through dangerous rapids in flimsy canoes filled with provisions and children, and portaging hundreds of kilograms of supplies. In 1935 a Hudson's Bay Company employee described how the Innu travelled to his post at Davis Inlet:

> Once the load is on their backs they can travel thus for hours over what is probably among the roughest country in the world, barring actual mountain territory. All their hunting is done either on foot or in canoe, by far the greater part on foot, and in winter, on snowshoes, they rival the caribou in speed and endurance. . . . They are no strangers to hunger and are inured to great physical effort from early childhood, since even toddlers must carry their share when the tribe or family is in motion.

The film crew of *Hunters and Bombers* was travelling with fifty-seven-year-old Maniaten and her sister Tshaukuesh to the site of the largest industrial development in the Innu homeland, the Churchill Falls hydroelectric project. Maniaten had spent many years travelling through this territory with her family. She had not been back to the falls since the project was completed, and we wanted to film her reaction to what she saw. The old travel route is no more. Water has been diverted from important rivers like the Mishikamau-shipu, once used as a highway across Innu land, drying them up and rendering them useless to travellers. In other places, flooding has drowned islands over which the Innu once portaged.

We soon reached the perimeter of the Smallwood Reservoir. Fallen trees littered its stagnant waters. Hundreds of waterways were diverted and more than 1300 square kilometres of black spruce forest were flooded to make the reservoir, which is half the size of Lake Ontario. Politicians in the 1970s boasted that it was the third-largest artificial body of water in the world.

Maniaten started to speak excitedly, then with indignation, while Tshaukuesh and Nikashan, Maniaten's son, strained to see out their windows. Nikashan translated for us.

"She's talking about places where her brothers and sisters were born which are all underwater now, as are places where family members are buried. She told us that there used to be portage trails but they're gone now. There are many places she doesn't recognize anymore."

One important spot destroyed by the hydroelectric project was Michikamau Lake. Diverted into the Smallwood Reservoir by a series of dykes, it is unrecognizable today. The Michikamau had been a welcome sight to the Innu after months of hard travel overland; by canoeing from one end of the huge lake to the other they could cover 130 kilometres. Innu families from all over the peninsula met there in the spring and fall to make the last stage of their journeys together. Maniaten's father hunted and trapped the forests around Michikamau Lake; her family considered it home.

The Innu not only lived, hunted and travelled over land now underwater; they also buried their dead there, and carefully marked sites where children were born and where legendary and heroic deeds had occurred. The flooding of graves is considered a blasphemous act by many Innu. Archaeologists speculate that thousands of years of Innu history disappeared with those graves. The single archaeologist hired by the companies involved in the project surveyed the Michikamau area before it was flooded, and found campsites and bones a thousand years old. That was the first and last survey of one of the most important archaeological sites in Canada. Evidence needed to prove Innu land rights has been wiped out by those who now make claims to the land.

When the plane landed at the town of Churchill Falls we loaded our film gear into a rented truck and drove to the site of the falls. From there, we headed out on foot along a trail designed for tourists. The pleasant path is bordered by a mix of birch and aspen trees and thick stands of conifers.

Maniaten slowly made her way, weaving from side to side. She had once walked much longer distances with no trouble at all, but the fifteen children she has borne and the sedentary life she now leads have taken their toll on her body. As we walked along she joked quietly with Tshaukuesh, who collected boughs to make a comfortable seat for her older sister once we reached our destination. The closer we came to the falls, however, the more the trip seemed to tax her cheerfulness. At one point on the trail she stopped and motioned us to listen. We heard nothing.

"Maniaten says it's odd not to hear the falls," Tshaukuesh told me. "She says at one time you could hear the falls many miles away from here."

(In 1895 the geologist A. P. Low visited Churchill Falls and wrote: "The noise of the falls has a stunning effect and although deadened because of its enclosed situation can be heard for more than ten miles away as a deep, booming sound. The cloud of mist is also visible from any eminence within a radius of twenty miles.")

I was the first to reach a lookout that had a commanding view of the huge cavern extending hundreds of metres below. The long chute, twenty-five metres higher than Horseshoe Falls at Niagara, was once covered by turbulent, foaming water. Today it is barren and desertlike. The sisters stood beside me and looked on in silence, then Maniaten left the spot abruptly, shaking her head.

"We called the great falls Patshetshunau [steam rising]," she told us later. "You could see the mist going straight up when it was cold. It was like this all the time, that's why the weather was always bad around here. . . . You could still see the mist [and] you would say 'That's where Patshetshunau is.' And since it's been dammed you can't see the mist anymore. I never thought the falls would be like it is now . . . what a poor sight it is today. All Innu are deeply hurt when we think about this."

We moved to a second lookout and Maniaten began to tell us about her nomadic childhood. She was born at Machinipi, near Uashat. It was common for the family to spend summers on the coast while the men made new canoes and collected supplies for the winter ahead. Every fall the people set off on immense journeys. Maniaten's family travelled the 490 kilometres from Uashat to the site of what is now Schefferville, then sometimes 370 kilometres farther north to Fort Chimo (Kuujjuaq). From there they continued on to Utshimassit, 500 kilometres away; the last leg of the journey was the 300-kilometre trip inland to Michikamau Lake. These trips took many months, Maniaten recalls, and the travel was hard and dangerous.

We carried our canoes, supplies, and even put the children on our backs. Many times the babies would cry and Mother would stop, unload what she was carrying and breastfeed the child. The older children walked behind because they were slow. Mother would keep encouraging the children; she would say, "Keep it up, we're getting closer to the next lake." When we got to a lake or river we'd pile everything back in the canoe and paddle off.

I remember one very beautiful lake. It had islands on it; we called the lake Kanikuanikau. The islands had fir and birch trees mixed together. The Innu liked this place very much. I remember arriving there one winter after a long journey on snowshoes and towing our belongings on toboggan. We usually stayed there throughout the spring and then began our trek back to summer camps on the coast.

It was a big lake and we used a pole to push our canoe up the rapids. Paddling by the small birchy islands was a very beautiful sight. There were so many islands. Tshaukuesh was born near there early one spring when we headed back to Uashat. Rose was born nearby in the fall. Our father delivered them both. I have many good memories of that place. Now all those small and beautiful islands are underwater. . . .

While travelling from one place to another you sometimes got short of food because you didn't have time to hunt. We often met other Innu who gave us food.

It's hard to believe the distance we travelled to get to our hunting area year by year. The gear got smaller along the way, especially food, because we would have eaten most of it. We cached some of the basic foods high on tree platforms. That was the food we ate travelling back from the country. Today, all that land has been wasted.

Tshaukuesh listened intently to her sister, then told us some of her own memories of life on the land.

I can recall the happiness we had while living in the country. My father made the platform for storing all the caribou meat and my mother dried the meat. Father always told Mother to make lots of dry meat so that our gear wouldn't be so heavy when we travelled.

The Innu were always very hard-working. Our father was always going back and forth bringing all the caribou he had killed near our camp. He took the older children with him to bring back the caribou. The older girls also went with him because we didn't have many boys in our family then. I can remember the bountiful catches of furs we had in the country—beaver, marten, mink and so on. My father hung them inside our tent. He carried them in a huge bag and when he went out to get more supplies he took that bag with him. He never once thought about getting help from government social services when he went to get supplies at the store. We had a very good life in the country all the

time. . . . We never went back to the same place year after year because
we were careful not to overtrap an area. We moved once we knew fur
animals were getting scarce. When an Innu hunter finds plentiful traces
of animals in an area, he places his camp there. Innu were always on
the move, travelling in winter and summer.

As Tshaukuesh explained, neither the Quebec and Newfoundland governments nor the hydroelectric companies had consulted
the native people about plans to dam the great falls, which she calls
"a major crime against the Innu." Her parents were so unaware of
the projected development that they left their canoe, traps, tent and
other belongings near the dam site; all of it was lost when the water
rose in 1973. "We were really unhappy about what happened, all the
stuff that was flooded was valuable to us," Maniaten said. "Although
we were upset we couldn't do anything about it. The people had a
meeting and we all talked about how we felt, but in those years very
few people spoke English."

"I guess the government dammed the great river because money
could be made selling power and jobs were created," Tshaukuesh
continued. "But governments don't live off the land so they are not
hurt. On the other hand, we have been deeply hurt to see our land
destroyed, land which has sustained us for thousands of years. The
government acted like they were the owners of the land. This is Innu
land. They are stealing land that belongs to the Innu."

■

The Churchill Falls hydro project, with its output of 5.2 million
kilowatts, is one of the largest hydroelectric generating stations in
the world. A University of Toronto economist, Hugh Grant, estimates that $14 billion has been made so far from the project. Hydro-
Quebec received 88 per cent of that, with the rest going to other
investors and to the province of Newfoundland.

All of the profit made from flooding Innu land helped to dispos-
sess the James Bay Cree, according to Grant. "The huge returns gar-
nered by Hydro-Quebec from Churchill Falls have played a large
role in financing the James Bay hydro development," he writes. "The
conclusion to be drawn, therefore, is that the revenue obtained from
the exploitation of hydro-electric resources has deepened and accel-
erated the rate of future resource exploitation in the area."

In a book commissioned by the developers, author Phil Smith says
that no one suffered a loss of land or livelihood as a result of the

Churchill Falls project. (Smith, like the developers, seems unaware of the existence of the Innu.) The hydro companies have not compensated the Innu in any way for the losses they suffered as a result of this large-scale development.

Smaller hydro projects have been just as destructive to Innu communities on the lower north shore of the St. Lawrence River. Laval University historian Paul Charest says that permission to flood land was often given by a missionary without the knowledge of local Innu. In 1948, for example, a priest gave his permission for a hydroelectric project near the reserve of Betsiamites, on the condition that local Innu were given work on the project. No one, neither priest nor engineers, thought to consult the hunters and their families. "Their traditional economy never survived the hard blows it received," Charest says. "To give an example, half of 80 family hunting territories were damaged by the water diversion following these projects."

Hydro-Quebec owns ten hydroelectric stations in Nitassinan, on the Manicouagan, Outardes, Betsiamites and Magpie rivers. This power has made the company one of the lowest-cost producers of electricity in North America, and other companies have benefited as well. Alcan provides cheap electricity to its aluminum smelters in Arvida and Île Maligne from hydro power generated in the Saguenay–Lac Saint-Jean region, also part of the Innu homeland. Aluminum smelters, pulp and paper mills and other industries consume vast quantities of hydroelectricity generated on Innu land. As Paul Charest puts it, "The Montagnais' hunting territories have been used as the main water-works for the rest of Quebec."

The flooding that accompanied these projects has destroyed the river habitats of beaver, muskrat, otter, mink and marten. A species of salmon disappeared from the Péribonca River, and Atlantic salmon have vanished completely from the Betsiamites River, which once sustained a thriving commercial salmon fishery. At one time, thirty people on the reserve harvested up to 6800 kilograms of salmon each year. In 1962, they earned $100,000 in this way. The hydroelectric project that replaced the fishery provided only a few dozen short-term jobs for Innu workers, who received salaries below what the non-Innu were paid. Once construction at the hydro site was complete, there was no more work.

Reservoirs created by hydro projects also flood thousands of square kilometres of forests, obliterating fish spawning grounds and changing the feeding and migrating habits of aquatic life. And access roads built by the hydro companies have made it easier for non-natives to trap and fish, so that the Innu now compete for reduced resources.

Woodcutting and forestry operations in Nitassinan have also been destructive, driving hunters and their animals off productive hunting land. In the Saguenay–Lac Saint-Jean area, the demand for wood by eight pulp and paper mills in northern Quebec has led to the cutting of twenty-six square kilometres of coniferous forest each year.

Rivers used to move pulpwood are polluted, fish stocks depleted. Economist Hugh Grant says that hydroelectricity created on the Manicouagan River fuels one of the largest paper mills in the world, the Quebec North Shore Paper Company (QNSPC) at Baie-Comeau. The American-owned company supplies newsprint for the *Chicago Tribune* and the *New York Daily News*. Although Grant was denied access to the company's books, he has learned from other sources that the Quebec government has profited handsomely by allowing the American company access to Innu land: "After World War II, QNSPC purchased the 2,357 square mile timber limits on the west of the Manicouagan River such that by 1950 the firm controlled about 6,000 square miles of timber land. During this period, QNSPC was cutting approximately 200,000 cords annually and paying stumpage fees of $1.80 a cord plus an education tax of 15 cents a cord. Thus the Quebec government was receiving in the order of $400,000 annually in stumpage fees."

The Baie-Comeau mill, which produces 460 000 tonnes of newsprint a year and 100 billion board feet of lumber, is the only successful pulp and paper operation in the Innu homeland. Various other projects were attempted (notably the doomed Labrador Linerboard Mill near Goose Bay), but failed because of the high costs of producing and moving an acceptable grade of lumber to the south. Hundreds of square kilometres of trees were sacrificed in the process and the wood left on the ground to rot.

Mining operations have also displaced Innu hunters. In 1949 the Iron Ore Company of Canada (IOC), a consortium of a Canadian gold-mining company and five U.S. steel companies, was formed to develop the ore deposits in the Schefferville–Knob Lake and Labrador City–Carol Lake areas. Ironically, it was an Innu hunter who led geologists to the site of the rich ore deposits. Mistanapeu (Mathieu André) received the Order of Canada for his naiveté, but he says he had no idea what all of this would mean for the future of his people nor did he understand the destructive capabilities of the technology involved.

The Quebec, North Shore and Labrador Railway began to transport ore from mines in the interior to Sept-Îles in the 1950s. The railroad, designed to carry ten million tonnes of ore a year south from Schefferville, covered a 573-kilometre stretch, and at one time 7000 workers were fed and housed along its route. Some Innu sought work at the mines, but they were treated as marginal and lived apart from other workers in ghettolike reserves. In 1967 there were 700 Innu living at Schefferville; another group arrived with their tents to look for work in Labrador City but were expelled by Iron Ore Company managers because they didn't want an Indian "shantytown" near their brand-new town site. A small group of Innu families began to camp alongside a lake near the town, as they had done for generations, but IOC forced them to leave and prevented their settlement at another location.

Innu land had become the property of huge multinationals with head offices in the United States. The aboriginal inhabitants were swept aside in the rush to scoop up riches. Economists forecast that by 1980 the iron ore mines would lead to the creation of a vast industrial complex with scores of major industries—steel mills, aluminum and copper smelters, an oil refinery and a heavy water plant—and predicted a population of a quarter of a million people in the boom town of Sept-Îles.

The forecasters were wrong. By the 1980s markets for iron ore had declined, and the dream of untold wealth and prosperity faded. Mines closed and thousands of people were uprooted. In 1983 the mine at Schefferville was shut down. A year later 4000 people left the mining town of Gagnon, and soon afterwards 14,000 people, a third of its population, left Sept-Îles to return south. The companies vanished overnight. Hugh Grant's conservative estimate is that $257 million was made between 1975 and 1980, when mining operations were at their peak, most of it ($220 million) by IOC.

A few of the Innu forced from the land by these projects worked for a time in the mining towns as labourers and janitors. Although they are now out of work, there is nothing for them to return to since their traditional economy has been destroyed. The Innu in the two reserves at Schefferville now live in a ghost town, and the reserves near Sept-Îles at Uashat and Maliotenam are in a similar

situation. Teen suicides are common, as are alcohol and drug addiction.

Proposals have been made to open more mines in northeastern
Quebec, at St-Augustin, St-Paul, Coxipi and Brador, with little or
no regard for how these operations will affect the area's aboriginal
inhabitants. According to Paul Charest, Hydro-Quebec has spent millions of dollars studying the energy potential of rivers on the lower
and middle north shore of the St. Lawrence. The company has am-
bitious plans to develop the La Romaine, Moisie, Magpie, Nutashkuan
and Little Mécatina rivers. Charest's forecast for the area is not good:
"Hydro-Quebec has conceived projects to dam all the hydraulic ba-
sins of Quebec, even those of the most remote areas, in the Arctic
tundra zone. So the industrialization actually going on in a part of
the Montagnais territory could eventually extend to all the hunting
territories still used by the native populations of Quebec."

In 1983 Innu hunters from Mingan, La Romaine, St-Augustin
and Nutashkuan provided their communities with 108,700 kilograms
of meat and fish, while trappers brought a further $164,000 into
their home communities from the sale of fur, an indication of the
successful hunting that is possible in areas not yet affected by industrial projects. These figures, however, tell only half the story. It is
harder to put a value on what this way of life means to Innu self-
esteem. In the autumn of 1983, more than eighty families in Unaman-
shipit (La Romaine)—500 out of a population of 650—lived in camps
in the interior of their homeland, living as their families have lived
for generations, far from the alcoholism, idleness and serious health
problems that too often characterize village life.

A proposed hydroelectric project on the Lower Churchill, the second phase of the Churchill Falls hydro project, has been delayed by a
political dispute between Newfoundland and Quebec. The project
cannot go ahead unless Quebec gives Newfoundland the right to
put transmission lines through its territory for power sales to U.S.
customers. The Innu hope the squabbling between the two prov-
inces will give them more time to press for public recognition of
their land rights before more damage is done in their homeland.

■

When our interview with the women at Churchill Falls had ended,
Maniaten and Tshaukuesh wandered over to inspect a monument on
the site, a large stone with a brass plaque imbedded in it. The words

on the plaque say: "The Falls were first visited by John McLean in 1837."

Tshaukuesh remarked bitterly, "It was probably an Innu person who showed him how to get here."

The history packaged for tourists visiting the Innu homeland begins with the arrival of Europeans. The existence of the indigenous peoples is ignored, their heroic struggle for survival treated as if it never happened. In this version of history, the Innu are a shadowy people who mistakenly survived the Stone Age and are headed for an early extinction. The Innu are painfully conscious of this misrepresentation and talk of feeling invisible, as though they and their culture are of no consequence. Maniaten had this to say about what has happened to her people as a result:

So much of our land has been taken from us, we are being pushed to spend longer and longer periods of time in the community, it's like a gate has been put over us. We're told not to leave the community. They want us to live in shame so people from the outside can say: "They're just drunken Innu people, they're not worried about their land." But it wasn't like this not too long ago. When we were in the country it was peaceful, not like today, younger kids attempting suicide and taking overdoses in the community. The Innu people are poor while the government and others are making riches from our land, they're making lots and lots of money from our land.

In the film series *La Mémoire Battante*, Pien Vachon, an Innu hunter from Schefferville, stands near a huge dam on the Manicouagan River. Hundreds of kilometres of the land Vachon once hunted on are now underwater to create power for four hydroelectric generating stations (Manic 1, 2, 3 and 5). Vachon, saddened to see his ruined hunting grounds once again, lapses into a reverie and recounts a dream of happier times.

I was with an old man and my son. We were walking on a frozen lake. It was wintertime. In the middle of the lake caribou were seated; we wanted to shoot at them. All of a sudden I heard singing. The old man in front of me wasn't singing, neither was my son who was behind me, none of us were singing. I listened. The tree branches made a sound in the wind. The noise wasn't continuous, I still heard someone singing. I

finally located the sound. It was coming from below. The caribou were
singing. There were five caribou seated on the frozen lake, singing. I
couldn't speak. I tried to understand what they were saying. We kept
walking, following the lakeshore. We were still going to kill the cari-
bou. We walked along the shore but we could no longer see them. . . .
The caribou sing no more, they have disappeared.

"The Manicouagan shelters no more spirits, but kilowatt hours,"
the film's narrator adds. "The trees are no more a source of life, but
of dollars. Megaprojects, megaproductions, the myth of untold progress have replaced ancient myths of survival, sweeping everything
out of the way, leaving in its wake disorder and anxiety."

Sheshatshit

*"We, the Indians, just as the Africans and whatever race you are
talking about, must be respected and informed and consulted when
anybody wants to use something that we own, something that is ours."*
INNU ELDER

I don't know what I had been expecting to see in Sheshatshit the first
time I went there for a holiday in 1978. I was twenty-three and,
aside from one year of college in Ontario, had spent most of my life
in St. John's. The only Indians I had learned about in school were
the Beothuk, the ill-fated tribe wiped out by early settlers on the
island of Newfoundland. In our geography books there were pictures of Indians in tepees, and I remembered reading about the struggle
the Jesuit priests had with the Huron. I was very ignorant of native
people.

I had become interested in the lives of northern indigenous peoples after seeing old photographs a friend had collected in Labrador.
Images taken early in the century showed Inuit families posing stiffly
in mission clothes and proud Innu men at trading posts in Utshimassit
and North West River. I wanted to know more, so I eagerly jumped
at the chance to visit Labrador soon afterwards.

That first day in Sheshatshit was like being in a foreign country. I
vividly remember the little girls who peered in at me through the
window of my rented car, which was parked in their schoolyard. They
were chattering in their own language, not a word of which I understood, and overcame their shyness by approaching me as a group.
Whenever I singled a child out, she would back away shyly. One girl

touched my nose; she said something I didn't understand to the others, and they all broke out laughing. I was astonished that this foreign culture existed so close by and yet I'd heard nothing about it. Before long the school bell rang and recess was over.

I took a stroll around the village. My birthplace, Newfoundland, is the poorest province in Canada. Poverty when I was growing up was defined by the wooden row houses of my working-class neighbourhood, or by the lives people lived in remote fishing villages. In Sheshatshit I saw Third World poverty for the very first time.

Shacks that were supposed to serve as houses stood unsteadily on the sandy soil, many with broken steps and missing windowpanes. Roads in the village were dusty and unpaved. There was obviously no running water. I watched an old woman fill two pails of water from an outside tap and then labour up a steep hill with them. There was no landscaping to give relief to the ramshackle buildings. It looked as though bulldozers had just gone in and cleared a large space for the hastily constructed housing. The most prosperous-looking buildings in Sheshatshit were the school and the houses that surrounded the church, which I later learned were for the priest and schoolteachers. I sat on swings in the tiny playground near the church to gather my thoughts. I had many questions. I wanted to know more about these people and this place.

Sheshatshit is an Innu word meaning "the great outlet," and it refers to the channel where water from Grand Lake spills into Lake Melville, on the east coast of Labrador. The Innu live on the south side of the channel. A community of non-Innu (some Inuit, Metis and European-descended settlers) live across the river in the town of North West River. When I was there in 1978 the two communities were connected by a rickety cable car that transported people back and forth across the river. Today the towns are joined by a paved bridge, and a modern highway (one of the few stretches of paved road in all of Labrador) links both communities to Goose Bay, forty kilometres southwest.

North West River is a pretty town: the gardens are landscaped, the roads are paved and the homes are well built. It is the sort of neat little town you would find anywhere in Canada, while Sheshatshit looks like a typical Indian reserve. All the houses are the same, and they look as though they were built in a hurry. It is very rare to see anyone from North West River on the Innu side, with the exception of taxi drivers or someone making a delivery. The two communities live side by side as two solitudes.

The people of Sheshatshit are part of a very fluid Innu population with roots all over the Quebec-Labrador peninsula. The Innu did not see themselves as belonging to bands; that kind of classification was more for the convenience of non-Innu administrators, fur traders and government officials. Individuals shifted from one place to another quite freely, and today Innu families are identified by the trading posts their families frequented early in this century.

Archaeologists have uncovered evidence of an Indian presence at North West River that is 5000 years old. There is still some debate over whether these remains are Innu, but Innu presence in North West River has been conclusively dated back a thousand years. Despite this, the Innu were driven away from their ancient campsite about sixty years ago by hostile settlers.

At the turn of the century the Innu who used trading posts in the Lake Melville–Sept-Îles area were prosperous. Their furs were in great demand and a string of competing trading posts lined their travel route between the Atlantic coast and the north shore of the St. Lawrence River. Innu hunters and trappers had been coming to North West River to trade since 1743, when a Frenchman named Louis Fornel established the first trading post there. In 1831 the Hudson's Bay Company had opened a post on the north side of the river, where many Innu congregated during the summer, to take business away from Fornel. Another French trading company, Revillon Frères, opened up shop across the river in 1901. As a result of all this competition, the Innu were paid increasingly higher prices for their furs, a trend that did not pass unnoticed by the settlers (many former Hudson's Bay Company employees who had married Inuit women) and by some Newfoundlanders who began to realize they could make more money trapping the Labrador interior than fishing on the coast. Before long, the settlers had extended their trapping area past the Hamilton River valley to the extensive raised plateau that comprises most of the interior of Labrador.

The settlers expected to own the land they trapped. When they weren't using their traplines, they rented them out to other trappers for a fee, and they bequeathed them to their sons. The Innu were astounded that one person or family could claim exclusive use of the land and its resources. Innu livelihoods were threatened, and the peo-

ple grew increasingly bitter when they discovered they were not welcome on lands they had once travelled so freely.

At one time there was an understanding that the Innu could hunt
and trap on settler-claimed land, but this magnanimity dried up as
the number of settlers increased. To make matters worse, over time
the settlers changed their method of setting out traplines in a way
that took up more and more land each year. Traplines had once radi-
ated out from a central point like spokes in a wheel, but they were
later set out in vertical lines that stretched for miles. The Innu, on
the other hand, were scrupulous about conservation and moved to
different territories each year to avoid overtrapping or overhunting a
particular area. No individual Innu was associated with a particular
area, a fact that made it easier for settlers to appropriate native land.

Every year the number of settlers and their greed for land and fur
grew, creating more and more conflict with the indigenous inhabitants. It was a process well known to Innu in other parts of Nitassinan.
In 1866 the Jesuit Father Louis Babel reported that whites had forci-
bly taken the north shore of the St. Lawrence from the Innu, pushing the people farther into the interior and eventually hemming them
in all across their homeland. Raoul Thevenet, the Revillon Frères
manager at North West River from 1920 to 1921, complained that
the settlers were making the Innu poorer each year. In 1921 Thevenet
stated that the situation was becoming very serious and he expected
trouble between the Indians and white trappers to break out "any
year."

The issue of Innu land rights was discussed during the Labrador
boundary inquiry in the early 1900s, although it is clear that neither
Quebec nor Newfoundland ever took these rights seriously. Stuart
Cotter, a trader with the Hudson's Bay Company at North West River
from 1893 to 1901 and again from 1904 to 1906, complained that
the settlers "were trapping country that was really old Indian hunting grounds." He added: "Prior to 1893 the Indians were the chief
fur hunters and they brought the bulk of their furs to North West
River. At this period there were no more than ten half-breed hunters [English-Inuit] on all the principal streams which were wooded
and where marten could be trapped. During my stay at North West
River many young half-breed boys were growing up to manhood. All
the nearby trapping grounds were taken up, and these young men
commenced to go farther afield."

A settler named Thomas Blake told the inquiry in 1909:

I never heard of any claim of Canada until four or five years ago, when there was a dispute between some of the trappers amongst our people and the Indians residing in the interior in connection with the fur ground, which the Indians claimed to have been their fathers' and grandfathers' and they now wish to exclude us. For the last year or so it has been getting more pronounced and this year I heard they are threatening to shoot some of our settlers if they go in on their [the Indians'] hunting grounds.

No settler was ever shot in the dispute, however. The Innu tried peaceful means to resolve it. They appealed for help to their priest, to the Hudson's Bay Company and to Sir Wilfred Grenfell, a British physician and philanthropist who founded a medical mission that bears his name. Grenfell asked Newfoundland's Commission of Government to study the matter, but no study was ever undertaken. In a letter to Commissioner Sir John Puddester in 1929, Grenfell expressed sympathy for the Innu, but he was not prepared to suggest that the settlers retreat. "There is no question whatever that the competition of our white trappers means great impoverishment of the natives, and yet you cannot curtail the fur paths of increasing numbers of trappers." Instead of guaranteeing Innu self-sufficiency by respecting land title, the Newfoundland government handed out welfare relief, a practice that has continued ever since.

As the number of settlers grew, the Innu were increasingly unwelcome in their old summer camping place. Pressure was put on the Church and the Grenfell Mission to have the Indians removed, and in 1930, Father Edward O'Brien, the itinerant Catholic priest who served the Innu from 1920 to 1946, persuaded the people to move across the river, where he converted the abandoned Revillon Frères trading post into a little church. This is where Sheshatshit is located today. Many Innu are still bitter about this dislocation.

Forced to accept the loss of their trapping and hunting territory because no one was prepared to help them defend it, the Innu began to travel farther and farther afield to avoid charges of trespassing and theft on land claimed by new settlers. Their move coincided with a cyclical decline in the number of caribou in northeastern Quebec and Labrador. The fur trade collapsed as markets for fur in Europe continued to decline.

These changes were very hard on the Innu economically and physically. The more time the people spent on relief in the village, the more frequently they came into contact with diseases like tuberculosis that took many lives, weakened the Innu social fabric and resulted in greater dependence on Church, hospital and government charity, a dependence many Innu found repugnant.

An important witness to the dispossession of the Innu in the Lake Melville area is John T. McGhee, whose thesis was published in 1961. McGhee lived for more than three years at North West River, first in 1942 and later in 1951. He writes:

> *Since the Northwest River Band of Algonquians are not treaty Indians, de jure, they owned no land. . . . From their own point of view they once owned the whole area over which they moved, hunted, fished, picked berries, and trapped. In the course of time much of this land, including the better fishing and trapping places in the immediate locale of Northwest River, was pre-empted, or in most cases, simply taken over by whites, some of whom have not been a bit bashful about describing how they succeeded in getting Indians off "their" land.*

McGhee tells the story of several Innu hunters who were accused of stealing a settler's bear. They had shot the bear while travelling through the woods, but the settler asserted that it was his because he had set a trap for it.

In the 1940s the Hudson's Bay Company closed many of its small trading posts in the Labrador interior, requiring the Innu to concentrate their trading at North West River. They became more dependent on the company's credit and on welfare. In spite of all this, however, the people continued to spend up to ten months of the year inland, coming out to the coast during the summer to trade and visit their priest. At those times, Sheshatshit became a busy tent village with lots of traffic between the trading post and the mission. Once the trading was done, people fanned out along the river to spend the rest of their time fishing. Some of the older settlers at North West River say it was a beautiful sight to see the Innu emerge from the bush each spring paddling their canoes, looking happy and strong after a winter of living off the land. One elderly man told researcher Evelyn Plaice, "Awful good, them Indians, to help. They'd do anything for you! You'd go across to their tent camp . . . and they'd . . . offer you anything to eat, cup of tea, and anything." Another said, "Some of them would come from Nutashkuan, some more from

Musquaro. Some from St-Augustin, Mingan, Seven Islands. All up that way, with the little small children. Little tiny things, walking . . . very good people, awful kind!"

But to some of the settlers the return of the Innu was not a welcome sight. In 1940 a group of non-Innu placed their salmon nets on the Innu side of the river and then complained when the Innu set their trout nets in the same place. A law officer was asked to intervene. He listened to both sides and concluded that the Innu trout nets, which were placed much deeper in the water, were not affecting the salmon fishery at all. The settlers were warned not to put their nets on the Innu side of the river again. It was a short-lived victory for the Innu, however. Forces outside their control, and outside their understanding, conspired to make things worse.

By 1942 construction of the American military base at Goose Bay, a sandy plain at the mouth of the Churchill River where it enters Lake Melville, was in full swing. People streamed in from all over the Labrador coast and Newfoundland. Many trappers moved to Goose Bay to find work, and there was a huge influx of American servicemen. The population tripled overnight, and the town that is today Goose Bay was created. As David Zimmerley writes in his book *Cain's Land Revisited*, "In the space of a few short years, the fur-trade culture became submerged and engulfed by the onslaughts of the expanding war machine fabricated for World War II."

Non-Innu trappers happily gave up their old livelihood for salaried work in Goose Bay because fur prices had declined drastically. Settler Isaac Rich had this to say of the heady days that brought Labrador into the twentieth century: "We were jumped from the dog team age to the machine age, all at once. All the machines were new to us, the bulldozers, airplanes, tractors, everything was new. It was all excitement. Then too we were a people used to going wherever we felt like whenever we felt like it. But the construction company had signed us on and expected us to work regularly."

Soldiers on leave flocked to Sheshatshit in the summer to take pictures of the Indians and their tents. Some Innu tell of their fear of seeing black people for the first time; one middle-aged Innu woman shyly told me of a romance she had with one of the black American soldiers. In the fall most families packed their belongings as usual and went back into the interior, oblivious to the war and its aftermath.

Newfoundland's entry into Confederation in 1949 had a greater effect on the Innu than did the Second World War. By some quirk in the terms of Newfoundland's union with Canada, the indigenous people became wards of the province and not of the federal government as they are elsewhere. As a result, many programs that provided native people with housing and services in other parts of Canada were denied to those who lived in the new province. To this day both governments pass the buck when money has to be spent on aboriginal people in Labrador. Ultimately the federal government has paid most of the bills, but money earmarked for native people in Labrador is spent on the salaries of bureaucrats in St. John's and Goose Bay who duplicate work done by Indian and Northern Affairs officials in Ottawa. The Innu did begin to receive old-age pensions and family allowances from the federal government, and this must have seemed a windfall. But they paid a high price for these benefits. The people had come to rely on a growing number of European goods that could only be obtained with cash. Since they could no longer make this money by selling furs, the Innu became dependent on welfare.

In 1952 Oblate priest Father Joseph Pirson, a native of Belgium and a strong proponent of assimilation, went to live in the village year-round. He felt the time had come for the Innu to join the mainstream of Canadian society, to put aside their customs and traditions and become like the strangers around them. He believed this could be done by sending the younger generation to school, where they would be taught the same curriculum as children elsewhere in Canada. He knew that keeping the children in school would force their parents to abandon hunting and settle down in the village, and he thought this would be a good thing. The Innu had come to depend on the Church more and more to act as intermediary between them and the confusing number of non-Innu who now tried to direct their lives, and Pirson had tremendous moral authority, as illustrated by this account Tshaukuesh provides of the priest's visits with her parents:

The priest would go to my mother and sit close by her, talking for a long time. He lectured her on how to bring up her children. He would say to her, "If you take your children into the country they will be hungry and cold, it's better for you to stay in the community year-round, your children will be schooled." And of course he was obeyed because he was treated like Jesus. Many Innu thought it was wrong not

*to obey the priest. I guess we never knew or foresaw how the future
would be for us once we lived permanently in the community.*

There were other forces that weakened Innu resolve to continue
practising their way of life. Tuberculosis hit hard after the war, and
the Newfoundland government began demanding financial help from
Ottawa to pay medical expenses. In 1954 the International Grenfell
Association hospital was enlarged at North West River, and a fed-
eral-provincial health agreement for Labrador's indigenous people
came into effect. Now there was even more money available to rein-
force Innu ties to the village.

At the suggestion of the priest and the local doctor, the first houses
in Sheshatshit were built for the elderly and the disabled. Father Pirson
seems to have had a great deal of pull with government officials. In
1959, under his direction, a two-room schoolhouse was built at a
cost of $76,000, at a time when substandard houses were being built
in Sheshatshit for less than $2000 each. The effects of Pirson's influ-
ence on the people were gradual, but each year more and more Innu
began to abandon nutshimit for life in the village. In 1962–63, fourteen houses were built, ten of them inhabited year-round. They had
no running water and were heated by small wood- or oil-burning
stoves. Father Pirson continued to put pressure on Innu families to
stop going to the bush and to send their children to school. Maniaten
remembers the kinds of arguments he used.

> *The Innu were told that houses would be built for them and they had
> to school their children in return. It's like bribing the Innu. The Innu
> were not to leave the community when their children were schooled.
> Not even to go into the country while their land was being destroyed
> through exploitation. That was the idea the governments must have
> had. And many Innu were led to believe all this. We were told the
> children would eventually find proper jobs once they finished school. It
> was never like that. All those promises.*

Innu who persisted in taking their children to the bush were told
they would lose their family allowances, the small amount of cash
many now depended on to provide them with some necessary staples.

No attempt was made to schedule the school year around the Innu
hunting cycle. Classes ran from September to June, the period tradi-

tionally spent hunting and trapping in the country, instead of during the summer, when people were camped at Sheshatshit. Some men went into the bush without their wives and children but found this enforced separation from their families hard to endure.

School was one of the main tools in a program of assimilation, considered the best solution to "the Innu problem." This position was forthrightly stated in government agent Walter Rockwood's 1959–60 annual report from Labrador: "Indians must be taught the three R's, and will also need vocational training, but it would be naive to think that this will automatically solve all the problems overnight. As with Indians elsewhere there are deeply rooted psychological problems to be overcome before the process of integration is complete."

In 1963, two anthropology students from the Université de Montreal, José Mailhot and Andrée Michaud, spent a summer doing fieldwork in Sheshatshit. They noted that despite the Innu's long occupation of the Quebec-Labrador peninsula, the people seemed to have no legal right to the land where they lived and worked, and were treated as nothing more than squatters. "In the last century the Hudson's Bay Company bought from England the rights to all the land used by the Innu at North West River. When the Newfoundland government started to build houses for the Indians . . . they had to buy back several portions of land . . . from the Hudson's Bay Company."

Mailhot and Michaud recorded the decline in the number of Innu men who hunted and trapped during the period they studied. In 1962–63, fourteen men did not go caribou hunting as usual, nine men trapped without their families, and six gave up trapping altogether. School, poor health and pressure to give up life in the bush had begun to have a serious effect on the number of people who returned to the country each year.

Innu men tried salaried work, and some even moved to Goose Bay to live, but language and training were big barriers to their success in these ventures. "Most of these Indians do not know enough English to understand supervisors or bosses," observed John McGhee. "Even for very simple jobs, where the principal requirement is brawn, such as digging ditches and spreading gravel on roads, the same problem comes up, as it did when I got jobs for two Indians at the Airbase. In this case a white resident who had picked up a few words of Indian had to act as liaison between the foreman and the Indians. For this reason and others, they rarely last as much as a couple of months on the same job."

Life in the village created new strains on Innu social patterns. The Innu had no experience with the type of political, social or economic organization that life in the village and contact with non-Innu institutions required. The nuclear family replaced the extended family as the central social unit. When a man brought home a salary it was not shared in the same way meat had been shared in the bush. These changes created strains within families that the Innu were not equipped to resolve.

People suffered new health disorders. Sanitation is not a problem when small numbers of people frequently move camp, but it becomes a serious problem when hundreds of people live in the same spot year-round in shacks with no water or sewage facilities. Richard Budgel has studied government accounts of this period and writes:

> *In 1966 the Director of Northern Medical Services for the International Grenfell Association, Dr. Tony Paddon, wrote to Newfoundland's Deputy Minister of Health stating that gastroenteritis, impetigo, and related infections were rampant in the Indian village at North West River. Paddon said the Innu needed a clean water supply (this, nine years after the first Indian homes were built there). Paddon describes conditions in the village as "filthy", "perfectly horrible," and "an unsanitary mess."*

There was widespread confusion over what should be done for the Innu. Ignorance of Innu history and their way of life led to remarkable misunderstandings. Dr. Fred Rowe, the Newfoundland cabinet minister responsible for Premier Joey Smallwood's program to resettle Newfoundland outports, identified Innu tents as a major factor in the spread of tuberculosis and coined the phrase "tent syndrome," which he claimed threatened to cause the Innu to "go the way of the Beothuks."

In fact, in 1967 the Utshimassit Innu were still living year-round in tents and had the lowest mortality rate of all people on the Labrador coast, comparing favourably even with the Canadian average at the time (8 per thousand in 1960, compared with Utshimassit's 9.6 per thousand). Innu patients who were treated for tuberculosis at Sheshatshit were encouraged to stay behind in the village despite the widely acknowledged unsanitary conditions. In all likelihood, the disease would not have been as widespread had Innu families been travelling and living in the bush. But the newcomers to Nitassinan perceived life in nutshimit as too troublesome to authorities, and the Innu, worn down by the loss of so much of their land, by brainwashing by their priest and by illness, were losing their will to resist.

One government agent tried to help. Max Budgell watched in horror as Innu society seemed to be collapsing under the weight of non-Innu interference. He agreed with those Innu who believed they would be better off on the land, so he set about encouraging a return to nutshimit. He orchestrated an ingenious system of airlifts to take hunters and their supplies to good trapping areas, and it worked well until the Newfoundland government axed the program because it was considered too costly. When Budgell overspent his budget by $2000, he was told to collect the money from the Innu.

Budgell eventually quit his job with the Newfoundland government and fired this salvo at how the Innu were being treated: "The Indian is not dumb, he has seen the different men responsible for his well-being come and go, his position has not improved. Can the Indian be blamed for viewing the white man with distrust and hearing his utterances with cynical indifference?"

Each year the condition of the Innu deteriorated further, and more money was required to support them. Few government officials knew what to do. Government agent Rockwood wrote in exasperation:

> For the Indians, and many of the Eskimos, there is no easy short term solution, unless it be the solution found for the Aborigines of Newfoundland more than a century ago. They, the Beothuks, have been no bother since June 7, 1829. The writer does not advocate this solution for the Labrador Indians, but it would almost be kinder than to allow them to live off garbage dumps, and become a prey to unscrupulous persons. The Montagnais . . . have given up their propensity to die out.

Rockwood continued to puzzle over "the Innu problem," later writing to his superiors: "The Eskimos and the Indians cannot continue to exist as isolated minorities but must ultimately be integrated into the general body of our Society. A vigorous program in Welfare and Education, particularly the latter, is required to match the Health program already underway, and to prepare these minorities for the Society of the Future."

The Society of the Future was clearly a society with no room for a people like the Innu. Not only were their rights to the land disregarded but they were also denied self-determination, a right Canadian society purports to support for minorities in other parts of the world.

Government and Church authorities remain committed to assimilating Innu children. An even bigger and better school was built for the Innu in 1967. Peenamin McKenzie School, named after a respected Innu woman who was a devout Catholic, has an operating budget of $1 million a year ($800,000 for teachers' salaries). School attendance has dropped to 40 per cent because this Cadillac of a school fails dismally to serve the Innu as it might. Parents complain that their children are being taught the wrong things and want the curriculum changed to better reflect their culture. The parents directly link the emotional breakdown of their children with loss of pride and self-respect.

The government policy most regretted by Innu today is the enforced schooling of Innu children. "We longed to go into the country but the children were taught in school," Maniaten says. "The priest wanted the children to remain in school. He said that a school would be built and it would be a beautiful school. He said to the Innu, 'Do not take your children into the country because your children are getting smart.' And look at most of my children today. They finished school, but they don't have jobs. We were saddened and longing for the country but the priest was adamant, insisting we not go in the country because he was the one who taught the children." In the fall of 1990 angry Innu parents padlocked the doors of the school and kept their children home until Newfoundland government officials agreed to give them a more direct say in how their children are educated.

Many Innu bitterly argue today that little of what was done for them by the Church and Canadian governments was done in the name of philanthropy. Rather, they feel they were housed and their children schooled so that the colonial governments could move in and develop Innu land. In the 1960s, though, the Innu did not know much about colonialism nor about how it was affecting them. Despite what was happening around them, some still looked to the future with optimism.

"Not the Government's Children"

"They came to us and called us savages and sought to change us. Now they can really call us savages."

AN INNU WOMAN

By 1970, most Innu children in Sheshatshit were attending school regularly and most families had new houses, which were little more than small, uninsulated shacks with two bedrooms, a kitchen and "bathrooms" that lacked toilets. Only the non-Innu elite—teachers and clergy—were provided with running water.

Life in the village was not at all what the Innu had thought it would be. The first winters seemed more desolate than they had ever been in nutshimit. There was no planning done for the new community and no consultation with the people for whom the houses were built. Government officials operated from the racist assumptions that the Innu did not know what was best for them and that any house was better than the tents the people had lived in for thousands of years. Bureaucrats in St. John's spent federal government money as they saw fit, and decisions were made on the basis of expediency.

Innu expertise in choosing a good dwelling site for the subarctic climate was overlooked while southern contractors, eager to make their money and leave, bulldozed trees indiscriminately. As a result, flimsy houses were built in neat, tidy rows on a hillside overlooking the river, with nothing to shelter them from bitter winter winds. In the bush, family connections determine where Innu tents are located, yet such factors were disregarded when the first homes were built in Sheshatshit.

Water had to be hauled by hand uphill from the priest's house. Lack of sewage facilities for the 600 residents of this new town created a health hazard and caused the smell of feces to permeate the village when the snow melted in spring.

Once the Innu had been housed it was easier for the government to control them. A people with strong ties to the animals and the land found themselves abruptly cut off from what had once meant so much to them. Their life on the land became criminal; new hunting and fishing laws were enforced with great vigour. And, as anthropologist James Ryan has written, from the 1930s on Innu families received more financial incentives to stay in the village than to go out hunting. "Those who stayed by the mission throughout the winter would receive a steady cash income, while those who travelled into the bush would obtain an outfit [of supplies] . . . [which] amounted to considerably less than the regular welfare payments." Newfoundland welfare officials even threatened to withhold federal family allowance cheques if parents did not send their children to school.

The Innu residents of Sheshatshit now had to purchase all their food. Reliance on cash was something new to them, and people had a hard time managing money. The small amount that came from welfare, family allowances and pension cheques was often spent before new cheques arrived. Children and adults went hungry for days until the priest or store manager granted them credit. Stripped of their autonomy and the pride they once enjoyed by providing for their own families, many hunters turned to alcohol.

Sebastian Pastitshi's family moved from a tent into a house in 1968, and Pastitshi says that's when his troubles began.

I was born and raised in the country. I was happy then. No one tried to stop me from living the life I wanted. My family was in the country the whole year round, and we never had to eat store-bought food. I ate all sorts of good country food.

The Innu were free before, they could hunt anything they wanted, they weren't stopped. Now you make a little trek to go hunting and the police are on your back. Nowadays we Innu hunters are reluctant because we are scared of what might happen to us. We turn to alcohol.

Many are like that. I am like that. I have been drinking now for twenty years. I've been in this house for twenty-one years.

When I am in Sheshatshit I have a multitude of problems. I can't hunt, I don't like being there. It's not the same feeling as when I'm in the bush where all my problems seem to go away. When I'm in Sheshatshit my problems reappear, I feel emotionally troubled.

Once a respectable and proud people, the Innu now became the objects of local derision. When the people crossed the river to get food, welfare, health care and other services, settler children jeered at them, and many recent newcomers to Labrador stared curiously, even fearfully, at the impoverished Indians. Some of the older settler families, who were accustomed to seeing the Innu in better times, felt a sense of futility as they watched the rapid deterioration; others were complacent. Many said that what was happening was inevitable: the Innu had to join the twentieth century and there was no gentler way to make them do it.

School textbooks confirmed what Innu children were hearing from their neighbours—that their parents were backward and poor, their way of life impractical and primitive. A kind of collective depression took hold in Sheshatshit as people saw little hope of improving their situation. Now their lives were controlled by institutions and individuals who, however well meaning, instilled fear and self-loathing in Innu hearts. Social workers and police delved into the most intimate details of family life and made decisions, including the removal of children for adoption outside Sheshatshit, without consulting respected elders and relatives. Most Innu adults could not speak English and were therefore unable to communicate with the authorities who were suddenly controlling so many aspects of their lives. None of these authorities, not even social workers or teachers, bothered to learn Innu-aimun.

Perhaps the starkest effect of forcing the Innu from their land was observed by Montreal anthropologist Remi Savard. When the Innu of Pakuat-shipit, near St-Augustin, gave up their nomadism and moved into houses in 1972, all their newborn children died. There is no ready explanation for this; Savard suspects it had to do with poor sanitation and collective despair. Dr. Kay Wotten, a community medicine specialist who lived for a time on the Labrador coast, says the higher mortality and illness rate occurred because the Innu were "forced to live on reservations or in settlements with inadequate sanitation and housing; left without traditional medicine, which was scorned and rejected by Whites, and provided with a diet poorly suited to their needs."

The effects of year-round life in Sheshatshit were exacerbated by Newfoundland game laws, which are the most restrictive in Canada. The province persists in treating its aboriginal inhabitants "like any other Newfoundlander," and that means the Innu must abide by laws that apply to sports hunters and anyone else who might want to snare the occasional rabbit or hunt a moose on the island. Newfoundland's hunting laws also affect Innu on the Quebec side of the border.

In February 1990 I sat in court in Goose Bay when a hunter from Pakuat-shipit, his wife and two sons, and a third young man were tried for illegal hunting. Before their court appearance Jean-Baptiste Malec and his family had spent a night in the Goose Bay lockup. They came into court looking tired and frustrated. Malec wore knee-length caribou skin moccasins, which were stained with blood. His face was weather-worn; this was indisputably a man who had spent his life on the land. His family seemed confused as they filed into their seats in front of the judge. The thirteen caribou they intended to bring back to share with their community were confiscated by police, along with skidoos, rifles, furs and traps. A woman from Sheshatshit sat beside me in court, and when the judge announced that the hunters' goods would be held until their trial months later, she turned to me and said: "The judge has just sentenced that man to many months of heavy drinking."

The Innu risk arrest every time they go out on the land. Once I accompanied a friend who was distributing meat that had been flown in from one of the bush camps to relatives in Sheshatshit. People were so excited to get these bundles of fresh meat that it felt like Christmas. As we rounded a corner in the village we saw an R.C.M.P. truck, and my friend ordered me to cover the meat bundles with my coat. Only then did I realize that what we had been doing was against the law.

The game laws are enforced in the name of conservation, but the Innu find the government's position hypocritical. Conservation was not a consideration when the land was flooded to create hydroelectricity from the mighty Churchill Falls, and it never seems to be a factor when great sums of money can be made off the land.

The province's wildlife regulations display incredible insensitivity to the Innu way of life. Newfoundland is one of the few places in

Canada where it is illegal to hunt porcupine—and one of the few places with a people who like to eat it. Provincial wildlife authorities admit there are no studies that suggest the porcupine population is in any danger, yet the law remains on the books and the Innu continue to face prosecution for eating a favourite food.

Sheshatshit hunter Shinipesh looks over his shoulder in fear every time he does anything he and his ancestors once did freely in nutshimit. He says:

> They even stop us from cutting trees for use as firewood. Not only that, Innu are heavily regulated from all kinds of things. It's only after we have bought the proper licence, then we could get wood heat for our homes. Sometimes you are brought to court. I was in court once for cutting wood. To me that wasn't necessary because I don't waste wood. I use wood to heat my home. I agree with being incarcerated for committing a crime but cutting wood to heat my home is no crime at all. It's also very wrong to incarcerate me for hunting. It's wrong to put me in jail for hunting, it has always been my way of life.

It is clear that the government does not value the life of native hunters in the same way it does the subsistence life of a Newfoundland inshore fisherman, for example. When Newfoundland joined Canada in 1949, an exemption was made in the Canadian Wildlife Act to allow outport Newfoundlanders to kill as many "turrs" (a seabird considered a delicacy) as they wanted. No such exemptions have been made for the Innu. Maniaten watched what happened shortly after Sheshatshit was founded.

> Even in the community out in the open river here, there were many canoes with Innu going after ducks and geese before the authorities put a stop to that, the same with caribou hunting. Many hunters would bring out the caribou meat to their families but the government stopped that too. They were jealous because the Innu were still hunting caribou. People nowadays are reluctant to go into the country because they're up against all kinds of game laws. What we always hunted is now off-limits to us because of government restrictions. And when the Innu go out hunting along the brooks, along the road, there are cabins there owned by English people. They always want to be the first to hunt in areas where the Innu have always hunted.

The restrictions drove Maniaten's husband to drink, and he died prematurely as a result.

The Innu are, in fact, a colonized people: their lives have been taken over by others. Their land rights are consistently ignored and violated. In Labrador, the descendants of European fishermen now dictate how the Innu must live. Powerlessness, loss of control, and spiritual and cultural impoverishment are facts of life today in Sheshatshit.

Sociologist Bill Horswill uses the term "anomie" to describe what cultures like the Innu have gone through in the last century. He defines it as "the emotionally and morally devastating experience of losing one's traditional values and beliefs, yet without gaining a meaningful new set in exchange."

Franz Fanon, a psychiatrist born in Martinique, writes of the psychological pressures created by colonialism in his book *The Wretched of the Earth*. He says that when a nationality is denied the right to its own cultural expression, mental confusion and anxiety follow. "Because it is a systematic negation of the other person and a furious determination to deny the other person all attributes of humanity," Fanon writes, "colonialism forces the people it dominates to ask themselves the question constantly: 'In reality, who am I?' " He says one cannot deny a distinct people their language, culture and traditions without causing psychological harm. "The negation of the native's culture, the contempt for any manifestation of culture, whether active or emotional, and the placing outside the pale of all specialized branches of organization, contribute to broad aggressive patterns of conduct in the native." Violence is created, Fanon says, when the native person sees his own "social forms disintegrating before his eyes," and because "the settler considered him to be an animal and treated him as such."

The Innu, like people elsewhere who have been colonized, are self-destructing at an alarming rate. The Goose Bay Correctional Centre, as the local jail is euphemistically known, is filled with Innu and Inuit prisoners. Most of their crimes were committed under the influence of alcohol. Spousal abuse and child abuse are common, and the suicide rate, particularly among youths, is extraordinarily high. As Franz Fanon points out, colonialism "depersonalizes" the individual and destroys indigenous social structures so that the colonizers can take over native lands successfully. "Railways across the bush, the draining of swamps and a native population which is non–existent politically and economically, are in fact one and the same thing," he says.

Alcohol abuse swept through Sheshatshit like a brushfire in the 1970s and is now an ingrained feature of daily life. A kind of cultural and spiritual schizophrenia has been created. People who are respected hunters and survivors in the country are often the most despised drunks in the village. Many Innu who were raised in the bush say they are themselves only when they are back on the land. Shinipesh describes his experiences:

> *I would go everywhere around the community from house to house looking for alcohol, knocking on doors. Sometimes I would find it around somebody's place and many times, when I overdrink, I would go home looking for food to eat, country food, but it would rarely be there. And when I don't have this my wife and I fight and shout at my children. This is the main reason I don't like the community life. Because I know once I am in the country I never have to shout at my wife, and when I go hunting all day for my children, I come home and everything I want is there and this is not the same in the community. My father didn't need alcohol in the country, and the same with me. I want my children to have a good lifestyle in the country.*

Shinipesh was drinking when he decided to take his skidoo out onto the soft ice between North West River and Sheshatshit some years ago. The snowmobile fell through the ice and his daughter, who was riding with him, was drowned. Her body was never recovered. Shinipesh became almost hysterical with remorse and grief, and he may never recover from the guilt.

Many diseases, including measles, chicken pox and tuberculosis, have hit the Innu in epidemic proportions since European contact. But alcoholism is even more destructive, because it is passed on from one generation to another. Family life has become dysfunctional, and Innu children grow up without the inner strength they need to resist the temptation to deaden their own pain and unhappiness with alcohol.

In the 1970s the message from priests, school officials, store managers, the R.C.M.P., welfare officers and medical professionals was hard to ignore—they said the Innu way of life was a thing of the past. This is what forty-year-old Raphael Gregoire heard at school.

With the school they taught us all the wrong things about being people. First we were taught to forget about our language, to accept the white man's language in order to be able to function at their level, and they told us to abandon a lot of things our old people have taught us.

I was the first student with another young fellow to go to high school in St. John's. The person that handled us said, "You're going to the white man's country and you'll have to do things that they do. At mealtimes you have to act a certain way." One of the things that stuck in my mind was that he told us we had to speak English. "You have to forget about talking in your language because these people will be offended if you speak your language in their presence." I've never forgotten that, you know, being told, "Forget who you are and try to be what the other people want you to be," and I could never accept that.

It's one of the things that still holds very true for the school located in our community today. Young Innu are being encouraged to abandon their culture because it's not a good enough culture. The good enough culture is the white culture and that is the culture you should be following.

I haven't really been a part of the kind of life that my father used to live when he took his family into the bush to survive by living off the land. I won't be able to do that because I was forced to go to school until I was sixteen years old and then I went to university and I've worked all the time since then. I feel pretty inadequate that I am not able to be an Innu, a true Innu.

In the mid-1970s the Innu themselves realized that something drastic had to be done to alleviate the crisis. They demanded that some of the money provided for community services in Sheshatshit be used to airlift families into the bush for extended periods each year. It was their first exercise of self-government, and this program continues today. Residents of Goose Bay criticize the money spent on the airlift, but they overlook the fact that the Innu now have to travel greater distances to find wildlife.

"The daily life of some people in Sheshatshit," Raphael Gregoire says, "is doing nothing at all most of the time. And when they're doing nothing they're mostly drinking to get away from the boredom. You see almost daily people just walking around aimlessly with no purpose in life. That's mostly what this community is."

The promises that settlement life would be better for her children have a hollow ring for Maniaten today. "Look at the young people who finished school," she says. "Do they have proper jobs? We were told once they finished school they would have jobs right away. Instead my children were robbed of their way of life. They were schooled to lose their way of life."

Rose Gregoire is an Innu social worker whose lined face bears witness to all the pain she has seen in the village where she has spent most of her life. Her compassion for everyone in Sheshatshit—she calls them her brothers and sisters—is great, but she knows that their problems are beyond her best efforts to correct.

"Sometimes a woman doesn't want to drink," Rose says, "but because she's frightened and scared she thinks she has to drink with her husband so she wouldn't feel it when she gets beaten up."

Like her cousin Raphael, Rose was educated in the village, and like him she suffers because she feels she has lost something essential to her well-being.

I always think about my mother, I think, "Why didn't I learn the traditional things from her?" Today I can't make moccasins, I can't make anything. That wasn't good at all. I feel very unhappy for not being able to learn the things that are traditional in our lifestyle. And I have always wanted help from the white people, I was always looking for help. I always wondered why I was having headaches, then later on I took pills the doctor gave me. I was sick from them.

I find that very difficult to talk about. I took pills all the time until I was almost killed from taking them. And now when I look back I believe going to the doctor was wrong, that's not where help should have come from. I very much preferred the help that I was getting from my mother when she was living. There were times when we were alone, we talked about things. She always suggested I leave the pills alone because they would kill me if I didn't stop taking them. She always asked what I needed them for.

I feel so depressed at times, I really don't know what to think. Sometimes I feel my lifestyle was robbed from me. And then you tend to think you are nothing, not a person and not an Innu.

The casualties of assimilation in Sheshatshit span every generation. Self-destructive behaviour is widespread. The story is the same everywhere across the north where native people have been dispossessed of their homelands.

The number of Innu and Inuit in jail is far out of proportion to their percentage of the total population. Rose sits in the back of the court sometimes, watching and listening.

I went to court yesterday, the court was full, but no white person was there, only Innu. Only one white was tried in court. And there again, Innu who care for each other pity their people in court. It was very sad. Two Innu were sent to jail yesterday. None of them had been sober when they were involved in crime. They were drunk when they were involved in crimes. And one of those fellows said, just before he was put aboard the police car, he would always try not to remember things he would miss while away in jail. He said, "I will always try to sleep, not wanting to remember what's happening to me." I didn't get a chance to talk to the other fellow.

The suicide rate for native people in Labrador is five times higher than the national rate among Canadians and twice as high as that of other native people in Canada. Most often the victims are between the ages of fifteen and twenty-four. In 1988, twenty-one teens in Sheshatshit tried to kill themselves. "It is the plight of a people whose social framework has been gravely damaged," Kay Wotten writes, "and its fragile economy ruined, leaving the young with a stultifying sense of worthlessness; a culture whose customs and traditions have been mocked."

The Innu see only one way out of this crisis: they want to reclaim their self-respect and their dignity. "What we want is to control our own lives, our destiny on this, our own land, because we came out of that," says Pien Penashue, a respected elder in Sheshatshit.

We'll continue to be hunters and maintain our survival here. We will not live the way you want us to live. The English governments are a new thing, we did not get any money from them to survive on our land. The only money that existed came from the furs the Innu trapped.

At one time a group of us were charged for killing caribou that our families depend on. We were each charged $500 in the provincial court. We feel it was unnecessary and we were banned from hunting caribou for five years. Of course we didn't believe in it. A five-year ban would not deter us from hunting what our ancestors have always hunted. Our hunting way of life ends the day of our death. That's what we told the *judge at the court. It's unnecessary the way governments have treated us, bringing us to court every time we are supposedly breaking their laws.*

Out here in the country there's no such thing as persons hating each other. We all help each other. We, the elderly people, teach and pass down our skills to our young people. But life in the community is very different, people tend to hate each other. The young people that we teach like the way of life in nutshimit. And when they are back in the community, they are involved in all kinds of trouble. But out here they have a problem-free life, they are happy.

Nobody has the right to control people who have hunted for thousands of years. We have the right to control our lives, to control hunting. That's why we don't like foreigners controlling everything we do. We are not children. Yes, for a child who doesn't fully think what is right and wrong, there is a right to control, but we are not the government's children.

CHAPTER

7

One Family's Story

*"To attempt to civilize them or in any way hinder their nomadic
form of life would undoubtedly finally destroy the Labrador Indians,
for they would degenerate to mere hangers-on at the settlements,
losing their self-reliance and dignity."*

RICHARD WHITE, TRADER

In the summer of 1963 Tshaukuesh Gregoire was living in Sheshatshit in her parents' tent and working part-time in the kitchen of the Grenfell hospital in North West River. She was engaged to be married to Francis Penashue, the only son of Matthew Penashue, a widower known among his people as Kanatuakuet, "porcupine hunter." Like Tshaukuesh, Francis had been raised in the bush and was excited at the prospect of the great future that lay ahead. Once married, they would qualify for a new house in Sheshatshit.

Their wedding was a time of great celebration. Half the community came to see Father Pirson perform the marriage ceremony. When the couple came out of the church, guns were fired with great fanfare. The wedding reception was held in the school, where tables were laden with food provided by relatives of the newlyweds. There was salmon, partridge, porcupine and caribou as well as "English" food like cakes and sweets. The supper went on until eleven at night, then the tables were cleared away. Some of the old men played their drums and sang while people danced the Innu way, hopping around in a circle. Francis and Tshaukuesh believed, as they began their new life together, that they would have the best of both worlds, the world of their parents and that of the new society that had sprung up around them. Unfortunately, they were not given a choice. One world had to go.

Tshaukuesh and Francis Penashue had their first child in 1964, a son they called Peter. There were six more children after that. Tshaukuesh adjusted more easily to village life than Francis did. Her work had not changed significantly; she still cared for the children and prepared family meals. It was odd, though, to have the children in school all day. In the camp, they were in and out of the tent, watching their parents and grandparents at work. Tshaukuesh felt badly as her children toiled away at homework and puzzled over questions she couldn't answer. She missed nutshimit and, like others in Sheshatshit, had trouble feeding her family the new diet. She was used to preparing the wild meats she'd grown up eating and had been taught to cook. The only meat she could buy in the village was ground beef, hot dogs, chicken and pork chops, which were expensive and lacked the rich flavour of the caribou, rabbit, porcupine, beaver, goose, partridge and fresh fish that are staples in the bush. Tshaukuesh had to make do with high-starch foods like bread, macaroni and potatoes to fill up her hungry family.

Francis took jobs here and there, but there was only one job he really enjoyed doing: hunting. He occasionally left for the day and came home with rabbit and partridge, but it was hard to find game and firewood close to the village because there were so many people now living there. The welfare money was never enough to buy the things his children pestered him for—new clothes, schoolbooks and junk food. There was constant conflict in their home. Francis tried to persuade his wife to abandon the village and return to the bush, but she was afraid to take the children out of school. She heeded the priests' warnings that if her children didn't get an "akaneshau," or English, education, they would be swallowed up by the tide of newcomers.

Francis disagreed. He'd had an akaneshau education and it had only confused him. Whenever he thought of his years in school, powerful emotions engulfed him—disturbing feelings of self-hatred and disdain. He preferred to remember the freedom he had had on the land with his father, learning to survive in the cold, procuring animals for food.

Francis had been hand-picked by Father Pirson in 1958 to attend school at Mount Cashel Orphanage in St. John's. Francis's mother had died of tuberculosis, and his father was a respected hunter who still practised Innu religion. Kanatuakuet had trained his son in nutshimit and Francis was known as Kanatuakueshis, "little porcupine hunter." Father Pirson felt that if the fourteen-year-old could be successfully assimilated, he would serve as a fine example to others. The priest was very persuasive; Kanatuakuet could not have known how the experience would harm his son. Francis was sent to the city with another boy from Sheshatshit, but once they arrived at the orphanage they were forbidden to socialize with one another in order to prevent them from speaking their own language.

Life in the orphanage was highly structured and the boys had little time to themselves, a change Francis found difficult since he came from a society where children enjoyed great autonomy and were encouraged to explore the world for themselves. The boys rose at daybreak, went to Mass, ate breakfast, cleaned their rooms, attended classes, did chores, ate supper, studied and then slept until the resumption of the next regimented day. Francis was physically abused at Mount Cashel. On one occasion his hands were beaten so badly he was unable to hold his pencil for days. Francis was not surprised to receive such harsh treatment from the Church: on one occasion Father Pirson had beaten him repeatedly on both wrists with a heavy chunk of wood.

Francis was racked with homesickness. Besides missing his family and friends, he missed other things: the smell of caribou frying over a fire, snowshoeing, the thrill of finding a rabbit in his snare. He found the ways of the people around him strange and unfamiliar, and his own ways were scorned. When he returned home a year later Francis could speak English, but he refused to return to the orphanage. A rage burned inside him, and it surfaced when the pressures of marriage, children and the aimlessness of life in the village became too much to bear.

Tshaukuesh watched in horror as married life became a nightmare. The more time they spent in the village, the more Francis drank. Tshaukuesh was the most frequent target of his anger. She and the children sought shelter with friends or relatives in the community but were sometimes turned away. "Many times we were put up in a house where I wasn't related to the people," she once told me, "because my relatives were afraid of my husband and I knew this, that's why so few people would open the door for me. I was very depressed, saddened to see my children in that state, watching the fighting and beatings because of my husband's drinking. My young boys were too small to fight for me. But ever since they have gotten bigger they can stop their father from fighting with me. What I'm talking about has really hurt me and always does when I think about those days."

To escape her terror and unhappiness Tshaukuesh drank as well and the couple thus conformed to the self-destructive pattern of life around them. They drank every day, neglecting their children and their marriage. The only peace they knew in those years was when they were airlifted to nutshimit. When the village called them back—principally for their children's education—the chaos returned. Tshaukuesh stopped drinking when she feared her husband's brutality might one day kill her.

"He broke all of my facial bones around here," she told me, pointing to the right side of her face. "There are metal wires attaching my bones. My jaw was broken and one side of my face was pretty well injured."

Tshaukuesh spent a week in St. John's recovering from her injuries. When she came home her youngest child, a little girl, pulled away from her mother's embrace. "She was scared of my eye because it was still full of stitches," Tshaukuesh explained. "And it really hurts me to remember all these things that were done to me ever since I got married."

I find it hard to reconcile the Francis I know in nutshimit with the man described in the village. Once while I was camping with his family, Francis brought an orphaned beaver back for his young sons to play with. The little beaver delighted the children. Francis intended to put it back in the water when it was old enough to live on its own. I watched him patiently explain to his youngest son how the beaver lives. On another occasion Francis helped save my life. I had an asthma attack in the bush and my usual medication failed to assuage it. Tshaukuesh held me and tried to keep me relaxed as I gasped painfully for air. Since it was winter, Francis alternated his time between the woodpile and the emergency radio, cutting wood like a maniac to keep us warm and then shouting himself hoarse radioing for help. Although he is a heavy smoker, he didn't light one cigarette during the long four hours we waited for an aircraft to evacuate me to hospital. During the worst moments, he knelt with his wife and they prayed together for me. That's when I saw the teamwork that make Francis and Tshaukuesh such an inseparable pair in the bush. Their upbringing has prepared them to cope with emergency situations that threaten survival on the land. They know discord can mean the difference between life and death. On the land, Tshaukuesh and Francis are like a well-oiled machine.

Life in nutshimit is certainly a far cry from life in the village, however, as Francis explains:

In Sheshatshit all you do is get up in the morning, have a breakfast, turn on TV, sit down with a cup of coffee, or go out for a little walk. But when you're in the country you're trying to support your family. You have to hunt for food every day, you get more exercise, and you show your family how to hunt or set a trap, how to survive in the country. I know no end to what I have to do in nutshimit because the way I look at it, it's healthy, you're busy, you're moving almost every day and you're doing things, like cleaning a beaver or an otter, drying meat.

I show my children how to light a fire when it gets wet. If you're in the country you need to know how not to go through the ice or how to be careful in a canoe. I show my sons how to handle a rifle because when you're out hunting you have to be ready all the time, have your shells handy by you.

I don't have much to do down in Sheshatshit because I have more family problems down there. My kids will be out to the movies or to the game halls or anywhere, probably they may be involved in something like shoplifting because they don't have money to go around in the community. As for ourselves, there's nothing to do. Probably you'd have a drink with alcohol or something like that because you don't have nothing to do, nowhere, no place to go. There's always the clubs, or maybe have somebody into your house. But stepping in here [to nutshimit], there's a lot of difference, I find, it's quieter. I find it better to go in the country because I learn from listening to people. I learn more from my father about my culture in the country. I know how to go by myself and how to handle everything dangerous, like the axe, canoe and gun. This is what I have to show my family so they can continue when I'm gone.

Additional pressures were put on Francis when he became chief of Sheshatshit in 1980. The notion of chiefs and elections is foreign to Innu society, where it is the height of rudeness for one person to impose his or her will on others. After setting up the village, however, the federal and Newfoundland governments ordered that a band council be established. Elections were held, and a chief and band

councillors were chosen to act as the main liaison between outsiders
and the community. A working knowledge of English was required.
There was no place for the expertise and wise counsel of parents and
grandparents in this new government, because the elders did not
speak English. The segment of Innu society that had traditionally
guided and led the people was thus excluded. Apathy grew within
the community. There was no vigilance or supervision of those elected, and they rarely had a real mandate from the community since
voter turnout was low and loyalty could be bought with beer. It
wasn't long before unscrupulous outsiders realized that money could
be made from the Innu in the same way.

Businessmen from Newfoundland or Goose Bay wanted to get
their hands on some of the government money allocated for new
housing and services in Sheshatshit, but in order to do so they needed
the chief to sign construction contracts. Francis says he was often
invited to meet people at hotels in Goose Bay, and inevitably a bottle
of booze would be put on the coffee table in front of him. The liq-
uor eased his nervousness and enabled the businessmen to get what
they had come for—his signature. Instead of enjoying the prestige
that should have come with the chief's job, Francis's self-respect was
further diminished and he became more depressed.

Tshaukuesh and Francis have learned life in nutshimit is the anti-
dote to their family troubles, and they take their children to the bush
whenever possible. Francis regains his pride and his life has more
meaning because he is able to feed his family from the animals he
hunts. Life in the country is not what it used to be, however. Now
the long arm of the law extends even there, and wildlife officers are
regular visitors to Innu camps, instilling fear in the people who go
there to find some peace from the turmoil of the village. Nutshimit
becomes less and less of a refuge every year, and very recently alcohol began to be consumed in some of the camps. The oppression of
village life now extends to the bush, as Tshaukuesh explains:

> *Today when the Innu are in the country they feel very uneasy, they are*
> *afraid wildlife authorities will raid the camp, so they hide the animals*
> *they kill. This was never the case before. An Innu hunter always con-*
> *trolled his own hunting and was careful never to overkill the animals.*
> *He was happy because he had a sense of accomplishment, he was pro-*
> *viding for his family, and that felt good. His children were very happy*
> *because they ate very good food. How does the government think the*
> *Innu can survive in the bush if we can't kill the animals we find, and if*

our tools are confiscated? To me this is also a crime done to the Innu because we have been hunters all our lives and down through our ancestors. We were never treated like this before.

Tshaukuesh believes a vibrant life in nutshimit is the only way out of her people's disintegration.

Life is important in the country because you don't have to worry about the children, you know they're close somewhere in the camp. But in the community I start worrying. I worry my children will drink, then get involved in vandalism and have to go to court. There are so many things that keep me worrying all the time in the community. My children try to commit suicide when they drink, they give up on themselves, they're totally confused. Whereas in the country they're busy all the time. They might go in the canoe with their father, or hunt with him. They're doing something in the country. But in Sheshatshit the children find it so boring, there's nothing for them to do there. They feel the only thing they can do is drink alcohol to let out their frustrations. I find it helps my children when I talk about life in the past and when I take them to nutshimit to get them to see what their culture is really all about.

In 1982 Francis and Tshaukuesh's son Peter boarded at my home in St. John's, where he had been sent to finish high school. At that time, Peter constantly worried about his family. As eldest son, he felt responsible for protecting his mother from his father's drunkenness. One week Peter sank into a depression after receiving a letter from one of his brothers recounting events back home. He prepared to leave right away, but his mother wanted him to stay in school. That spring Peter began to relax as he learned that his parents were "going to the country"; peace was restored. He finished high school and returned home soon afterwards.

Thanks to the time Peter spent in the country as a young boy, and the many hours he spent listening to his grandfather's stories, he received a good grounding in his culture. Today he is one of the emerging young leaders of his community. He has given a lot of thought to what lies at the core of his people's troubles, and he articulates it well.

There's so much anger and fear in Sheshatshit. The people blame themselves for not doing well. But it's not their problem. If you put others in the same setting, take away everything they had—dignity, self-respect and an understanding among themselves—then everything collapses, and I think any people would collapse if they were put in the same situation.

When people go in the country, or as most of them say, back home, respect and the dignity is put back and everything they do is right for them. They go hunting, they shoot caribou even though it's illegal, and all the things that didn't make sense in the community start making sense in the country.

We're seeing more and more people go back to the country each year. But those who don't go in the country, it seems these are the people that are mostly lost.

Wife-battering, social collapse, all the child neglect we see in the community, derives from assimilation. But once people start putting their anger in the right place then I think it's very positive because it makes people respect themselves and start seeing that it's not them that is the problem, it's been brought upon them. As soon as you can start fighting back, things will start changing. That's why I think the days when people just let things happen to them are long gone, I don't think that will ever happen again. I think people have seen the light and I think they see that there is more light to come.

Peter Penashue and his brothers and sisters now struggle alongside their parents to restore what has been taken away from their people. But they have received no support from their non-Innu neighbours, because what they are fighting against threatens the established social and economic order in northern Quebec and Labrador. In fact, their efforts have been met with tremendous hostility, and all of the forces at Canadian society's disposal have been brought out to stop them.

The Turning Point

"The churches have two choices. We can choose to be advocates for the native people or we can pick up the pieces."
BOB BARTEL, MENNONITE CENTRAL COMMITTEE

During my stay at Penipuapishku-nipi in the spring of 1988, two social highlights brought everyone together in Sylvester Andrew's tent—bingo and Mass. Both events centred around Father Jim Roche, the young, energetic Oblate priest who, when I first met him that spring, had been in Sheshatshit for five years. He was then thirty-three years old. His diminutive stature is far out of proportion to the high regard in which he is held by the Innu. As I watched him come and go in the camp, it was easy to see why he was so well liked. In temperament he is very much like the Innu themselves: gentle and self-effacing. Despite the respect the Innu have for priests, Father Roche refuses to take himself and his position too seriously. Jim never lectures the people, and he strives to learn more about their way of life, rather than trying to change it as other priests have done.

Every day Father Roche made a point of visiting each tent, sitting quietly and unobtrusively, listening to whatever the people had to say. He was friend and confidant. He knit our little tent community together because he brought news with him—something he had heard on Sylvester's radio, or something someone had said that he thought was worth sharing with others. One day he came to our tent with a large hardcover logbook.

"Janet, I want you to tell me what happened the other day when the jet flew over your tent," he said. "I was not in the camp and I've only heard others talk about it. I want an eyewitness report."

He produced a copy of *Jane's All the World's Aircraft* and asked Janet if she could identify the jet that flew over our tent. He questioned her carefully, showing her pictures from the book and explaining the distinguishing features of each plane. After some discussion, he decided the plane had been an F-4 Phantom.

"That's five times our camp has been directly overflown in the last eleven days," he noted.

He then asked Janet to describe an event she had witnessed some time earlier. She had been collecting boughs one day when she saw something much smaller than a jet flying at great speed in the distance. Father Roche thought it might have been a missile. The military denies there is any missile training taking place, but Roche says he has seen fragments of missiles on the land. The priest carefully documents events like these to help the Innu present their case against low-level flying to government. He uses his literacy in English (something many Innu lack) to produce written documentation that carries more weight with Canadian officials than Innu anecdotal and oral evidence.

Even in the face of these threats to the Innu way of life, Father Roche always found a cheery note to end on, a joke or an invitation to "come to Sylvester's tonight for a bingo game."

Jim Roche was a bit sheepish about the bingo games, especially since gambling has become another addiction in Sheshatshit. High-stakes bingo games in Goose Bay are de rigueur among many Innu, a way to break out of the monotony of village life, and, for some, part of an effort to stop drinking as they trade an alcoholic high for the thrill of gambling. Father Roche participates in the bingo games in nutshimit because, like everything else in the country, bingo is different here.

After a large crowd has assembled in the tent and smiles and cards are exchanged, the young priest starts to call the numbers. Usually children get into a scrap and threaten to upset the numbers, which balance precariously on the bough floor. "Call in the R.C.M.P.," Roche shouts, and five-year-old ruffians pick themselves up and scurry over to the safety of their parents.

What makes bingo in nutshimit so special is that no money is exchanged. Instead, everyone brings some treasure from their supplies and offers it as a prize. Bingo in nutshimit provides another opportunity to share. The grand prize is often a pack of cigarettes, a precious commodity, for everyone's supply is low after a few months in the bush. Candies and other junk food are crowd pleasers as well.

The wealth of the camp was harmoniously and cleverly redistributed. If someone won something they already had in good supply, they traded it for something else. Everybody won something, and we all had a great deal of fun. The children provided a wild side show while Ben Michel and some of the other men kept up a steady stream of jokes, many of which I missed because the person next to me was laughing too hard to translate. When bingo was over families slipped out of the Andrew tent and made their way home under a night sky dripping with stars.

On Sunday mornings we gathered again, this time for Mass. Father Roche was dressed in a soft caribou-skin robe that had been made for him by Innu women. An overturned box covered with an embroidered ivory-coloured cloth framed on each side by two large candles made a fine altar.

The service was said in a mixture of English and Innu-aimun, and our Mass was linked to other Innu camps by short-wave radio. The community spirit that Mass creates was strong inside that tent. People came not from duty but because they wanted to celebrate a spiritual occasion together. Shinapestis, one of the hunters, knelt with one hand on a hymnbook, the other tenderly stroking the son who sat on his knee. In a clear, resonant voice, rising unselfconsciously above all of the others, he sang familiar Catholic hymns in the language of the Innu.

■

Father Jim Roche was born in Ottawa in 1955, the son of devout Catholic parents. His family, like those of many Roman Catholics of his generation, put a lot of pressure on him to seek a vocation in the Church. But it wasn't until he reached university that his own search for God began, taking him to a Trappist monastery in Kentucky, a religious order in Los Angeles founded by Mother Teresa and a posting in the Yukon, where he served with an Oblate priest. Roche returned to the south convinced that northern life was not for him. Somehow, though, he was drawn back to work with native people, and he came to Sheshatshit in August 1984 as a member of the Oblates. Roche didn't know what to expect and says nothing could have prepared him for his first few months as parish priest in this troubled community.

"Everything was completely the opposite of what I thought it would be, and in a very short time the full weight of the social chaos in Sheshatshit struck me hard," he says.

The first tragedy was the death of a twenty-two-year-old man after a Friday-night drinking spree. "I still don't know exactly what happened," Roche says. "It was kind of hushed up by the police, but the chaos was there and seeing what that was doing to the people, experiencing the pain, witnessing this night after night, really affected me."

Sometime later Father Roche got a call from police about a young woman who was threatening to kill herself. He waded into the river where she was standing to attempt to dissuade her from using the knife she was holding to her neck. He succeeded, but the toll life in the village was taking on him was immense. He might have left had Tshaukuesh and Francis not invited him to camp with them and other Innu families in the bush that autumn.

"Immediately I experienced the incredible difference of life in the country, where the people are truly alive, unlike what was happening in Sheshatshit, where life is being squeezed out of them," he said. Roche saw a people transformed. Families that lived in great distress in Sheshatshit were leading happy, fulfilled lives in nutshimit.

Later that fall, Innu from Unaman-shipit, near La Romaine, joined the Innu in Sheshatshit to discuss a joint protest campaign against the growing menace of low-level flights. Families from Unaman-shipit had had their fill of the bombers that spring and fall. One of their young women attributed a miscarriage to her shock following a jet overflight.

Roche says that as a result of this meeting he felt the seeds of Innu unity were sprouting. But he knew that it would take more than this rising sense of nationalism to counteract the individual self-destructiveness caused by Innu alienation from the land and their dependent position in Canadian society.

"It's the pattern of colonialism everywhere. When you undermine a people, their identity and way of life, you are going to have self-destructive behaviour," he says. "You are going to have alcohol abuse. That then allows for a silent kind of rage that's under the surface to be lived and expressed. All of it is actually quite simple, but the frightening part is, if you accept the answer [native self-determination] you know that change is required and it's the change which people most naturally resist."

Roche began to commit himself to working towards this kind of change. He brought his own brand of liberation theology to the Innu homeland. Fellow priests, politicians and non-Innu residents of Labrador have called him a freak and a troublemaker, and he has been ostracized in many quarters because of his outspoken political support of the Innu. Nevertheless, he continues to encourage Innu resistance to unfair laws and practices, and has taken part in actions that have led to his arrest many times. He was first arrested in March 1987 for illegal hunting in the Mealy Mountains, a beloved traditional hunting area.

The mountains had been off-limits for caribou hunting for more than fifteen years because of the poor condition of the Mealy Mountain herd. It had apparently been good sport for American pilots stationed at the base to make low passes over these animals to decapitate them and take the antlers for trophies. The Innu felt the herd had recovered enough by 1987 to allow for a limited hunt, but many in the village were afraid to defy a government order. One day a couple of men spotted caribou from the herd near the village and spread the word around. The community was starved for fresh meat. Jim Roche tells what happened next.

Pien Penashue wasn't living in a house then. He was still living in a tent all winter. I'd been in the village two years, but it was the first time I heard the older men talk about the pain of being treated as foreigners in their own land. They felt they had already lost so much. These are men fifty, sixty and seventy years of age, and they spoke sorrowfully of the profound changes in their lives. They were frustrated that they had to sneak around when they hunted caribou as though they were doing something wrong, when in their own minds they know it is the right thing for them to do. I think if I had any doubts before about the kind of pain that was in their experience, I didn't after that night listening to those older men.

The men met twice and then held a meeting with Innu women to hear their views. At the third meeting consensus was reached to do something people in Sheshatshit had never before done on a large scale. They planned to openly break the foreigners' laws by camping and hunting in the Mealy Mountains without permits. In March 1987, dozens of Innu families packed supplies and tents and headed to the mountains by skidoo to openly defy the hunting ban.

At first, wildlife authorities turned a blind eye to the illegal hunt, but residents of Goose Bay complained that the Innu were getting special treatment from police, and there were calls in the local press for the arrest of the native hunters. On 15 March police raided the mountain camp. Peter Penashue recalls what happened when he and several other hunters were stalking caribou and heard an R.C.M.P. helicopter circle above them.

We kept walking with our guns, leading the R.C.M.P. on a chase. We were afraid, we'd never done anything like that before, actually provoking arrest. In the past we would have hidden, but not any more, we're through hiding. It's time our rights are recognized on this land. So, when those Mounties finally caught up with us, you know, I felt they looked at us with some respect because they could see we were doing what we thought was right, and they could see we aren't afraid of them any more.

The experience of openly defying the authorities the Innu had once so feared spread confidence throughout the community. Women and children back at the "illegal" hunting camp also sought arrest.

"Take me," a young girl said to the police, "I ate the meat. I have illegal meat in my stomach." Yvette Michel sat on a caribou carcass and wouldn't get up when the police tried to confiscate it.

After the arrests were made, people began a campaign of civil disobedience. They failed to show up for court appearances, then refused to agree to conditions that would have released them from jail, and some even went on a hunger strike. The jail in Goose Bay became the site of regular candlelight vigils and demonstrations. In the end, Jim Roche and seven young hunters were sent to St. John's, where they spent three weeks in prison. It was a new experience for all of them, and it was a powerful one. The people were working together to resist unfair laws and by doing so were getting back their dignity and self-respect. Roche remembers an evening in prison when the lights were put out and one of the hunters asked the others to pray with him. The priest's eyes burned with tears as a chorus of gruff Innu voices prayed together aloud.

On 29 April 1987, Ben Michel stood before a judge in Goose Bay to defend what the Innu were doing. "We are a hunting people," he declared. "It is this form of living which lies at the core of our identity as a people, which gives expressiveness to our language, which animates our social relationships, and which for thousands of years breathed life into our people. Without exception those who have categorized our hunting existence as primitive are those who have not tried to live it."

The judge said that until Newfoundland laws were changed to exempt Innu hunters, his hands were tied. The men were found guilty and fined. Although the Mealy Mountain protest did not cause the Newfoundland government to change the legislation, it did accomplish something important: it encouraged the Innu to keep fighting back until their rights are recognized.

Jim Roche is not the first Catholic priest to help his parishioners resist Newfoundland's cruel wildlife restrictions. In 1975 a local wildlife officer, William A. Anderson, complained to his superiors that Father Frank Peters was advising Innu hunters in Utshimassit not to cooperate with him. The Utshimassit Innu had only been living year-round in the village for eight years, and Father Peters knew that respecting the wildlife restrictions would only exacerbate the crisis created by the abrupt change in his parishioners' way of life. He encouraged people to ignore the government's new rules and continue hunting as they had always done. At least two other priests have been arrested in Labrador because they were present at camps where the Innu were "illegally" hunting.

No priest, however, has gone as far as Jim Roche has. His activism has made him an outcast among non-Innu in Labrador and within his own church. He recalls the pain of meeting former acquaintances in the supermarket at Goose Bay and watching them turn away so they wouldn't have to say hello. "I am being shunned because I am identified so strongly for my support of the Innu," he says.

Roche has had to confront and violate the policies of many institutions he was brought up to believe in and respect. He says his life among the Innu has changed his outlook on many things:

It's not unlike coming to see all things anew. My own life, how I view history, law, how I view the concept of development, how I view education and even religion has very much been changed by my life and my years among these people. I believe that at the heart of the gospel by which I try to live my life is a call to justice, and I believe that what the people are struggling for is right and just, and I believe that the future of all of us is in some way dependent upon justice being sought for these people.

Roche says that his position is backed up by a pastoral statement published by a number of Canadian Christian churches. The "New Covenant towards the Constitutional Recognition and Protection of Aboriginal Self-government" states: "There exist in Canada many aboriginal peoples, and these peoples were self-governing with distinct cultural practices, self-sufficient economies, social structures and spiritual traditions." It urges government to protect the rights of indigenous peoples. Roche believes his actions are in line with this policy. "If you hold to the belief that this is Innu land, and that is at the heart of everything that is happening, then I think you have to act on that," he says.

In the months following the Mealy Mountain incident, the focus of the Innu and their priest shifted from protesting Newfoundland's hunting laws to resisting the escalating military presence in Nitassinan. The Innu reasoned that jet bombers posed an immediate and sinister threat. They feared that once the military was established in their homeland they would lose any chance of ever controlling what happens there.

The British started training pilots to fly Vulcan bombers from Goose Bay in the 1960s, but these aircraft were rarely seen by Innu hunters and their families in nutshimit. In the early 1980s, however, both British and West German bombers began to appear in greater numbers, flying at extremely low levels. In May 1985, Innu representatives from all over Nitassinan met and unanimously condemned the presence of jet bombers. Terrifying overflights of Innu camps had become a regular occurrence, and the Innu wanted them stopped. The Quebec government provided funding for an Innu delegation to visit Britain and West Germany to discuss their concerns but refused to get involved in the controversy, despite the fact that 40 per cent of the flights occurred on the Quebec side of the border and public opinion in the province, according to a 1988 poll, was against the practice. It was not an issue taken seriously by Quebec politicians, since only native people were affected.

Innu from Sheshatshit also travelled to various European countries and to the United Nations. They succeeded in finding allies in peace and environmental groups but had little success reaching the legislators. A turning point came when Canada signed bilateral agreements with Britain, West Germany, the Netherlands and the United States in 1986, allowing these countries to train pilots over the Innu homeland for ten years. Neither the Innu nor the Inuit of northeastern Quebec and Labrador were consulted, despite Canada's formal recognition of their land claims. (In 1977 Canada had advanced money to the Sheshatshit Innu to research their claims; negotiations were supposed to get underway once the research was completed.) After its deal with the Europeans was signed, the federal government ordered an environmental assessment of the project, thereby ensuring that the flights could be continued even if they were found to be environmentally damaging.

To make matters worse, Canada stepped up its efforts to attract a NATO tactical fighter weapons training centre to Goose Bay. The more the Innu learned about this scheme, the more their anxiety increased. Central to Innu thought is the belief that they are the caretakers of Nitassinan, placed here to safeguard the land for future generations. In their minds, Nitassinan and its resources exist to sustain life; jet bombers are built to destroy it. The Innu set out to stop construction of the NATO base because they felt it would forever alienate them from their land and thus destroy their culture.

There was much justification for Innu fears. With a NATO base, the number of flights would drastically increase, from 6300 a year (the 1986 figure) to 40,000 a year. Eleven bombing ranges would be established within 200,000 square kilometres of the Quebec-Labrador peninsula; three of the ranges were designed for the use of live weapons. A sea base off the Labrador coast would permit bombing over the ocean, and more than 60,000 pilot trainees would pass through the small town of Goose Bay each year.

The Innu had little faith in the government's environmental review process. It is administered by the Federal Environmental Assessment Review Office (FEARO), an independent government agency. FEARO appoints an Environmental Assessment Review Panel (or EARP) to study specific projects. The panels are made up of private citizens and experts in the area under review. The chairperson works for FEARO. As far as the Innu were concerned, it was the akaneshau seeking a way to justify the harm they were once again causing. Nevertheless, the people told their stories to the panel when it visited their communities in 1986.

Sheshatshit's chief, Daniel Ashini, was speaking for many Innu when he told the panel conducting the review that there was a lot of cynicism about what the hearings could accomplish. "We believe that even if you people determine, as we have, that the land where the military air combat training occurs will be made uninhabitable and will threaten the very survival of our culture, the federal government will ignore your recommendations and proceed with the military developments anyway," he said.

Greg Penashue of the Naskapi-Montagnais Innu Association (NMIA) told the panel that military expansion would "bring more non-Innu people along with non-Innu values and political institutions into Nitassinan, which will make it very difficult for us to achieve self-determination and to regain the kind of control over our lives that will ensure the survival of our hunting culture."

Father Roche told panel members that large sections of the Innu homeland would become restricted zones or be made uninhabitable by the military flight and bomb training. He pointed out that what was of value to the Innu seemed to have no value in the eyes of others. "Much has been made of the millions of dollars which would be invested in this area. This attitude fails to recognize that material well-being is only one component of a decent human life. Equally important is the ability of individuals to participate in the decisions that will affect one's life. This element has been notably absent in terms of the development in question."

"Whose lifestyles are more valued? Who as a people are more valued?" Lyla Andrew asked. "In the past, it has been quite clear that, as a people, the Innu have been the least important."

The panel encountered outrage and exasperation in every Innu village it visited. Ben Michel's mother, Manian, could hardly contain her rage as she spoke to the panel, whom she believed to be government representatives:

> Do you have any shame that you should come to our land and face us like you are now, requesting that we give up our land to you? We will never give it up. I am very angry when I see white people, such as yourselves, looking for us to give up our birthright. I am very angry today. How many times have the Innu come to you, for land, for anything? Even the Innu, in its despicable condition, in its wretched condition, never comes to you for anything. Do you hate the Innu, do you want to kill the Innu? You have killed us in many respects. We have nothing. There are no animals near us, and we cannot even drink our water, we cannot get wood without a permit.

In Utshimassit, William Katshinak told the panel, "We are hurt that there were no meetings held and nothing has been happening. I think it is too late for you guys to come around here. You are doing to our land what has been done in the past."

Martha Piwas, also of Utshimassit, testified: "People from outside native communities do not go to live in the country for long periods like the Innu. Therefore, they do not really know what it is like to hear the aircraft roaring over their camps and disturbing the wildlife." In the same village, Tshenish spoke of his fears that "all wildlife will be driven away, lakes will be polluted, fresh-water fish will not be any good to eat, there will be increased health problems."

In Schefferville, the panel heard that the Innu in that area wanted to establish a non-profit caribou harvest that would provide meat for the entire community and allow them to set up a tannery to produce clothing and other products for the Japanese market. Pauline Vollant said that these plans would be jeopardized if the jets exterminated caribou herds and Innu rights to their land were not soon recognized. "We have lived on these territories for a very long time," she told the panel, "and it's because our fathers and our mothers took care of the animals, the land and the water that we are here today."

In the fall of 1987 a delegation from Sheshatshit travelled to a bombing range one hundred kilometres southwest of Goose Bay. Father Roche went along in his role as chronicler, taking his copy of *Jane's All the World's Aircraft* to identify the types of inert bombs being dropped. The group knew there were risks involved: bombing practice would be taking place, yet they couldn't alert the military to their plans. A chartered plane flew them to just outside the perimeter of the range, since the rest of the area is off-limits to commercial aircraft. The delegation was forced to walk the rest of the way—a thirty-kilometre hike. They travelled through incredibly rough terrain, across rivers and over bogs. Roche describes the trip:

> *We went in there on a Sunday morning, flew to a little lake, and it was some awful walk to get in there. We walked carrying two weeks' worth of supplies plus the stove, tent, guns and ammunition. We walked and walked through the worst bush I've ever seen. Even Mary Adele Andrew [Sylvester's wife], who at that time was sick, would not quit, no sir. We walked Sunday, and then Monday and again on Tuesday. We set up camp and Sylvester radioed out to three other Innu communities to*

*explain what he was doing and challenged others to come. It was pow-
erful to hear from them the strong sense that they are ready to sacrifice
for the future, for children yet to be born.*

What the people saw on the bombing range shocked them. A military awareness committee had visited their communities with a cold
smoke device that fits into the palm of a hand, saying that only these
devices would be dropped during bombing practice. But what the
Innu found was something quite different, as Jim Roche explains:

*We saw two simulated runways ripped up in the earth and the walls of
earth that had been pushed aside were as high as the walls of this
building [a hall in Sheshatshit]. The earth was stripped and many
trees had been knocked over. As we walked into the range we saw
thousand-pound bombs which had been dropped and can knock down
very large trees. There were huge craters in the ground. I stood up in
one of them and disappeared from sight, they were that deep. So there
is a real sense of being betrayed, lied to; and each time we came to the
boundary of the range, and the Innu saw a sign in their language
indicating this was a restricted zone, they cut the sign down and flung
it up into the air.*

The Innu set up a tent on the bombing range and radioed a warning to the base. The military had little choice; they closed the range.
Innu hunters from Unaman-shipit who were camped nearby visited
the Sheshatshit delegation and complained that their camps had been
overflown twenty-five times that fall. Ten days later the group returned to Sheshatshit, eager to tell their community what they had
seen. Roche wrote a letter to a local newspaper, the *Labradorian*,
telling readers that the base seemed to be violating its own flying
orders, which state, "The only ordnance [artillery] authorized at this
time are inert practice bombs up to 25 kg in weight."

"It was not uncommon," Roche wrote, "to find [450-kg] bombs
far from the actual target site, leaving a crater twenty feet in length
and approximately five feet in depth."

The military replied that they had received authorization from
government to use the heavier bombs. Roche found little comfort
in this explanation. "This decision was made with no public discussion and without any environmental review," he pointed out.

The bombing range became the central focus of Innu opposition to the militarization of their homeland. They paid another visit to the range a year later, a visit that became the catalyst for events unparalleled in Innu history and in the history of aboriginal resistance in Canada.

A NATO survey team arrived in Goose Bay early in September 1988 to assess the town's suitability as a site for the proposed $555-million Tactical Fighter Weapons Training Centre. NATO had already chosen a site in Konya, Turkey, in 1984, but the Canadian government lobbied for a second chance to compete. The federal government provided $93 million to improve facilities on the base at a time when many in Labrador lived in shacks without running water and sewage. Newfoundland Premier Brian Peckford and International Trade Minister John Crosbie went to great lengths to convince NATO officials that Goose Bay was the best location for the centre. Crosbie told them, "It is indeed part of our new defence policy to promote the use of Canadian territory and air space for allied military training." He promised to spend more Canadian money improving the infrastructure at Goose Bay. "In short, gentlemen, we can provide an exceptional operational environment for the NATO centre, an environment in many ways similar to that of northern and eastern Europe," he said proudly.

For a week the survey team was wined and dined. An array of politicians addressed them, beginning with the mayor of Goose Bay and concluding with federal Defence Minister Perrin Beatty, who reiterated Crosbie's promise of financial assistance to upgrade facilities at Goose Bay.

The Innu also wanted a chance to talk to the NATO team, but their requests for a meeting were denied. Daniel Ashini and other community leaders were not invited to any of the public functions, nor was a visit to Sheshatshit on the NATO delegation's itinerary. Canadian politicians were determined that Innu opposition to the base would get no hearing. The Innu were angry but could not reach a consensus about what should be done. Then two Innu teenagers, Maniaten's eighteen-year-old son Eric, and Tshaukuesh's seventeen-year-old son Matshen, came up with a plan. They asked Father Roche if he would accompany them on a trip to the bombing range. They wanted to go, they told the priest, "to show the Canadian government this is still our land and to show them that we will never stop fighting."

A day later Roche once again found himself stumbling through

impossible scrub and brush with a load of supplies on his back. "Once
we arrived and the camp was set up," he recalls, "we were seen by
some of the aircraft practising over the target site, then most of the
flights began to stop. We had a camp radio with us and made communication with Sheshatshit."

A news release from Sheshatshit on 12 September 1988 alerted
the public and the military that there were people camped on the
range. Reconnaissance aircraft confirmed their presence, and the military called a halt to the bombing. The news release formally requested
that the bombing range land be returned to the Innu people from
whom it had been "illegally seized" and that no future bombing ranges
be constructed on Innu territory.

Many in Sheshatshit were encouraged, but they still wanted a face-
to-face meeting with the NATO delegation. On 15 September, the
last day of the NATO visit, word of a plan spread around the village,
and, despite miserably cold, wet weather, many people jumped aboard
open trucks and headed for the base.

Security guard Marilyn O'Dell stood watch over the entrance to
the West German hangar that morning. O'Dell looked on in surprise
as truckloads of Innu stopped in front of the open gate and then
began wriggling under the barrier, which was held in place only by a
rope.

By the time Sgt. Joe MacDonald of the R.C.M.P. arrived, more
than seventy-five men, women and children were walking towards
the runway. "I approached two of the Innu persons whom I recognized—Chief Daniel Ashini and Ben Michel," MacDonald remembers. "I asked them what they were doing but they just kept walking,
heading toward the runway with all the others. Other officers joined
me and I instructed them to arrest Ashini and Michel. There was no
resistance from these individuals. They went to the police car peacefully." MacDonald also instructed his men to arrest Peter Penashue,
whom he saw instructing the group to continue marching towards
the runway. (Tshaukuesh too was arrested, for allegedly kicking
O'Dell, but the charge was later dropped.) An alarmed base commander soon appeared on the scene. Col. Phil Engstad walked out to
meet the protesters, who refused to leave the airfield until they had
met with the NATO survey team. Engstad promised a meeting on the
condition that the Innu board military buses waiting to take them to
the Billy Bishop social centre. The people complied.

Engstad came to the centre some time later to say the survey team was unavailable, but the Innu threatened to go back on the runway, and then on hunger strike, if their demands were not met. Engstad went away once more, returning this time with the head of the survey team, who listened politely to the protesters. The NATO official was told that the land proposed for the training centre belonged to the Innu and that NATO would be joining Canada in an act of ethnocide by bringing its foreign air forces to Goose Bay. The man listened in silence, then thanked the Innu for their comments and left.

No one was sure what the NATO official had thought of their speeches, but they were nonetheless jubilant. The people of Sheshatshit had found a way to be heard, and they had begun to realize that their power came from within themselves. Tshaukuesh describes walking onto the runway as though it were a religious experience.

Once we had set our minds to it we weren't afraid, we had to do everything in our power, we had to take our protest right down to the runway. Going inside the gate made us feel like heaven is opening up for us to come in. And the reason we have to struggle is because we know what the future has in store for us if we don't do something about it. The struggle is for every Innu, the old people, adults and children, every Innu is a part of it. Everyone just rushed to the gates. It felt like heaven opening up just for a few minutes, everyone rushed to get in.

Sylvester and Mary Adele Andrew packed their belongings and headed out to join Father Roche and the two teenagers on the bombing range. They planned to stay long enough to shut down bombing for the rest of that year's flying season, and they knew that if they were removed by force other Innu families would take their place. Colonel Engstad told reporters that the bombers could practise elsewhere. But the Innu knew that the Europeans wanted a state-of-the-art bombing range and that the Canadian military establishment was embarrassed it couldn't assure them of the use of the one they had constructed.

Father Roche experienced profound emotions as he camped a second time on the bombing range. He began to understand that what was planned for the Innu homeland had implications that went beyond Innu land rights. "It struck me then what was happening out of Goose Bay, what was being rehearsed, meant destruction, death and violence," he wrote to a friend. The priest reflected on a saying

of Mahatma Gandhi's—that the "failure to resist, expose or protest
evil is to be part of it"—and he resolved to do everything in his
power to oppose the militarization of northern Quebec and Labrador, not just for the sake of the Innu but for the sake of world peace.
He decided to fast, something the imprisoned Innu hunters had done
after the Mealy Mountain protests.

The news that their beloved priest was not eating caused great
concern in Sheshatshit. A group of women made a trip to speak to
him and see for themselves what it was like on the bombing range.
Tshaukuesh was among them.

> We saw the damage that was done to the land. We saw the craters made
> by those mock bombs. Trees were damaged, bombs dropped on the pond.
> Some of the bombs were very huge that fell on land and in the water.
> Once we got back to the community we held a meeting. We told the
> Innu what we saw out there. There were many people present. At the
> outcome of the meeting it was planned that we would once again pro-
> test inside the fenced perimeter of the base runway. That morning we
> ran inside the gate.

Even more Innu participated in the second runway protest. On
22 September 1988 a hundred of them walked through the open
gates of a private aircraft company hangar and calmly strolled about
on the tarmac. They sang hymns and waved placards that said "NATO
Go Home," "This Is Innu Land" and "Save Nitassinan."

The people fell passively to the ground when military police in
riot gear and the R.C.M.P. arrived to arrest them. Two fire trucks
were also called to the scene to hose down the protesters if they
became violent. The protesters were dragged one by one to waiting
buses. One onlooker, Mennonite Central Committee worker Bob
Bartel, said Dutch pilots took pictures and mocked the protesters. The
Labradorian quoted an Innu woman who angrily told the Dutch air-
men, "Stop laughing. This is not a joke. There is nothing funny about
this." It took several hours for all of the Innu to be removed.

The protestors were taken to a local arena, where the R.C.M.P.
noted the names of all those arrested. People grew tired of waiting
for a promised court appearance, and one woman suggested to the
crowd that they end the waiting by walking to the courthouse themselves. Bob Bartel remembers, "The movement of the people was
uncontrollable, and a police officer roughly took the lady, pinned

her against the wall of the arena, handcuffed her and brought her to a patrol car. The people headed towards the courthouse anyway and entered one by one as community leaders called out their names." Sixty-three adults and fifteen juveniles were charged and released unconditionally until their trials.

As the protestors began to leave the courthouse they saw a strange procession coming towards them. The two teenagers were back from the bombing range, their faces burned after days of walking through the bush. An emaciated Jim Roche was with them, accompanied by Greg Penashue, who had carried the priest out of the bush to a waiting airplane. "The reunion in front of the courthouse was a moving one, with applause and tears," Bartel recalls.

Later that day an Innu camp sprang up on base property, just beyond the fenced perimeter of the main runway. It was a camp somewhat in the style of Greenham Common—a peace camp founded by women to protest the presence of American cruise missiles housed at an RAF base outside London, England—although the Innu did not know anything about Greenham Common or the peace movement at that time. Over two hundred people, a quarter of Sheshatshit's population, began living in the camp. Base officials posted military police nearby to keep twenty-four-hour surveillance, but people came and went as they pleased, undisturbed by the scrutiny. Raoul Vollant, an Innu reporter from Sept-Îles, began broadcasting news of what was happening to Innu communities on the north shore of the St. Lawrence River. Before long the chief of Ekuanitshit, a north-shore reserve, arrived with a delegation to lend support.

Reaction to these events among the non-Innu in Goose Bay was quite negative, not surprising given the coverage CBC provided. Local television made the Innu look violent and unruly. Father Roche was portrayed as uncooperative since he had insisted on being visited on the bombing range by his own doctor rather than a military one, and the CBC broadcast comments from the Catholic chaplain on base who said Roche had become "a victim of the people he served."

When I next saw Father Roche he had been fasting for two weeks and was living in a tent with Ben Michel's parents at the runway camp. He had lost a lot of weight; his jaw and cheek bones protruded. Shocked by his appearance, I challenged him, thinking he was going too far. "Are you trying to make a martyr of yourself?" I asked.

The young priest smiled back at me weakly and replied, "This is not a fast where I'm threatening to die if nothing is done to change the situation. It's a prayer fast, a sacrifice for my Innu friends that the people be strong, that they be united, that they be peaceful in their actions."

Father Roche's fast, the occupation of the bombing range and the runway demonstrations brought the Innu together in a way that few ever thought possible. The priest was eventually nursed back to health by Innu elders who had experience with starvation and knew exactly what he should begin to eat. They started him on broths and small quantities of animal grease and fat. I knew he was well the day I peered inside the Michel tent and saw him ravenously eating a breakfast of fried salmon and boiled rabbit as Manian and Shimun Michel looked on in delight.

There was a noticeable improvement in the Innu as well. The people were proud and defiant. The runway camp became a vital community as Innu resistance grew stronger. There was no turning back now that they had come so far in their struggle to preserve their homeland for future generations of Innu hunters.

Outwitting the Akaneshau

"They [the Innu] have been here for 9000 years and they still can't earn their own living."

HANK SHOUSE, FORMER MAYOR OF GOOSE BAY

I had joined the Innu at their runway camp on 23 September 1988. I was once again living in the Michel tent, but the setting this time was incongruous; there were moments when it was almost surrealistic. The camp was set up beside a road that bordered one of the main runways in a deciduous forest of birch and aspen trees, a reminder of the natural beauty that had been destroyed to build the base. The site on which the base now stood had once been a popular summer camp for Innu families and a great place to pick berries.

The entrance to the camp was signalled first by the presence of a police surveillance car, then by a sign that assured me the Innu sense of humour was still intact. "No Trespassing by Order of the Innu Defence Minister," it warned. Buried in amongst the trees, a gathering of about twenty or thirty tents sat under a bright canopy of fall leaves that glittered in the sunlight like copper and gold. Caribou roasted on outdoor spits, people chopped wood, Innu elders sat around serenely talking and smoking their pipes. People spoke about the usual things—the weather, the likely prospect of a successful fall caribou hunt—until conversation was forced to stop midsentence by the deafening roar of jet bombers taking off from the nearby runway. Then, as though nothing had happened, the thread of conversation was picked up again. The Innu were living at the runway camp as though in nutshimit, yet alongside the very technology they were fighting to get rid of.

I arrived in the camp the day after the Innu's second entry onto the runway, and people were still buzzing with excitement. Ben Michel chuckled as he told me how they had openly walked through Labrador Airways' hangar and infuriated the owner, who is a staunch supporter of military expansion.

We were awakened at night by the eerie sound of huge cargo planes as they sat on the runway with their engines idling. The ground shook when they eventually took to the air. Occasionally guns could be heard firing at a nearby shooting range.

Innu children made a game of throwing stones at jet bombers that passed overhead, and, more disturbingly, fashioned guns out of sticks to aim at the pilots. Their parents spoke of nonviolence and peaceful resistance, but the children seemed too young to understand this. They just knew that their parents were sad and angry, and these machines were to blame. School was held each day in a tent, taught by an Innu teacher who had joined the protest despite warnings from the school board that she might be fired.

Sheshatshit was a ghost town; anyone not at the runway camp was in nutshimit, and many even abandoned their bush camps to join the protest. A common purpose united the Innu, as daily survival on the land once had. A collective effort was being made to protect nutshimit and to break out of the morass of daily life in Sheshatshit. I never saw any alcohol at the runway camp; in place of it there was a great deal of clear thinking and creative action.

Tshaukuesh Penashue emerged as a strong leader during this period, and this made her husband uneasy. Politics had been a man's business since the village was established, and her activism was not in keeping with the role assigned to Innu women. But Tshaukuesh had come back from the bombing range filled with new purpose. She became more outspoken, and she mobilized other women to become a driving force behind the protests. For the first time in years Innu women took command, injecting badly needed political energy into the community. Francis wasn't the only one concerned about Tshaukuesh's determination to drive away the jets. Her son Peter was also worried. "Mom doesn't know what she's up against," he told me.

Tshaukuesh spoke little English and had not travelled outside her homeland, so she had little knowledge of what the NATO alliance

was. But she did know what was good for her family—life in
nutshimit—and she knew that this was now threatened. In the months
ahead Tshaukuesh demonstrated a strong instinct for survival and a
mettle of steel. Many underestimated her political adroitness and
shrewdness. She eventually learned just how powerful the forces lined
up against her people were, but she continued to come up with creative tactics to outmanoeuvre her opponents.

Tshaukuesh had become involved because she was disillusioned
with the way the political organizations in Sheshatshit handled community problems. She watched the elected men leave the village time
and again for meetings with Canadian and Newfoundland officials,
yet nothing ever changed. Obviously, cooperating with outside government authorities was not working, so Tshaukuesh and other
women sought new ways to achieve their goals. They knew it was
only when Innu rights were recognized in Nitassinan that their children could feel whole and secure again.

"We always thought politics was the men's job," she told me. "After the women became involved in the struggle we realized how much
power women have to do things. We always thought it was the job
for the chief and councillors and the Naskapi-Montagnais Innu Association to get involved in politics. The more we women talked,
the more we realized what the future held for the Innu if we didn't
do something."

On my second day in the camp I helped Tshaukuesh, Janet Michel
and other women collect boughs to spread out in the large tent they
were setting up for meetings. Preparations were underway to receive
the Roman Catholic bishop of Schefferville, Henri Goudreault.
Sheshatshit was one of his parishes, and the bishop was reportedly
alarmed by Father Jim Roche's active participation in the protests.

Bishop Goudreault arrived on 25 September. After he had toured
the camp, he was brought to the meeting tent, where many had gathered to speak to him. Father Jim, still pale and weak from his fast, sat
next to the bishop, while a priest from Goose Bay crouched on the
floor beside them.

Speaker after speaker told the bishop that the time had come for
the Innu to stand up for their rights and protect the land and animals
from jet bomber training. Many spoke in defence of their priest,
who they knew was in trouble with his superiors.

Those gathered before the bishop that day also talked about something else, something few would have dared to bring up before. They

criticized the Church for its lack of political support and for the part
it had played in encouraging them to adopt a European style of living. Kathleen Nuna, a schoolteacher who has always been a very
obedient follower of the Church, surprised everyone when she told
Goudreault:

> *Before the priests came we felt we were closer to God because we lived
> on the land and in harmony with nature. We respect all the animals
> because they come from God. God gave us this land to live from. We
> think Father Jim understands how important the land is to us. I left
> my job and came here to join my people because I don't want my
> children to be like white children, I want them to stay Innu children.
> It's not that I don't like white people personally, it's just the way of
> life. I don't want to lose that, I don't want my children to lose that. There
> is no way that they can become like white people, or that white people
> can become like us. We're Innu and we'll stay Innu.*

Goudreault, a kindly French-Canadian who has spent many years
working among native people, seemed genuinely moved by what he
heard. He promised to talk to the Pope about the situation when he
went to Rome the following month for meetings. (Later the bishop
arranged for a group of Innu to meet the Pope in Rome.) Goudreault
then prepared for Mass. He put on his robes, and the other two priests
stood on either side of him while an altar boy shook incense around
the tent.

"I think I should tell you," the bishop said during his homily,
"that your strength is not only your involvement in these protests,
but also in the fact that you do not use violence. Involvement through
peaceful means, prayers and solidarity are the secret of success. Always
trust in the Lord and ask him to keep you active and peaceful. Seek
to obtain your rights without a sentiment of revenge in your hearts."
Many took this to mean the bishop was giving his blessing to what
they were doing, and the mood was upbeat in the camp for the rest
of the day.

After Goudreault left, the occupants of the runway camp received
news that ministers and deputy ministers from across northern Canada
were gathering in Goose Bay that weekend for the eleventh Annual
Interprovincial Northern Development Ministers' Conference. The
Innu were ready to act again. On the day most delegates were sched-
uled to arrive, a large group of Innu gathered near their vehicles at

the runway camp, shouting and waving Innu flags and signs that read "Stop Bombing Innu Culture" and "We Will Always Struggle for Nitassinan." About a dozen cars and trucks were soon filled to overflowing and the Innu headed towards the base, brazenly passing the twenty-four-hour police guard as though they were taking part in a parade. The surveillance officer radioed an alarm to his superiors, and within minutes the boisterous band of protesters was followed by a convoy of R.C.M.P. and military police vehicles.

But the Innu weren't planning to go on the runway that day. Instead, they marched around the public streets of the base carrying banners and signs while a couple of teenagers played Innu music over loudspeakers. "Tshinanu" ("We Innu"), a song by the popular Innu duo Kashtin, became the theme song of the Innu resistance.

No one from Sheshatshit had been invited to any of the official functions of the conference, so the Innu were forced to figure out another way to make the representatives aware of their opposition to military expansion. When people at the camp learned that Newfoundland premier Brian Peckford was going to be in Goose Bay for the event, they gathered in the meeting tent to decide how best to get the attention of the premier and the outside media who were expected to accompany him. Innu protests had still not received much media attention beyond Labrador.

After a great deal of animated and passionate discussion, Mani May Osmonde, who had gone to the bombing range with Tshaukuesh, spoke emotionally to the crowd. People applauded enthusiastically when she had finished, and the elders moved their heads up and down in assent. After the meeting I asked Mani May what she had said to resolve things.

"We plan to make a hole in the wooden fence by the camp here so we can get on the airfield again," she told me. "But our parents say we should not be destructive. They don't want us to damage military property. I told them that compared to the damage the military has done to our land, removing a few boards from a fence is nothing."

At dawn the following morning the camp awoke to the sound of helicopters. The noise went on for hours as dozens of the aircraft, participating in a search-and-rescue exercise, buzzed over our heads on their way to and from the base. Anxiety at the camp was high; it seemed to be a bad day to try getting back on the runway. Strolling outside among the tents, I began to think I'd been transported to the set of "M*A*S*H." Ben Michel had another movie in mind. Jocularly poking his head outside the tent door, looking for all the world like an Innu version of Jerry Lewis, he yelled, "Good morning Viiieeeeeeet Naaaaammmmmm!" Laughter erupted in neighbouring tents and much of the tension lifted. His joke became the rallying cry of the day.

Shortly before noon Innu adults and children once again gathered with their flags and protest signs. They climbed aboard trucks that formed a line as though headed once again towards the base. I was puzzled, for the plan had been to go through a nearby fence. The surveillance officer began talking into his walkie-talkie, but without the urgency of the day before. It looked as though the Innu were just going to march around the base again.

Suddenly a great shout went up. The Innu, carrying flags and banners, jumped from the backs of their trucks, raced down the banks of the adjoining hill and squeezed themselves through a hole in the fence, while a couple of teenagers, holding axes and looking very pleased with themselves, stood nearby. The diversionary tactic had worked.

There was much laughter as stouter protesters got stuck in the hole, but everyone managed to get through somehow, and they were soon racing towards the jet bombers parked several hundred metres away. Father Jim was one of the last to go through. Two elderly women tightly grasped his hands, as if to draw strength from him, and the three walked slowly towards the crowd. The surveillance officer looked on in amazement, then scrambled to alert officials that the Innu were once again on the airfield.

Soon the protesters were surrounded by the flashing lights of police cars, three fire trucks and a couple of military buses from which the riot squad emerged, holding sticks and shields which they brandished protectively in front of the jets. Dominic Pokue proudly held the Innu flag high over his head and continued to march along. The blue-and-green flag, which has a snowshoe in the centre and caribou antlers on each side, had become an important symbol of Innu pride and nationalism.

Old men, women, mothers with babies, teenaged girls and young men rarely seen sober in Sheshatshit were all on the runway that day, marching forward as police picked them off one by one and arrested them. The known leaders were apprehended first, but new leaders emerged until it became clear that this was a movement that everyone led. The bravery shown by even the youngest child seemed to touch the arresting officers. Once everyone had been removed from the airfield and placed in buses, the R.C.M.P. courteously drove the elderly Innu back to the runway camp some distance away.

■

I found it very moving to watch this small, defenceless group of people pit themselves so coolly against the military, one of the most powerful institutions in any society. A young CBC television reporter who stood beside me that day, however, felt something quite different.

"Come on, let's go," she told her cameraman, who was trying to take pictures through the fence. "There's no story here, they're just using us again."

It was the third time the Innu had been on the runway, and the local CBC was already tiring of the story. It was not until the Lubicon Cree in Alberta started making headlines with their blockade against oil exploration that fall that the national press became interested in what the Innu were doing. The two stories together made sexy headlines about a possible native uprising in Canada.

The only news outlet in Goose Bay with national connections is the CBC, and since most of its staff socialize at the base they were under a lot of pressure to downplay Innu protests. The Innu complained repeatedly to CBC officials about biased coverage from a senior radio reporter who is an officer in one of the military auxiliary units, yet nothing was ever done about these complaints. There was even talk in Sheshatshit of a collusion between the CBC and the defence department, but David Suzuki, a CBC celebrity and outspoken environmentalist, put the matter in perspective at a public meeting in Sheshatshit in December 1988. "It's not a conspiracy in the way you mean," he told the crowd. "The CBC is run by white middle-class men and women who don't care or understand where you are coming from."

At the department of defence headquarters in Ottawa, I was shown a documentary produced by CBC's "The Journal." The program suggests that the Innu have a "secret agenda" for opposing the military flights—land claims. By characterizing the protests in this way, the program dismissed Innu concerns about the environment and presented the people as opportunistic money-grabbers. This point of view played so well into DND hands that the documentary had become part of the department's public relations package.

"They want money. They're not after fifty million bucks any more,"

Lt. Col. Robert Jodoin, an official at the base, told a Labrador news-paper. "They're after ninety million bucks."

The defence department tried to counteract the emotional im-ages shown on TV of Innu elders, women and children peacefully marching in front of jet bombers by stepping up its own public rela-tions campaign and playing hardball with journalists who covered the issue sympathetically.

An official at the defence department sent a letter to the Montreal *Gazette* complaining about an article I'd written following my expe-riences at Penipuapishku-nipi. Then the same official tried to block publication of a piece I was writing for *Peace and Security*, a magazine published by the Canadian Institute for International Peace and Se-curity, by contacting the editor with unfounded accusations about my credibility. Not until I challenged the defence department with a lawsuit were all allegations dropped and a formal apology issued.

The Mackenzie Institute for the Study of Terrorism, Revolution and Propaganda, a right-wing think tank with links to the National Citizens' Coalition, published a study of media response to Innu protests. It accused newspapers like the *Globe and Mail* of being bi-ased and "blinded by morality," and reported that the best coverage of the issue came from Labrador. The Labrador press was in fact hope-lessly biased against the Innu; even the Mackenzie Institute had to admit in its report that coverage provided by the *Northern Reporter* was often racist.

■

Shortly after they had been removed from the runway, the Innu who had been arrested were released from police custody. By the time I returned to camp, everyone was getting ready to move again. This time the plan was to demonstrate outside the banquet hall where Premier Brian Peckford was going to speak to the northern minis-ters.

The weary protesters formed a line in front of the only entrance to the hall and jeered whenever anyone of local prominence passed through. Government representatives from across northern Canada entered the hall, but there were few aboriginal people among them. Finally the premier arrived with his entourage and the protesters began to shout: "Go home, Peckford. Go home, Peckford. We don't want NATO. We don't want NATO." Peckford rushed through the human barricade, looking brash and arrogant, without turning to acknowledge the people who were so obviously displeased with him.

"When are you going to meet with us, when are you going to listen to us?" someone shouted.

The demonstration continued until all the guests were inside. I felt a little awkward when I entered the hall. I had changed from the jeans I usually wore in the camp to a skirt and high heels. I recalled how two years ago three Innu delegates, Ben Michel among them, had been invited to the same hall for a banquet in honour of several visiting NATO ambassadors. The Innu never got past the front door because they weren't wearing suits and ties as required by military dress code. The men stood outside for a while, feeling humiliated, while inside John Crosbie, then Canada's international trade minister, announced that he was giving $150,000 to the Mokami Project Group, a pro-military lobby, so that they could step up efforts to convince NATO to build its massive new base in Goose Bay. At the same time Crosbie tried to reassure his European guests that Canada respects the rights of its native population. "You can be sure this country is not ignoring its aboriginal peoples," he said.

Inside the banquet hall I sat beside a young Inuit woman who was on her first assignment for the new radio station in Nain. Raoul Vollant, the energetic Innu reporter who was still broadcasting news of the protests to Innu on the Quebec north shore, was seated beside her.

Several hundred people were packed into the room. Anyone who was anyone in Goose Bay had come to rub shoulders with the premier and the visiting government leaders.

As we finished our first course of smoked salmon and arctic char, Deputy Minister of Northern Affairs John McGrath, Newfoundland's top bureaucrat in Labrador and emcee for the evening, began to speak. He had to shout to be heard above the protesters outside because they were making a racket on the other side of the prefabricated walls, playing loud music and occasionally chanting, "Go home, NATO. Go home, Peckford." But McGrath is a big man with a big voice, and he soon captured his audience. He told some jokes, including a few about the Innu. He tagged one of his stories with this: "And if you believe that, I've got some recreational land for sale in Sheshatshit." Then, turning to the small, mustached man in uniform beside him, he said, "I'd like to introduce this man, Col. Phil Engstad, the new commander of Canadian Forces Base Goose Bay. Let's give him a big hand."

The crowd obliged.

"I offered to show Phil a few of the local sights today," McGrath continued. "I wanted to drive him down to Sheshatshit but he said, 'No thanks, I'd rather see Sheshatshit from the cockpit of one of my jet bombers!' "

McGrath paused for laughter, but there was only a titter from the local residents. Most of the outside visitors looked embarrassed. The deputy minister, who shortly afterwards obtained leave from the Newfoundland government to attend military college, had shown his contempt for the Innu in countless ways during his time in office. He had used divide-and-conquer strategies to get his way within the native communities to which he administered funding, and had played politics irresponsibly in communities that were dysfunctional because of widespread alcohol abuse.

Although he put on his Irish accent to play the stereotypical Newfoundlander, he showed no sentimentality about the aboriginal cultures he lives beside. He once told me during an interview that "languages and cultures come and go" and that the Innu must be prepared to lose theirs.

We started on our main course, caribou, another staple of the Innu diet. The next speaker was the guest of honour, who did his best to be heard above the shouting and music outside. The room was very hot, and it got hotter as Peckford spoke. His speech was riddled with platitudes, obviously written to please the government representatives from other parts of the North but horribly ill suited to the setting that evening.

"Northern development must be done in such a way that the customs and traditions of native people are respected," he said.

"We don't want NATO. We don't want NATO," the native people outside chanted, determined to protect their customs and traditions.

"We must give the native people a say in how the North is to be developed," Peckford went on.

The Innu outside continued to exercise boisterously the only voice they have been given by government—the voice of protest.

"We have to give institutional expression to the special interests and concerns that our native people possess," the premier continued.

I couldn't help but think that jail seems to be the institution of choice in Canada for responding to the expression of native people's interests and concerns.

The premier concluded with a flourish: "I want our native people to know in no uncertain terms that we are going to come to know and understand their wisdom."

Peckford's speech was designed to please northern bureaucrats for whom it had become fashionable to acknowledge native rights. The premier, however, had demonstrated on several occasions that he did not have a firm grasp of the issues.

Peckford had made his attitude towards native people clear at the First Ministers' Constitutional Conference on Aboriginal Rights in March 1987. Before he left for the conference, the premier told the St. John's *Evening Telegram* that self-government might one day make native communities "big municipalities" with powers to pressure provincial governments for money, a statement that shows his deep misunderstanding of the issue. At the conference itself, Peckford told the native people gathered at the table, "I'm not sure you're being as smart as you think you're being." He compared the lives of the poor in Newfoundland with those in aboriginal communities, showing how little he knows of the deplorable destitution in northern Canada. "We are a welfare society just like the aboriginal people are, in some cases worse," he said, and then: "I almost feel like I'm the leader of an aboriginal people."

After Peckford's speech at the Goose Bay banquet, reporters peppered him with questions about whether he would meet with the Innu while he was in Labrador. Peckford said he would meet with them only if they came to St. John's, thereby upholding a longstanding tradition. (No Newfoundland premier visited Sheshatshit officially or socially, and none stepped inside an Innu tent, until November 1991, when Premier Clyde Wells met the Sheshatshit Innu at a camp near Grand Lake.) Peckford gave reporters the impression that he was conciliatory and the Innu uncooperative: "I've held out the olive branch to the Innu many times," he said, "and I'll do it again. If they want to meet with me and my officials, our door is open, it has always been open."

Peckford went on to defend his friend the deputy minister for his earlier remarks about the Innu. The premier told the *Evening Telegram*, "You had to be there at the time to put what Mr. McGrath said in context. He was just trying to take a different approach as an emcee. In my view the case is closed and there will be no repercussions coming out of it as it relates to the government vis à vis Mr. McGrath."

On my way out of the banquet hall I stopped to speak with Sgt.

Joe MacDonald, the R.C.M.P. officer in charge at Goose Bay. He was standing by the door as people left the building. The Innu protesters had returned to the camp, but they were the subject of a few parting shots. One local resident thanked MacDonald for protecting the citizenry from Indian attack.

Back at the camp, I stopped in at Tshaukuesh and Francis's tent for tea. Tshaukuesh put more wood on the fire, while Francis reclined beside her, drawing on a cigarette. Tshaukuesh's sister Rose was also staying in the tent with her children. I was surprised by their upbeat mood, quite a contrast to my own.

"Could you hear us inside?" Rose asked.

"Hear you? You couldn't hear anything else," I said. "Peckford had to shout to be heard above your music."

"That was Metshen's idea," Tshaukuesh said. "We thought the R.C.M.P. would make us turn the music down, but they didn't. We had a great time."

She and Rose described how the chief of Ekuanitshit, Pinip Pietashu, whose daughter is married to a Sheshatshit man, had shown up with his drum and before long had people dancing in a large circle to keep warm. It soon became apparent that they had had a much better time that evening than those of us inside. My spirits started to lift. At least the Innu weren't discouraged by the night's events. They felt victorious because they had exposed the government's hypocrisy.

When I got back to the Michel tent Ben and Janet asked for an account of what had gone on at the banquet. Ben chuckled when I read aloud parts of Peckford's speech. I told him how difficult it had been for the premier to speak over the noise outside.

I settled down to sleep, as did Janet, but Ben continued to read. After half an hour I looked up to see him puffing on a cigarette and staring into space.

"Shall I turn off the light?" I asked.

"No," he said, "I want to keep it on. We asked the premier for a meeting while he's in Labrador and I have to stay up until we get his response. He must be meeting now with his advisers to decide what he'll do. I want to keep the lamp on so they'll find my tent when they come with their answer."

I knew the premier wasn't meeting his advisers; he was probably having a few drinks at the hotel bar. If there was going to be a meeting it would take place in St. John's, as in the past. That meeting would be like all the others: nothing would change to improve the quality of Innu lives, just as Tshaukuesh feared. I decided to keep silent. Ben deserved to hear directly from the premier.

He kept the lamp on late into the night but there was no message. Peckford left Labrador early the next morning. Eventually he arranged a meeting in St. John's between the Innu and a minor cabinet minister who had no responsibility for native issues.

Peckford continued to insist in subsequent press reports that he has always made land claims a high priority. "We've been willing to sit down with the Innu for a long time," he was quoted as saying. "We are already meeting with the Inuit to discuss their land claims."

The Innu could draw little comfort from the Peckford government's dealings with the Labrador Inuit, however. The Inuit were invited to join the land claims process in 1977, but Newfoundland held up the talks by insisting that provincial and federal officials meet first without Inuit representatives. The Inuit objected, fearing the province was not prepared to bargain with them in good faith. The land claims policy that Newfoundland finally drafted in 1987 is considered by some to be one of the most regressive in the country. Aboriginal people are expected to give up title to their homelands forever in exchange for very little. All subsurface and water rights would revert to the province, and there would be no revenue sharing with the native inhabitants. Aboriginal people might be given an advisory role in the management of resources on their territories, but that was all, and it was not much more than they already had. The Labrador Inuit were actually at the bargaining table in 1988, but they were allowed as little input on the issue of military expansion as the Innu had. In an article published in *Northern Perspectives* in 1990, Judy Rowell, environmental adviser to the Inuit, wrote of the problem. "Between DND and the provincial government, the Labrador Inuit are repeatedly frozen out of the planning and review stages," she explained, "and are even denied access to the site selection process which identifies land for DND use in northern Labrador."

The Innu had no reason to believe they would be treated any differently.

Who's Training the Innu?

"We know what destroyed the Innu way of life. It wasn't low-level flying or the base or development or progress. It was interfering busybodies who couldn't leave well enough alone."
NORTHERN REPORTER, GOOSE BAY

Throughout the fall of 1988 the Innu went onto the runway seven times. Their motivation was always the same—to assert ownership of their land—but the timing was reactive. Spontaneous protests were prompted by the news that outside media were in town or by dissatisfaction with something Canadian politicians had said or done. Once the people went onto the runway to support an imprisoned friend.

On 7 October 1988, a young Innu mother, Naomi Jack, was arrested along with many others during a protest. For some reason, perhaps because her husband was a former band chief, she was the only woman jailed that day. A rumour reached people at the runway camp that Naomi wasn't eating. She was frightened that she might be taken to prison in St. John's as some Innu men recently had been. Naomi's relatives would not be allowed to visit her until her court appearance. Concern for her grew so great that a group of Innu women decided to go back on the runway themselves, hoping to get arrested and then keep Naomi company in jail. Their plan worked. Naomi was delighted to see them, and they were all released together a few days later.

From the beginning, the military's response to these runway demonstrations was extreme. The riot squad was called out, complete with helmets, clubs and shields which they wielded in front of unarmed Innu men, women and children. Shishin Rich, a young Innu woman, wrote me a letter describing a demonstration she participated in:

> *I watched my people being hauled out by the military police and the R.C.M.P. helping out—children clinging to their fathers and their mothers as they were taken away. And you can see the children crying. I was in tears and I was very moved by the whole thing. I was also arrested for watching. During my time watching and standing, seeing my people being hauled away, there were military squad teams holding their sticks and their shields and fire trucks surrounding us, ready to blow us with their hose "water" if we did not move. So instead they took us one by one, hauling us to the military bus. I watched and I cried as I see my people being taken away, plus the children clinging to their parents. It really tears me apart wishing there was something I can do, but all I could do was cry and wipe my tears with my hands. I said to myself—what is there to do when there are so many military police around? And I think along the way to being arrested, is it wrong to fight for your rights—for your land?*

Police thought that jailing those they considered ringleaders would stop the protests, but they didn't understand Innu politics and the grassroots nature of their leadership. Even with Father Jim, Daniel Ashini, Ben Michel and others in jail in St. John's, the protests never let up that fall. If anything, they intensified. Women were taking an unprecedented role in community action, and the elderly, so often shoved aside in village life, were deeply involved in the planning and implementation of the various actions. The social and political structures that have existed for centuries in Innu society came alive, and community self-esteem was restored.

"We're taking better care of ourselves," one young woman told me with pride. "We've woken up," said another. Tshaukuesh vowed, "We will never be silent again."

Innu courage also came to the fore. Father Jim Roche recalls how terrified the Innu were at first of being arrested. "It was their greatest fear," he says. "No one wanted to go to jail, especially when it meant long confinement from family and friends. They feared being alone in jail most of all. Once they overcame that, however, there was no turning back."

As the protests continued, the Innu gained the support of Cana-

dian Mennonites. The Innu struggle was a natural one for Mennonites
to champion, since it combined two of their major concerns—world
peace and native rights. Mennonite community development workers had lived in Goose Bay before, but they had kept a fairly low
profile. Bob and Dorothy Bartel and their two teenage children arrived in Goose Bay at the height of the Innu resistance, and they
eventually paid dearly for their public support of the Innu.

The Bartels' house on Tenth Street was the Goose Bay centre for
the protest movement. People at the runway camp often got their
water there, and Bob drove back and forth with Innu passengers to
Sheshatshit several times a day, while Dorothy wrote press releases
and provided newspaper clippings to outside supporters and journalists. During long court appearances, the Bartels provided lunch.
Bob and Dorothy made fast friends in Sheshatshit, but many enemies
in Goose Bay. The tires of the family van were slashed and the
windshield broken. Their daughter left to live with her grandparents
in Saskatchewan.

The Bartels' good works made them suspects in what some thought
was a plot to overthrow democracy. The suspicion came from those
who believed the Innu could not possibly be running such an effec-
tive protest campaign by themselves: they had to be getting direction
from either the Soviets or Middle Eastern terrorists. A Labrador member of the Newfoundland legislature, Jim Kelland, warned the federal defence minister in June 1989 that communists from the Eastern
bloc might have infiltrated the Innu resistance. "I was just going by
comments people were making in the community," the *Labradorian*
quoted Kelland as saying. "Even if there was the slightest chance of it
being true, I thought it should be looked into."

A rash of xenophobia struck Goose Bay. The town council sought
retaliatory measures against outsiders suspected of encouraging the
Innu to protest. One councillor suggested that hotel rooms and car
rental services be denied strangers thought to be Innu supporters,
and some car rental agencies refused to provide insurance for vehicles that were to be driven in Sheshatshit. A video camera was
mounted on the wall opposite the arrivals door at the airport to film
everyone who came to the town. Even the Canadian Security Intelligence Service (CSIS) launched an investigation.

One night Dorothy Bartel received a phone call at home from a
Roy Kearley, who said he was with the solicitor-general's office and
wanted to meet Bob that night at a local hotel. Bob arrived for the

appointment, and no sooner had they finished shaking hands than Kearley revealed himself to be the new head of CSIS in Newfoundland. Bob's first inclination was to leave, but curiosity got the best of him.

Kearley took a peculiarly direct approach to his investigation. He asked Bob outright if there was any foreign manipulation of the Innu, either from Iraq or the Eastern bloc. According to Bartel,

> He said that if this was a purely local issue there was no interest on the part of CSIS, even if the Innu sought national and international support for their cause.
>
> I replied, "Unequivocally no! There is no foreign intervention." I told him that the foreign manipulation was by the British, Dutch and West Germans, whose low-flying needs were hindering Canada's role as a peacemaker and hurting Canada's ability to look after the environment.
>
> Then he asked if there was any manipulation of the community that I knew about and I said that the military was manipulating the local town council. He then muttered something about being frustrated about the way I turned things.

Kearley told Bartel that four Innu supporters were also under close scrutiny by the spy network but would not say who they were.

The CSIS investigation of the Innu was part of a nation-wide spy operation to ascertain if aboriginal groups were plotting violent means to achieve their ends. CSIS got involved after a widely publicized speech by Georges Erasmus, then head of the Assembly of First Nations, warning that violence might break out if relations between native people and Canadian governments didn't soon improve. A parliamentary committee later investigated complaints that CSIS was tampering with mail and bugging telephones in its efforts to gather this information, but their report acquitting CSIS was never made public.

Few Innu took the spies seriously, particularly once Bartel's account of the bungled interrogation made its way around the runway camp. People were upset to think their phone conversations were possibly being monitored and their mail read, but they made the best of it. There was even cause for some amusement as it became apparent that the R.C.M.P. and CSIS worked against each other. A couple of R.C.M.P. officers tipped off Innu leaders that CSIS had posted a man named Weston in Goose Bay to keep an eye on them. The man

appeared at demonstrations with a video camera, but not much more
was heard from him.

The R.C.M.P. also actively gathered information on Innu protesters and their supporters. A Mennonite delegation from western
Canada came under close observation while in Goose Bay on a fact-
finding mission.

"It started when we came into the courthouse," Mennonite Ron
Mathies says. "The R.C.M.P. took a couple of minutes to give us a
visual going-over, talked to each other, took notes. Then outside
court there was an R.C.M.P. officer taking videos of all the people
coming and going. I've never had that done to me in Canada before."

The four-member delegation was later stopped and questioned at
a roadblock. When the Mennonites met with some Innu at the band
council office in Sheshatshit, half a dozen R.C.M.P. officers walked
around outside, taking down the licence numbers of all vehicles parked
there.

"Each time we went to the air force base, which has public facilities on it, we were tailed," says Mathies.

(Surveillance continued for some time. Peter Penashue travelled
to Japan in the summer of 1989 as a guest of the International
Youth Tour for Peace and Justice to take part in activities marking
the anniversary of the atomic bombing of Hiroshima and Nagasaki.
Upon his return, customs officials at Dorval airport searched him,
went through his papers and even read his diary.

"They went through all my stuff, my papers, everything," he said
at the time. "I understand they need to look for dope or guns, but
they don't need to look at people's diaries."

Peter told a news conference that his rough handling was another
episode of harassment by a paranoid government. "They seem to
think we're communists or something. We can't live with these flights.
It's not a myth for me, it's real," he said, his voice breaking. "I'm not
an Innu because my skin is darker but because I have Innu culture,
language and lifestyle. If the militarization continues, I won't be an
Innu any more. No one will. The Innu will be wiped from the face
of the map.")

The authorities were wasting their time looking for outside
agitators—the Innu were quite capable of developing their own strategies. The people did get some support from peace and environmentalists throughout the world. Representatives of Germany's Green

Party sponsored legislation to ban low-level flight training on both sides of the Atlantic. Dutch peace activists, following the example of the Innu, held sit-ins on runways in their country, while Survival International conducted a public education campaign in Britain. The Canadian Peace Alliance, Act for Disarmament, the Alliance for Non-Violent Action, Quebec Artists for Peace and numerous other Canadian groups supported the Innu by holding demonstrations outside defence department headquarters in Ottawa and other centres. In October 1988, Innu women at the runway camp received a telegram from Greenham Common women in England: "We gain inspiration from your struggle and see links that bind us to you. We too are involved in reclaiming land—common land meant for everyone to use—from the military who are practising nuclear genocide, poisoning us and trampling over our rights."

Although the Innu protests were undertaken to protect Innu land and culture, the people's contact with peace groups broadened their understanding of global issues. No one wanted to undermine democracy or deny the residents of Goose Bay a livelihood. Instead, those opposing the militarization of the Innu homeland wanted to ensure a healthier life for people in northern Quebec and Labrador, a life based on respect for the aboriginal people and their environment.

During one demonstration, Bob Bartel found himself beside the German commanding officer at Goose Bay. The commander called the Innu violent because he saw some of them pulling a wire fence off its supporting posts. Bob later speculated in a letter to supporters that "the dominant culture never sees violence in the denial of the rights of others, but is quick to denounce a struggle to regain those rights as militant and violent. To the dominant culture the only good Indian is a quiet, colonized one."

The Innu weren't acting like quiet, colonized Indians that fall. Their main weapon was humour, and their actions were most often carried out with brazen impudence. They took great delight in outwitting military authorities. One protest involved setting up a tent on the front lawn of the commanding officers' homes.

The three stately houses leased to the foreign base commanders stood beside one another and shared a large common lawn. On 26 October, about fifty Innu from the runway camp suddenly appeared in front of these houses and began emptying a loaded pick-up truck. They worked with military precision, and before anyone had time to stop them they had the tent up, a fire going and water on to boil. It took them thirty-seven seconds.

"Thirty-seven seconds flat is just a way of demonstrating to the military that we can do things very rapidly," Ben Michel explained to assembled reporters, "and without them knowing what our next move will be. By coming to the homes of the commanding officers, who seem nervous to come to our camp, we are hoping that they will see a small part of what Innu life is like."

Several Innu women made tea inside the tent and invited the officers' wives to join them, but none did. The Innu paraded back and forth in front of the houses, chanting and waving placards. When asked to remove the tent from defence department property, Ben Michel asked police: "How is it DND property when we were here first, when we have used this land for thousands of years? How was it that Europeans came fifty years ago and now it is their property?"

The Innu were determined to embarrass CFB Goose Bay, and they were succeeding. No amount of extra precautions seemed adequate to keep the determined Innu off the runway.

On 16 November base officials were on full alert. Peace protesters were planning a sympathy demonstration for the Innu outside department of defence headquarters in Ottawa as employees returned to work following the Remembrance Day weekend. The military assumed the Innu would try to get on the runway again to take advantage of national publicity. Security on the base was strengthened; checkpoints were set up and barbed wire was strung along fence tops. Undaunted, the protesters came up with a clever plan. While police were concentrating on demonstrators outside the runway fence, others gathered at an unattended part of the airfield, where they climbed over a 2.5-metre fence not protected by barbed wire back onto the runway. More than forty people were arrested.

In Ottawa, two hundred demonstrators protested outside DND headquarters. A member of the Alliance for Non-Violent Action was arrested for drawing a peace symbol on the building. Ben Michel had been invited to speak to the crowd. "For nine years the Innu have been protesting the militarization of our homeland," he said, "and that is why in the past two months we have occupied the bombing range south of Goose Bay and why we have on seven separate occasions disrupted or halted operations at CFB Goose Bay by sitting down on the runways. The experience of the last thirty years has left our people and society fragile and damaged. We will not survive what is now being done to our people and the land on which our culture depends."

The Innu got the headlines they wanted. Both demonstrations were well covered, and the following winter saw more international media in Goose Bay than ever before.

Innu actions were criticized as lawless and anarchistic, but Peter Penashue says the Innu had very little choice. "If the Innu people got stuck in their homes and waited for the governments to give them the things that they would like, such as self-determination, that's not going to come about," he explains. "It comes about when people start feeling ashamed. That's exactly what we've done to the government. We've shamed them to realize they have to do something, because we've said 'no' to low-level flying."

Consciences were being stirred all over the country. "Isn't anyone offended by the morality of this situation?" asked Thomas Perry of Vancouver in a letter to the *Globe and Mail*. "Each night's television news brings us fresh horror stories of famine or disaster from Bangladesh, Sudan and Ethiopia. Yet our government still wants to spend hundreds of millions of dollars training pilots for a war we all know the world cannot survive. In the bargain, it is destroying what is left of Labrador's native culture and its splendid wilderness."

Innu support spread to Toronto, where about two hundred demonstrators gathered one evening outside City Hall. Daniel Ashini was asked to address groups across Canada, including Physicians for Nuclear Responsibility and the Union of BC Indian Chiefs. Citizens' groups throughout Canada and Europe were inviting Innu representatives to come and speak to them. "I think we have been quite successful considering that Canadians have always described us as a backward and primitive society," Ben Michel told the St. John's Sunday *Express*.

By December the Innu had violated base security seven times. One hundred and fifteen charges of mischief had been laid, and twenty-one Innu had spent time in jail, some up to two weeks. Flight training had stopped for the season because of cold temperatures, but construction continued on a $40-million hangar for the West German air force. There were rumours that the Italians wanted to train at Goose Bay in the spring and that the number of flights would increase. Despite a warning from the Canadian Public Health Association, a limited number of laser-guided weapons were being used on the bombing range, and there was talk of allowing supersonic

flights. Alarmed by this escalation, the Innu agreed to hold explora-
tory meeti: ¸s with federal and provincial Indian Affairs bureaucrats,
but the meetings bore little fruit. The top politicians in Ottawa were
too busy seeking re-election that fall to bother with the Innu.

On 8 December, Innu at the runway camp heard shocking news
from West Germany. An American air force jet had struck an apart-
ment building in Remscheid, exploding into flames and killing six
people. The A-10 Thunderbolt 11, designed to support ground forces
and fight tanks, was carrying 1000 rounds of training ammunition
when it crashed.

More than ever before events in other parts of the world affected
Innu lives. Opposition to low-level flying was growing daily in West
Germany, where there had been twelve military air crashes since the
spring of 1988. *Jane's Defence Weekly* reported that ninety-seven NATO
combat planes had crashed that year. Political parties in West Germany promised to do everything in their power to reduce flights and
talked of an "evacuation to Labrador."

Meanwhile, the strategy of pro-military lobby groups in Goose
Bay had changed. Ian Strachan, head of the Mokami Project Group,
made an impromptu visit to Ben Michel's tent in the runway camp
one morning that December. He clutched an essay he'd written, entitled "Whose land is it anyway?" Strachan's essay called the issue of
Innu land claims the "single greatest issue in central Labrador." He
adopted an uncharacteristically conciliatory approach, urging government authorities to settle Innu land claims as quickly as possible.
His motivation for this new approach was not to seek justice for the
Innu but to stop the embarrassment suffered by CFB Goose Bay. "If
the Innu's claims are given their rightful attention their protests will
surely cease," he wrote eagerly.

Goose Bay officials were running scared. Support for the Innu
was growing, and the town was getting a lot of bad publicity.

On 10 December, David Suzuki visited the runway camp. He was
then taken to meet Francis's father, Kanatuakuet, and his uncle Pien
at a bush camp in Kenemou near the Mealy Mountains.

"If the low-level flying does damage and pollutes the atmosphere—
there goes the medicine and the caribou that we depend on," explained Pien, a thin, lithe man in his sixties. "That is why we are
always concerned about what is happening and why we ask so many
questions about the low-level flying and its effects."

Suzuki asked Pien how the land has changed in the last hundred years. Before answering, Pien thought carefully, and with a creased brow said: "The government thinks it's doing a good job, being a manager all these years. It has put all kinds of restrictions on us regarding hunting because the government thinks we will endanger the animals, yet government goes ahead with all kinds of development that endangers the animals more than our hunting. The Innu were always better game wardens than the government," he concluded.

Pien's wife quietly cleaned rabbits while Kanatuakuet, a scholarly looking man wearing round wire-rimmed glasses, made a wooden frame for stretching beaver skins. He became visibly interested when Suzuki asked how the low-flying jets are affecting the animals.

"We are used to seeing more lynx around," he told the visiting scientist. "Since the jets came the muskrats are gone and the caribou are not in the same places they were when I was brought up by my father and grandfather. The caribou travels and can go for days without stopping to eat. If they are frightened they will keep moving and may eventually lose weight if they don't stop to eat."

"There are those not concerned about the health of people and the environment because they care more about their greed," Pien added. "In Innu culture there is no such thing as greed. We are different. Fur is money, but you can only go so far to get fur. You need animals more importantly for food. That's the difference between white society and the Innu. If an Innu is too greedy it could cost him his life."

Suzuki asked about the scaffold of animal bones he had seen in the camp. Pien said that luck in hunting comes from the care taken with animal remains, especially the skull, which must be treated with extra care and always hung somewhere out of reach.

Just as Suzuki was preparing to leave, Pien's wife Lizette spoke. "The government is killing people of one human race. You can't turn us into your people, and we know we can't turn you into what we are, because it can't work that way," she said sadly. "We won't run our house the way you run your house. You would find it hard to live the way we live out here. It's hard to understand. Alcohol is creating a younger generation that is lazy. It's fun living out here— they think it's easy, but it's not. You have to work hard to survive here. We base things on the pride people have in providing for their own families."

Suzuki needed little persuasion. He was converted to the Innu point of view before he arrived in Labrador.

"I have come in support of the Innu," he told a public meeting in Goose Bay the following evening. He spoke of the need to safeguard what remains of Canadian wilderness and its indigenous peoples, whom he calls "local experts" on the environment. "There were a people here before the base," he said, "and this was their land."

To my surprise, he received a standing ovation from the three hundred people present, most of them non-Innu. This support was never reflected in the local media, who preferred to report instead what was said by politicians and businesspeople who stood to gain the most from military expansion.

Suzuki issued a warning to the hundreds of Innu who gathered later to hear him speak in the school gymnasium at Sheshatshit. "If you lose your land, you will lose your way of life," he warned. "You may still look Innu, but you will no longer *be* Innu." It was a warning many understood. He had voiced their greatest fear.

A defiant Maniaten holds her protest sign outside the courthouse in the fall of 1989. Her daughter Natash and grandson sit beside her; Tshaukuesh is in the background.

LOUISE OLIGNY

Demonstration at CFB Goose Bay.
Left to right: Manimat Hurley, Lyla
Andrew, Natash Hurley and
Tshaukuesh, accompanied by
children.
ROBERT BARTEL

German F-4 Phantom bombers
lined up on the tarmac at CFB
Goose Bay, 1989.
ROBERT BARTEL

Innu women and a local doctor inspect damage at the bombing range. *Left to right:* Dr. Jane McGillivray, Mani May Osmond, Rose Gregoire and Tshaukuesh (*touching dummy bomb*).

JIM ROCHE

Innu elders are arrested for trespassing on the runway. Manian Michel helps Mary Pasteen board a military bus.

ROBERT BARTEL

Top: In Europe to campaign against low-level flight training, Yvette, Jamie and Ben Michel hold the Innu flag. Behind them are Innu men from villages on the Quebec side of the border.
CAMILLE FOUILLARD

Bottom: Innu mother and child surrounded by military police during a runway protest.
LOUISE OLIGNY

Top: The first Innu go on trial: (*left to right*) Peter Penashue, Ben Michel, Daniel Ashini and Tshaukuesh, April 1989. They were acquitted by an Inuit judge, but the acquittal was later overturned.
ROBERT BARTEL

Right: Father Jim Roche giving out Holy Communion during Mass in a tent at Penipuapishku-nipi, April 1988.
MARIE WADDEN

Bottom: David Suzuki (*far right*) visiting an Innu bush camp, December 1989. Beside him are Kanatuakuet (*left*) and Pien Penashue (*right*).
MARIE WADDEN

A Historic Trial

*"We've been fighting back with everything we've got. We've made
great sacrifices. It has been emotionally draining and very stressful for
us all. But I am proud to say that our efforts have paid off.
For the first time we have succeeded in making Canadians aware of
who we are."*

GREG PENASHUE, SHESHATSHIT

By mid-December 1988 the time had come to dismantle the runway
camp. Jet bomber training was suspended for the season and would
not resume until spring. One by one, tents started coming down.
People were tired of protesting, and Christmas was seen as a good
time to return to the village. Tshaukuesh and Maniaten were the last
to leave, and they did so reluctantly.

"People will go to sleep again," Maniaten predicted. She and
Tshaukuesh dreaded the inevitable drinking binges that characterize
Sheshatshit during the Christmas season. Tshaukuesh was particularly worried. Francis had gone to a detox centre in Halifax earlier
that month, but it hadn't stopped his drinking. He was staying at a
Salvation Army hostel in the city until he had enough money to
return home. Tshaukuesh and Maniaten lamented leaving the runway camp for another reason. They were afraid they might never be
able to come back—in April 1989, the military was expected to tri-
ple security on the base once it had officially taken control of the
facility from the province's Public Works Department.

The Sheshatshit Innu faded from the headlines that winter, but
others took up the cry against low-level flying, mainly Europeans

subjected to the practice in their homelands. On New Year's Day the *Washington Post* reported that opposition to low-level flights in West Germany was growing every day, prompting Chancellor Helmut Kohl to promise that his government would export more flights to Canada or Turkey. A poll on German television revealed that 71 per cent of West Germans favoured a total ban on low-altitude flights. Almost a hundred deaths had occurred in that country as a result of low-level flight training in 1988. Seventy people had been killed in August at an air show in Ramstein, and a few months later a U.S. ground attack jet had crashed in a densely populated neighborhood near Düsseldorf, killing five civilians and destroying a block of homes. In January 1989 the *New York Times* ran a story from Landau, West Germany. It described the response of citizens there to the low-level flights.

> *A screaming jet comes out of the sky, shattering the picture book tranquility of this town of half-timbered houses that slumber, seemingly lost in time, in the verdant southern palatinate. Two U.S. F-16's are practicing for war low over the sun-drenched vineyards.*
>
> *"It's hell, isn't it?" said Erich Hepp, 37, a schoolteacher. Mr. Hepp decided to try to do something about NATO noise after his one-year-old son Stefan was terrified, falling to the ground in trembling panic, by two fighters lowering over Landau.*
>
> *"He was so frightened that he wouldn't come outside for the whole summer," recalled Mr. Hepp, a founder of Landau's Citizens' Movement Against Low-Flying Jets.*

Rupert Scholz, West Germany's defence minister, pledged to reduce Luftwaffe flights by 1000 hours and to cut another 1300 hours after 1990 by having more pilots train over Goose Bay. Reports like this sent shock waves through Sheshatshit as the Innu envisioned their homeland hosting more unwanted European jet noise and danger.

On 12 January 1989, two more West Germans were killed when an Alpha Jet and a Royal Air Force Tornado collided near Hanover. The country's Green Party called for a complete ban on low-level flights, and Walter Kolbow, a defence expert with the opposition Social Democratic Party, said the crash was "deadly proof of the urgency in finding a new defence-readiness concept."

It soon became clear that exporting the problem to Canada was an important part of the solution, and Canada was rolling out the welcome mat. On 18 January, Defence Minister Perrin Beatty wrote to a concerned citizen in Cookshire, Quebec: "Although the 850 Innu of Labrador have concerns about flying training, the vast majority of the 30,000 Labradorians support this activity. This support is reflected by endorsement from the regional and national offices of the Public Service Alliance of Canada, by the Labrador Federation of Munici-palities, and by Newfoundland's House of Assembly which, in each of the past two years, has passed resolutions approving this activity."

In reducing the issue to a numbers game, Beatty distorted the facts. More people than the "850 Innu of Labrador," opposed the flights: the Utshimassit Innu, the 9000 Innu on the Quebec side of the border and another 5000 neighbouring Inuit had all spoken out against them. And the 30,000 Labradorians allegedly in favour of the flights included members of the Labrador Inuit Association, which was also publicly opposed to the training. If the numbers had been added properly, they would have shown that more than 15,000 ab-original people in northeastern Quebec and Labrador strongly ob-jected to low-level training in the region. It was obvious, though, that with Canadian politicians the concerns of non-natives took prec-edence.

As spring approached, Tshaukuesh and Maniaten's fears were borne out. An attempt by the Innu to return to the runway camp in March of 1989 failed. Military police blocked the road leading to the site. When a determined group of Innu walked past the barricade and began to set up a camp, police moved in quickly to dismantle it. Twenty-one people were arrested and tents, stoves and vehicles seized. Nine people, including Tshaukuesh, were thrown in jail.

A few days later Canada's new defence minister, Bill McKnight, arrived for a long-promised meeting with the Innu. McKnight's visit was prompted by an unusual bail condition set for a number of jailed Innu in fall 1988 by local provincial court judge James Igloliorte. Igloliorte had insisted that the accused be granted a meeting with the ministers of defence and Indian Affairs, but the politicians had been too busy with a fall election campaign to comply. Now, with public support building for the Innu, McKnight could no longer afford to delay the meeting. He and his entourage made local history when their helicopter touched down in North West River and they continued on to Sheshatshit: it was the first time a federal cabinet minister had ever been to the community.

McKnight faced an angry crowd in the gymnasium of Peenamin

McKenzie School that day. He listened for an hour and a half to a long litany of complaints, starting with historical grievances and concluding with the recent incident at the runway camp. The minister was polite at first, but as more and more people rose to speak he became visibly irritated. He kept warning Innu organizers that he would have to leave, and his temper got the better of him when crying children came to the microphone to ask him to release their parents from jail. Without further warning, he turned heel on the gathering and walked out. McKnight explained later to reporters that he had "run out of time," yet he spent another half-hour doing interviews outside the meeting hall and then attended a cocktail party on the base.

Angered by the minister's response, the Innu tried to set up tents at the old runway campsite the next day, and once again police moved in to stop them. One of those arrested was Abenam Pone, a thirty-seven-year-old Innu sculptor who had come back to Sheshatshit from Windsor, Ontario, where he had lived for thirteen years, to participate in the protests.

Pone and four others were held for eleven days at a jail in Newfoundland because they would not sign bail conditions requiring them to stay off the runway. They felt signing such an undertaking would compromise their position that the runway was on Innu land and they were therefore doing nothing wrong by walking on it. Pone had been active at the Windsor Native Friendship Centre for many years, and the Windsor *Star* picked up the story. "We don't understand, we feel we haven't done anything wrong," Pone told the newspaper. "I truly believe it is our land and I would do it again. We don't want money, we just want our land and to be left alone—to live freely."

Twenty-six Innu were behind bars by the end of March. The mood in Sheshatshit was tense, and many were discouraged. The jets were still flying and people in nutshimit were still being harassed. Seven of those in jail signed their bail conditions because they feared their incarceration was accomplishing nothing.

But Innu women who remained in custody showed great determination. The women, who included Tshaukuesh, her sister Rose, several of Ben Michel's sisters and members of many prominent families in Sheshatshit, had at first been placed in the lockup at Goose Bay, which was poorly equipped to handle a large number of prisoners. The cells, usually used to keep drunks overnight, were overcrowded and dirty. The women slept on thin mattresses on the floor and ate near the single toilet that served them all. They continued to refuse bail conditions, and eventually they were moved to the women's prison in Stephenville, which had more comfortable facilities but was located across the water on the island of Newfoundland, hundreds of kilometres from family and friends. The experience built solidarity among them, but it was also very traumatic, as Tshaukuesh explains:

> *Twice one night I had trouble breathing in my nightmare. I woke up and looked at a book, hoping it would help me sleep. I fell back to sleep and had this nightmare. I dreamt that my house was on fire and all my children were inside screaming. I tried to run in but I couldn't. Then I woke up one of my friends in the cell. I told her I couldn't sleep, I'd had a nightmare, so she stayed awake with me for a while.*

On 3 April the women were brought back to Goose Bay for trial. Canadian Press reporter Penny MacRae described their return:

> *A group of Innu children howled a tearful greeting as their mothers, jailed two weeks ago after natives protested against low-level NATO flights, arrived at a police station on the eve of their trial on public mischief charges.*
> *The children sobbed and clutched at their mothers as the women were hustled into the station by R.C.M.P. officers. Later, family and friends hoisted the children on to their shoulders to get a glimpse of the women and wave at them through windows covered with wire mesh. Shouts of "Free the Innu" rang out from a crowd of about 40 people as the police wagon arrived carrying the women.*

The trial took place the next day. Since the protests had begun, police had filed 223 mischief charges against the Innu under the provisions of Canada's *Criminal Code*. Four individuals were chosen to be tried first: Tshaukuesh, her son Peter, Daniel Ashini and Ben Michel—all considered to be ringleaders. Lawyer John Olthuis, who had first defended the Innu in 1985 after the Mealy Mountain caribou hunt protest, had come to Labrador to act in their defence.

Early in his legal career, Olthuis had become involved with the Citizens for Public Justice, a Toronto-based group that believes in using the law as a vehicle for social change. The group intervened in

the Mackenzie Valley Pipeline hearings in 1975. They argued that
the chairman who had been appointed to an energy board panel
deciding the fate of the project was in conflict of interest, and succeeded in convincing the Supreme Court of Canada that he should
be removed. They also managed to stall the project until Thomas
Berger's widely known report on aboriginal northerners and their
opposition to the pipeline was published.

"I remember my first meeting with Georges Erasmus at that time,"
Olthuis recalls. "He was a staff person with the Dene nation. He
welcomed our solidarity but said what was most needed was for us to
change our own society. I realized then the real issue is changing the
way we live. We need to work towards a society in which native
people can be what they are, and we need to find a way to redistrib-
ute wealth and focus less on resource development when it threatens
their way of life."

Olthuis did some legal work for the Dene, and then became involved in the horrendous plight of the Grassy Narrows people, whose
homeland had been destroyed by mercury pollution. He watched
both levels of government pass the buck until finally the wrong decision was made. The injured Ojibway were given a cash settlement
and a monthly allowance of up to $700 for life, but not the land base
that would allow them to continue their traditional economy.

"There's a structural racism built into our society," Olthuis says.
"The government was saying, 'What we will do is give them compensation because money will help them assimilate into our society.
If we give them land it will mean they can continue their traditional
way of life and we don't want that.' " The Grassy Narrows people are
still negotiating with the Ontario government for the return of 3260
square kilometres of their traditional territory, retaining Olthuis as
their legal counsel.

Olthuis's strategy for the Innu being tried at Goose Bay had been
carefully worked out at a series of meetings in Sheshatshit. He told
the people he wanted to use a defence that had never before been
tried in an aboriginal rights case: his plan was to argue a legal princi-
ple known as the "colour of right," formally defined as "an honest
belief in a state of facts which, if it existed, would be a legal justification or excuse." Olthuis wished to prove that the Innu were inno-
cent of mischief because "of their honest belief the land is theirs"
and their belief that title had never been legally transferred to the
defence department.

The Innu had little confidence of winning, but they were willing
to give it a try. They knew Canadian authorities were against them,
and the courts were an arm of those authorities. However, they welcomed a chance to air their feelings in public and they trusted the
young judge who was hearing the case.

James Igloliorte, then thirty-nine years old, is from Hopedale, on
the Labrador coast. An Inuk, he is Newfoundland's first and only
native judge. Tshaukuesh had known Igloliorte since he was a boy at
residential school in North West River. She had never spoken to
him—their languages are different—but they had a nodding acquaint-
ance and she admired him as a gentle, understanding man before
whom Francis and some of her children had appeared in court. Other
Innu had had similar experiences with Igloliorte.

Dougald Gillis, the mild-mannered Crown prosecutor in Goose
Bay, received backup from St. John's in the person of Ron Stevenson,
a lawyer with the province's Office of Special Prosecutions. The Newfoundland government wanted to put an end to the Innu protests
and prevent the trial from becoming a platform for aboriginal rights.

The trial opened with several procedural arguments. Olthuis asked
that the prisoners be released from custody and the trial be moved
closer to Sheshatshit so that more Innu could attend. The Goose Bay
courthouse was too small to contain the number of people who
showed up for the trial on the first day, so Igloliorte agreed to hold
the hearings in a large hall in North West River.

On 5 April, hundreds of Innu crowded into the North West River
Lion's Club hall. The young judge sat at a simple table in front; a
chair propped beside him was the witness stand, and a second chair
served the translator. The accused sat with family and friends throughout the room. Children roamed about at will, and people squirmed
restlessly, unaccustomed to sitting still for long periods, particularly
when it required listening to a language many did not understand. The
packed room soon became unbearably hot. Smoking was not allowed
in the hall, so a constant flow of people made their way to the front
steps. Igloliorte bore all the noise and restlessness with grace. He
knew that this trial was important to people in Sheshatshit, and he
wanted them to see justice done. Few non-Innu sat in on the trial
unless there in some official capacity.

Olthuis began by telling the court that his clients did not recognize the jurisdiction of Canadian courts because they have never
signed a treaty giving their land away or giving the courts personal

jurisdiction over them. He said the Innu had agreed to cooperate because they had little choice and because they wanted to tell their story. Igloliorte set a sympathetic tone from the start with his reply.

Canadian law is founded on the English common law and here the Innu are saying they have never agreed to accept this kind of law as theirs. English and Canadian law has . . . omitted to include those who were without a written set of laws. That includes not only Innu people but a large part of aboriginal people in Canada.

While the social injustices against aboriginal people are obvious from the deterioration of their culture across Canada, and here for the Innu as well, the proper framework for this court to hear criminal trials does exist. There is absolutely no question that the Innu have been left out of decisions made which affect their lifestyle and adversely affect their unique society. This court will reply to these issues if they are brought forth as evidence and for consideration during the trial.

The Crown presented its case first. The base security guard, Marilyn O'Dell, described what had happened on 15 September, the first time the Innu went on the runway. Although the Innu were not denying that they had been on the runway, the Crown continued to parade security guards and police to the stand to prove so. Then Allister Michelin, the descendant of a well-known settler family and the defence department's property manager, showed copies of a lease signed by the governments of Newfoundland and Canada in 1941 giving Canada the right to use a 120-square-mile area as a base for the next ninety-nine years. This was the extent of the Crown's proof that Canada and Newfoundland owned the land on which the base is located.

Olthuis then began the defence. He knew he would have no difficulty getting his Innu witnesses to speak, but he could not have known just how passionately and persuasively they would do so. Chief Daniel Ashini spoke first. Asked to explain why he had gone on the runway, the shy young man replied in a faltering voice: "I believe that the way of life of the Innu people, their health, the environment and the wildlife is threatened by low-level flying. I believe it is part of my duty as an individual to try to stop this activity."

"Is it your belief, Chief Ashini, that CFB Goose Bay is located on land owned by the Innu Nation?" Olthuis asked.

"Yes, it is my belief," Ashini replied. To support this, he produced a letter the Naskapi-Montagnais Innu Association had received from then minister of Indian Affairs Hugh Faulkner in 1978. The letter confirmed that the federal government accepted Innu claims to land traditionally used and occupied in northern Quebec and Labrador.

"Now, you've just heard some people tell the judge that Canadian Forces Base Goose Bay and the government of Canada own the land. How do you react to that?" Olthuis continued.

"Well, I'm quite disturbed about it," Ashini responded. "If I saw a document which had been signed by Innu people stating that they have turned over the land to DND or the governments of Canada or Newfoundland I would accept it. But I cannot accept the documentation that they have put forth here."

The chief told the court that none of the elders in Sheshatshit had ever heard of anyone before them giving up ownership of Innu land.

"Are you aware of the fact that Canada has offered Nitassinan to NATO as the location of a full-fledged tactical fighter weapons training centre?" Olthuis asked. Ashini said he was well aware of this. "How do you react to that?" his lawyer queried.

"Well, I don't think that they should have done that without the authorization of the Innu people," Ashini replied. "The Innu people really believe that it's their land and that they never turned over the ownership of the land to any government. It's still their land. The government of Canada has no right whatsoever to turn over the lands to West Germany, the Netherlands or Great Britain for such activities."

Olthuis then asked what Chief Ashini thought might happen if the NATO base was established. Emotion had obviously been building up inside Ashini with each question. At this one, he looked down at his lap, trying to maintain composure, but it was no use. When he looked up tears streamed down his cheeks, and he brushed them away in embarrassment. When he spoke again, his voice was steadier.

"I firmly believe that the land will be destroyed and will be a wasteland. The Innu people will be destroyed. They will be forced to live in the community of Sheshatshit, and other communities, where there are many social problems—alcoholism, child neglect and so on."

There was a hush in the large hall as people stopped moving about. Language had failed to hold the crowd's attention, but emotion now gripped them.

Olthuis next asked if the federal government had ever offered to negotiate a land rights agreement with the Innu. Ashini produced a letter the Naskapi-Montagnais Innu Association had recently received from the Department of Indian and Northern Affairs explaining that the government could hear only six land claims at a time and that the Innu would have to wait their turn. Ashini added that Canada's Constitution Act of 1982 officially protects aboriginal and treaty rights, yet the government failed to abide by this provision.

"Their strategy seems to be to give away our land to third party interests for logging, mining and so on," he continued. "Most recently to the governments of the Netherlands, West Germany and Great Britain. It appears that their strategy is to empty the negotiating table even before sitting down with the Innu people. Our land will be a wasteland and the people will be destroyed before we even get to the negotiating table."

Ashini looked relieved when he gave up his seat on the witness stand to the next speaker, Ben Michel. Michel, his long hair tied back in a ponytail, is a seasoned public speaker, and he comes alive before an appreciative audience. Like Ashini, however, he spoke from his heart. Olthuis began by asking where he got his belief that the land belongs to the Innu. Michel answered, "I was taught by my parents that I'm Innu. I was taught by a foreign school system nothing of my culture, nothing of my people, nothing of my people's history, nothing of my religion, nothing of my rights or our rights as a collective people." Pointing dramatically to a homemade map showing the Innu homeland, Michel said: "My grandfather's dying words were: 'Never sell this land, never surrender it, it is ours, it will always be ours.' And this court is foreign, you who are defending me are foreign, the Crown is foreign, the R.C.M.P. are foreigners to this land. And I truly believe it because there were no white men here when my ancestors were here. So, by what right does Canada say it is theirs?"

Michel had been to the United Nations several times while an elected representative in Sheshatshit, and he quoted from the United Nations Covenant on Economic, Social, and Cultural Rights with some familiarity. "All peoples have the right to self-determination," he read. "By virtue of that right they freely determine their political status and freely pursue their economic, social and cultural development."

The Innu are a people according to criteria established by the

International Commission of Jurists, Michel added, because they have a common history and are tied together racially, culturally, and linguistically, as well as by religion, ideology and common territory.

The defendant sparred humorously with the prosecutor from St. John's, who tried to prove to the court that Michel and the others knew they were involved in wrongdoing when they walked onto the runway.

Stevenson:	*If you went to a store in North West River and picked up a can of Pepsi, for example, and walked out the door without paying, would you anticipate resistance?*
Michel:	*If it were my store I wouldn't, no.*
Stevenson:	*If it is not your store would you expect any resistance or reluctance upon the part of the store owner to allow you to exit that store with a can of Pepsi?*
Michel:	*Without paying for it, but charging it—probably he would let me go without resistance.*
Stevenson:	*I'm sorry I didn't get that.*
Michel:	*If I charged it. If the bill could be forwarded to me at a later date, I wouldn't expect any resistance.*

Stevenson never got far with his can of Pepsi analogy, but it provided the courtroom with a little comic relief. The prosecutor then pursued another line of questioning, hoping to prove that Michel and the others had known it was illegal to enter the runway.

Stevenson:	*Mr. Michel, if a non-Innu person entered your house and damaged or stole your property, would you complain?*
Michel:	*I would complain to the rightful authorities, yes.*
Stevenson:	*And they are?*
Michel:	*The Innu people.*
Stevenson:	*Would you consider complaining to the police?*
Michel:	*They are the very instrument of oppression.*
Stevenson:	*If you were assaulted would you consider complaining to the police?*
Michel:	*As I said, they are the very instrument of Canada's oppression of a people such as ourselves.*
Stevenson:	*Mr. Michel, did you anticipate being arrested when you went onto the runway?*

Michel:	As far as civil rights and civil disobedience are concerned we anticipated removal by our oppressors from what they allege is their property.
Stevenson:	Did you anticipate being arrested?
Michel:	September 15th?
Stevenson:	Yes.
Michel:	At that time anything was possible to be done by our oppressors because in their view we are subjected to their laws and forced into those laws without our consent.
Stevenson:	Were you aware that there was a Canadian law saying that you couldn't go on that runway?
Michel:	I was aware of it but I didn't care very much because it didn't have any authority or jurisdiction over our land.
Stevenson:	So you simply disagreed with that law.
Michel:	It's not my law.
Stevenson:	No, but you disagreed with the law?
Michel:	I can't put it any simpler than that. I don't agree with the laws of Canada. They are colonizers and oppressors. They are an oppressive regime, so I don't agree with their laws.

At the end of the day people filed out of the courtroom feeling purged. They finally had a public forum for their feelings, and Canadian authorities were being forced to listen to them.

Father Jim Roche was called to the stand on the second day of the trial. His presence caused a certain excitement, and people listened intently as he spoke. Here was a church man, an authority figure, who had taken the Innu side against other non-Innu authorities. Roche explained that he had come to Sheshatshit in August 1984 to be community pastor but that his role had since changed: he was no longer pastor, but lived outside the "mission compound," as it's known, and among the people of Sheshatshit in a log cabin where he spent his time reading, studying and praying.

"Could you tell the court what led to the change in the way you were present in the community?" Olthuis asked.

"A process has been undertaken by government, by business, by Church, to bring these people into a western civilization and European culture," Roche explained. "I think it's blatantly obvious now that this can only be done by first destroying the people's former way of life and replacing it with something else. I suppose I began to see

my own role as one of further sustaining, and in some ways further-
ing, that assimilation and oppression."

Roche said that Innu aspirations to take back control of their lives
are shared by many other indigenous peoples in Canada. He denied
that he is a "romantic." He said he had grown to love and respect the
Innu, and so could not sit back and watch what was happening to
them. He told the judge:

> *I think when you look at what is planned for this area in the years to
> come you will see that a life on the land will not be compatible with live
> bombing ranges, more restricted zones, supersonic flight, and other
> ranges. . . . What will happen, I believe, is that their homeland will
> become a vast military playground and an uninhabitable place. . . . And
> if the government is prepared to do so I think they best be prepared to
> build larger jails, a mental institution, more homes for young offend-
> ers—because I think if all this goes ahead we will witness the social
> breakdown of a people to a tragic degree with all of its pathological
> results.*

Roche attacked the misconception that the Innu were protesting
simply to get money from a land claims settlement. The Innu are
struggling for something more important than money, he said—their
lives and their land. The priest suggested that mediators from some
internationally recognized organization be used to resolve Innu differences with the government of Canada. He warned that a solution
will come only when Canada officially recognizes Innu ownership
of the land and agrees to halt low-level flying. In conclusion, Roche
read a very moving statement, and as he spoke not a sound was heard
from his audience.

> *Over the past five years I've held in my arms young Innu people who
> were dying and some who died from an overdose of pills. Young people,
> so confused that they didn't know any longer who they were. I've sat
> with old Innu people in their last days and in their last hours. Men
> and women who died in the fear that who they were, that what they
> believed in, what they had lived for, would be lost. And they died in
> the fear that the land on which they had lived, on which they had
> walked, many of them thousands of miles, would be taken away and
> destroyed. And I've experienced in my own life here and felt in my*

*own heart, the anguish of families—mothers and fathers, sons and
daughters— torn apart by the social disintegration and by the violence
that is done to these people. And I've seen and felt the spiral of deep-
ening chaos and disorder that afflicts them. The violence that is done is
not done by these people. It is done to them.*

*And I am proud to see Innu people who walked upon that runway
. . . ready to act on what they believe is right and just. And I am
proud of a people ready to sacrifice their freedoms, their comforts, their
very families for what they believe in. And I conclude by saying that
what is happening to these people must stop. And the sources of injus-
tice, the sources of destruction, must end. No matter how long it takes,
no matter how many times they must walk upon the runway, or camp
on the bombing range—no matter how long they must stay in jails, or
come before this court—they must not stop struggling for their land,
because if they stop struggling they will die and with them will die the
better part of ourselves.*

When Father Roche finished speaking, people applauded, even
though many had not understood exactly what he had said. The Innu
could read from the faces of the non-Innu that his words were having an emotional effect. Igloliorte, visibly moved himself, adjourned
court.

When Father Roche got up from his seat, he was immediately
surrounded by Innu well-wishers. In a rare show of public emotion,
some Innu hugged the small man, while others were content to simply shake his hand. Roche burst into tears, and so did several of the
people beside him.

■

The Labrador press covered the trial dutifully, but it was the work of
Canadian Press reporter Penny MacRae, describing the trial's emotional highlights, that captured national headlines. Defence Minister
Bill McKnight was asked in the House of Commons what his government was prepared to do to help the Innu. McKnight revealed his
ignorance of the nature of Innu leadership by complaining that he
had been unable to meet Innu leaders on his recent visit to Sheshatshit.
He had wanted to assure them, he said, that no new foreign air forces
would train at Goose Bay until the environmental impact assessment
was completed. But he quickly shifted the emphasis away from the
issue of Innu rights. "There are other individuals who live in Labrador," McKnight reminded the House. "There is an economy there

that depends on expenditures that take place in the region from the Goose Bay defence establishment." And Assistant Deputy Defence Minister Robert Fowler told reporters that even if the Innu were to win their aboriginal rights argument in court, the planes would fly because "if we're talking air, that's federal government jurisdiction."

Reaction to the trial was subdued in Newfoundland and Labrador because so few people felt threatened by it. Most believed the Innu would be convicted no matter what they said. More support for the Innu came from outside the province, however. Halfway through the four-day trial a dozen members of the Alliance for Non-violent Action were arrested for blocking the entrance to national defence headquarters in Ottawa by setting up their tents on a busy downtown thoroughfare.

■

On the third day of the trial, Maniaten nervously took her place on the stand. Her son Eric and nephew Matshen held up a map while she described in Innu-aimun her nomadic childhood. Another of her sons, Nikashan, translated her words into English.

"My hopes for my grandchildren is for them to have the land that they own and that it not be destroyed by military or other developments," she said. "I hope that they can enjoy their lives in the country as our forefathers did while hunting and trapping."

She then spoke directly to the judge: "Six of my children are here today facing you, to answer charges of mischief. . . . I have told you about the destruction of our land and this is more criminal than what we are doing, fighting back peacefully. . . . So today the court should be the other way around. Your government and the military, and the R.C.M.P. as enforcers of these foreign laws, should be facing an Innu judge."

Tshaukuesh took her turn on the witness stand following Maniaten. She said she went onto the runway for her grandchildren's sake. "We will lose our culture if the land is destroyed," she said. "We will lose our identity as Innu people and will not survive in the country any more if the wildlife is demolished by development. For you people, European people, white people—you can take your meals from the store. You can survive that, but our people have to depend on the land."

Tshaukuesh said she could not understand why she and others had been jailed for their protests.

While we were in jail we women tried to figure out why we were there, what crime had we committed? Just because we were trying to protect our land which is ours?

Those who are doing low-level flying . . . why can't they use their own land? Why do they have to come here and destroy our land and our lives?

Before anything was developed here we had good lives in the country. There was never any disturbance, only the breeze in the wind, the waves on the lakes. Now you hear tremendous booms, jets flying over you. You just can't live the way our forefathers lived. We can't do it. Everything is destroying us.

Tshaukuesh spoke of her children's future. She spoke of her fear of losing her children, of the tears she and other Innu have shed over this issue, of the pain and suffering of the elders. She pleaded with the court to do what it could to help. "We have tried very hard. We have done protests. We have gone to jail for the thing that we truly believe is ours," she told Igloliorte. "From our hearts, from the elders to the newborns, we believe that this is our land."

The next witness called was Tshaukuesh's father-in-law, Kanatua-kuet. When asked to describe his childhood, Kanatuakuet tersely replied: "As far as I can remember there wasn't any white people telling us what to do." He acknowledged that he too had been on the runway, and added he was doing nothing wrong. "We are not foreigners," he said. "We didn't come over to settle our homes here. We were here before you people and I strongly feel that the land we call Nitassinan belongs to Innu people. The government should not put laws, like for example a partridge licence. I went to court one time for killing a partridge and it took two years to settle in court what I had done. As a young man I was a hunter, a good hunter, and I have killed lots of animals to help my family survive. How many crimes, how many laws did I break then?"

Kanatuakuet's grandson Peter Penashue was the last witness to appear. He began by describing a visit he had recently made to Anchorage, Alaska, a visit that left a lasting impression. "I can't explain the feeling I had when I walked downtown in Anchorage, when I saw Iñupiaq people drunk on the streets begging for money. I think we've seen in Sheshatshit the social collapse that I saw in Anchorage but what I saw there is much, much more advanced than what I'm seeing today."

Peter had been watching the trial unfold with growing anger.

I've been here I guess, what, a couple of days now. And I've been sitting in the corner watching the Crown. I watch them and I see that every time that someone, some of our elders, old people, women— when these people had something honest from the heart to say, you turn around and crack a joke. And if we're going to . . . play a role in this conference, we've been beaten. Because first of all you've never taken us seriously. You've robbed us of everything that we've had.

The lawyers presented their summaries the following day. The Crown argued that the Innu had knowingly trespassed on base property, despite frequent warnings from security personnel. The prosecutors alleged that the Innu had known they would be arrested but had gone ahead with their actions anyway to get publicity.

Olthuis challenged the assumption that the base was DND property. In a dramatic gesture, he referred to the Innu packed into the courtroom as the "living title" of Nitassinan, and read out family names. People began to rise from their chairs as their names were called. "The first generation," Olthuis read, "Mary Adele Andrew, Germaine Andrew, Marty Andrew, three generations of living title. Mrs. Mary Ann Michel, Mary May Osmond, Geraldine Andrew, Melinda Osmond. Matthew Penashue, Francis Penashue, Peter Penashue, Jean Paul Penashue . . . "

One by one, grandparents, parents and children stood to face the judge. Olthuis proceeded:

This is the living title of the nation of Nitassinan here present in this courtroom and justice demands that this living title be recognized. Title lives in the hearts of these people, and it cannot be erased by some government somewhere waving a magic wand and saying, "Presto, Nitassinan now belongs to Newfoundland and Quebec." It is, I submit, your Honour, either madness or premeditated genocide for a so-called civilized democratic society to deprive the Innu of their homeland in defiance of the rule of law. The Innu have never signed a treaty or any agreement giving Canada any rights. But along about fifty years ago the government of Newfoundland gave Canada a piece of paper that said it was leasing the area where the base is now located to Canada. They have no right to do that. No more than Chief Ashini would have to lease downtown St. John's to the Cree of Quebec.

The trial was over. The Innu had stated their case with dignity, and many felt, no matter what the outcome, that something important had been accomplished. The only thing to do now was to wait until 18 April, the date Igloliorte would announce his decision.

The Judge Understands

*"And our children who are protesting with us will earlier understand
what we are struggling against.
They will be active at a very young age."*

MANIMAT HURLEY, SHESHATSHIT

Canadian Press reporter Penny MacRae and I were the only two
passengers on the DC-9 from Montreal the morning of 17 April 1989
who had Goose Bay as a final destination. I was going back to Labrador to do film research, while Penny was on her way to report on
Judge Igloliorte's decision. Penny's articles on the trial had been given
a lot of prominence in the country's leading newspapers, but she
confided that the verdict might not get the same attention.

"The outcome is a bit inevitable, after all," she said. "Everyone is
expecting them to be found guilty."

"But just imagine what a great story it would be if the judge ac-
quits them," I said. "What a precedent that would set."

"Yes, but it's so unlikely."

She was right. The Innu people deserved a victory, but the odds
were against them. They had been on the runway, and under Canadian law that was considered trespassing, even though the land in
question had never been ceded by the Innu to Canada.

The following day people from Sheshatshit lined themselves along
the sidewalk opposite the North West River Lion's Club building
where the verdict would be delivered. They carried Innu flags and
picket signs and banners that read "Innu Are Not Criminals," while
a ghetto blaster loudly trumpeted Kashtin and other Innu music.

At two o'clock we entered the building, and soon the makeshift courtroom was crammed with close to two hundred people. Judge Igloliorte took his place and called the court to order. Uniformed R.C.M.P. officers stood along one side of the room, while three of the four accused—Ben Michel, Tshaukuesh and Daniel Ashini—sat in front, facing the judge. There was a delay while we waited for Peter Penashue to arrive. Peter, whom I had seen earlier helping someone change a flat tire, came hurrying in a few minutes later, out of breath. The judge began to read his decision, reviewing first the evidence and then the charge. "On or about the fifteenth day of September 1988, at or near Happy Valley, Goose Bay, Labrador in the Province of Newfoundland," he read, "[the accused] did willfully interfere with the lawful operation of property, to wit, the Canadian Forces Base Goose Bay, contrary to . . . the Criminal Code of Canada."

Igloliorte dealt with business matters first. He suggested that the Crown consider applying his judgement to all of the people charged. He read in a taciturn, matter-of-fact way, creating cliffhanging suspense in the courtroom.

"Since we know [who are] the present users and occupiers of the land at the base, the Crown had little difficulty presenting a prima facie case," the judge said.

My heart sank. Most of the Innu standing beside me at the back of the hall could not understand what Igloliorte was saying, and they watched my reaction. It didn't look good.

Then, abruptly, this bombshell: "In my opinion, Mr. Olthuis has presented a valid defence and also a successful one. We are not dealing with any land which has been the subject of divestiture through treaties as under the Indian Act."

I couldn't believe my ears. It seemed too good to be true.

"Each of these four persons based their belief of ownership on an honest belief on reasonable grounds," the judge said. "Through their knowledge of ancestry and kinship they have showed that none of their people ever gave away rights to the land to Canada, and this is an honest belief each person holds. The provincial and federal statutes do not include as third parties or signatories any Innu people. I am satisfied that the four believe their ancestors predate any Canadian claims to ancestry on this land."

Max Gregoire, Tshaukuesh's younger brother, looked at me in alarm. I had tears in my eyes, so he thought the news was bad. I smiled and whispered, "No, no, it's good news, it's great news, the very best news possible. You won."

Igloliorte had written an eloquent judgement. His words were poetic, the sentiments profound. "Since the concept of land as property is a concept foreign to original people," he said, "the Court must not assume that a 'reasonable' belief be founded on English and hence Canadian law standards. The Innu must be allowed to express their understanding of a foreign concept on their terms, or simply to express what they believe."

Igloliorte was not satisfied just to vindicate the Innu that day—his judgement was made for the benefit of indigenous people everywhere in Canada.

All of the legal reasonings are based on the premise that somehow the Crown acquired magically, by its own declaration of title to the fee, a consequent fiduciary obligation to the original people. It is time this premise based on seventeenth-century reasoning be questioned in the light of twenty-first-century reality.

Canada is a vital part of the global village and must show its maturity not only to the segment of Canadian society that wields great power and authority . . . but also to its most desperate people.

The 40-year history of these Innu people is a glaring reminder that integration or assimilation alone will not make them a healthy community.

By declaring these Innu criminals for crying "enough!" the Court will have been unable to recognize the fundamental right to all persons to be treated equally before the law.

Both sets of the foregoing reasons are sufficient, in my mind, to have these four acquitted of any wrongdoing under s.387 of the Criminal Code of Canada.

Outside the courtroom, merriment swept through the crowd. The Innu were exultant—at last, a victory. How gratifying to hear someone in authority express so beautifully what they felt, deep in their hearts, was right.

A press release hastily drawn up by the four accused expressed their elation over the decision. "This is an historical day of great pride and joy for the whole people of Nitassinan. . . . By this decision the court has questioned the foundations on which Canada has

worked in dealing with aboriginal peoples in attempting to accul-
turate and assimilate them."

The country reeled with the news. The media didn't know how
much to make of the fact that Igloliorte was himself native, but the
Innu had no problem attributing some of their success to that fact. The
Inuit were experiencing the same social breakdown and oppression
the Innu were, and Igloliorte understood what a judge from the south
could not.

Native rights advocates were overjoyed as well. James O'Reilly, a
lawyer who had worked with the James Bay Cree, the Lubicon Cree
and the Mohawks at Kahnewake, phoned the band council office in
Sheshatshit and advised Daniel Ashini to make the best of the publicity provided by Igloliorte's decision. O'Reilly was certain the ruling would be overturned, but he optimistically told reporters that
the case would force the federal government to "come out of hiding" and recognize the Innu dispute with the military as first and
foremost a land rights issue.

"The Innu case is one of the best documented and strongest cases
in the whole country," O'Reilly said. "The government has tried to
ignore the real issue, and the court is bringing it back to the front
burner."

NDP Indian Affairs critic Robert Skelly was also pleased with
Igloliorte's ruling. "It's an excellent decision and it really shakes to
the foundation some of the rigid property rights views that judges in
numerous courts in the past have applied to conflicts between native
society and the dominant society," he told the press. "I would expect
the Crown now to drop the charges against the remaining defend-
ants."

"It's business as usual," base commander Col. Phil Engstad said
sourly when he heard the news. Engstad was convinced that the acquittal would be appealed long before the Crown made any move to
drop the outstanding charges.

Newspaper response to the decision was mixed. In an editorial,
the *Globe and Mail* suggested that low-level flights be suspended for
six months so that negotiations between the Innu and government
could get under way.

"The ruling . . . must be clarified by higher courts because it raises
more questions than it answers about Canadian sovereignty, native
rights, property rights and common justice," wrote the editor of the
Montreal *Gazette*.

Bob Nutbeem, a columnist for the St. John's *Evening Telegram*, scoffed at Igloliorte's judgement and suggested that the judge, "paid for by the government of Canada," be reprimanded for his decision. As for the Innu, Nutbeem said their claims to the land were spurious, and he encouraged them to stop "wallowing in history." "It's apparent to me," he wrote, "that history has passed them by, and unless they want to be captives in a massive aboriginal zoo, they will inevitably fall under the steamroller of time."

Brad Morse, a law professor at the University of Ottawa, told CBC Radio that the Crown would have little choice but to appeal the decision. "The stakes are simply so great from Ottawa's point of view, not only the implications for aboriginal peoples elsewhere but also for the impact on Canada's reputation with its NATO allies." He added that the judgement "tends to authorize" the Innu to continue sit-ins on the runway, something deeply feared by officials at CFB Goose Bay.

The Innu wasted no time in responding to the judge's decision. The following evening volunteers went door to door in Sheshatshit to collect signatures on a petition addressed to the base's air force commanders. It said:

> *We remind you that Canada has no legal claim to these seized lands, and as countries flying out of Goose Bay you are accomplices to this illegal activity. Our protests during the fall of 1988 have already shown that Canada is unable to guarantee the use of the practice bombing range and the security of the runways and ramps of CFB Goose Bay*
>
> . . . .
>
> *We have never given Canada, the U.S. nor any other European government permission to use our land. The airspace in which you fly is Innu airspace and the land over which you fly is Innu land. You are trespassing on our land and we are telling you to leave. We are defending our life and land and we will not stop.*

The next morning a convoy of trucks arrived at the hospital on base, and about a hundred Innu disembarked. Armed with their flags and banners, they began marching towards Canadian Forces headquarters. As soon as the protesters came into view, CFB employees locked the doors and peeked nervously from behind curtains, as though expecting attack. "We have a letter for Colonel Engstad," Daniel shouted through a megaphone. "We'd like to deliver it to him in person."

But too many military egos had been hurt by Igloliorte's decision.

Military police, the R.C.M.P. and the militia soon arrived on the scene in great numbers and began to assert their authority by clearing the area of reporters, TV cameras and newspaper photographers.

"This is DND property," one officer told me. "Leave immediately or you will be put under arrest."

"That's ridiculous," I retorted. "There's a civilian airport here, two schools, a hospital. The public uses these streets all the time."

"You heard what I said," he fired back. "Put that tape recorder away and leave the base immediately."

A second, more menacing warning came from a man who attempted to block me with his body, and I was about to obey him when I saw busloads of uniformed men with billy clubs arrive and begin to line themselves across the road. The Innu confidently proceeded towards the human barricade, proudly chanting, "This is Innu land." The military was being tougher than usual; what was it they didn't want us to see? Penny MacRae and I decided to stay. We ignored the intimidation and continued to follow the parade protectively.

Once again, the perceived leaders were separated from the rest of the marchers and put into waiting police cars. First they took Daniel Ashini, then Ben Michel, Greg Penashue, Tshaukuesh, Peter Penashue, and so on. The marchers continued to move forward. When the police took Lyla Andrew, she passed her infant son to Father Jim Roche, who, when he was arrested shortly afterwards, passed the baby on to someone else.

Then the flag bearer was taken, and I watched in surprise as Edward Nuna, the other high school student who had lived at my home in St. John's, rushed forward to take the flag. Edward was a timid young man who hadn't taken much of a part in the protests before this; now he was bravely standing in the forefront. He looked at the police unflinchingly as they hustled him aboard the bus with the rest of those arrested. Edward and other students in an adult education program had attended the trial. "My personal feelings as I listen to court," Edward wrote in his notes on the trial, "are that if I were the government of Canada, I would settle land claims, and let the Innu live in their homeland peacefully and support them to preserve their culture as the new age of technology creeps upon them. But the government of Canada hides behind the black curtain. Just waiting to see that Innu give up their land."

Before long, all of the adults had been picked out of the parade, leaving a small group of children. They continued walking forward, facing members of the Royal Canadian Regiment who held their riot sticks in front of them. The children kept going until they hit this human wall and could walk no farther.

Colonel Engstad felt it necessary to flex military muscle that day, letting the Innu know that the judge's decision had no meaning for him as base commander. All of those arrested were later released by police since the legal situation was too cloudy for charges to be laid. Engstad later acknowledged that his men had had no right to prevent the press from covering the event and apologized, but the damage had already been done. The public never saw this show of intimidation against a people who had come armed only with a sympathetic court judgement. Police had not interfered earlier that fall when the Innu delivered similar letters to the Canadian, British, U.S., West German and Dutch military headquarters on the base. Jim Roche speculated that the military reaction this time was "an attempt by DND and the Canadian government to show Europe they're going to be tough and no Innu are going to disrupt anything on the base."

There was a great deal of negative reaction in Goose Bay to Igloliorte's judgement. "If [the Innu] have gotten away with this, it means anarchy has taken over Canada," warned Goose Bay mayor Hank Shouse. He complained that Igloliorte was "too lenient" and should be removed from the bench.

The Innu waited for some response to their acquittal from Ottawa but heard little more than a promise that it would be "studied." Rumour had it that government lawyers were trying to find a way to override the decision.

Intrigued by everything that had happened, a West German television crew travelled to Sheshatshit, as did a team from "Pulse News," Montreal's most popular English TV news program. The Innu, angered at the way the base commander had responded to their successful court ruling, decided to take advantage of the national and international publicity by going back on the runway to once again assert their land rights. A community meeting was held on 24 April to decide how best to do this. Planning for the new demonstration was shrouded in secrecy, for many in Sheshatshit were convinced that their phones were tapped and that some people in the community were being paid as informers by the military.

The Innu had discovered a blind spot in military security. A "spy tower" was used to conduct round-the-clock surveillance of base property, but staff in the tower could not see the area directly beneath them where there was an unsecured gate to the runway. The Innu would use this fact to gain access.

A cavalcade of trucks left Sheshatshit early on the morning of 25 April. They were spotted by two R.C.M.P. officers a few kilometres from their destination, but the officers were powerless to prevent the Innu from going through the fence. There was no time to use wire clippers; in a split second a chain on the gate was axed and hundreds rushed onto the runway. The protesters resolutely sat on the tarmac until police reinforcements arrived and lifted them, one by one, onto waiting buses. The military tried to prevent news photographers from recording images of the Innu resistance by placing a number of large vehicles in a strategic spot in front of the fence.

This time protesters were charged under the National Defence Act, not the Criminal Code, because administration of the base had recently been transferred from Newfoundland's Public Works Department to the Department of National Defence. The Innu feared the change might mean that the new case would be taken outside Igloliorte's jurisdiction.

The next morning a bail hearing was held in Goose Bay. When police brought in the jailed Innu, families and friends cheered. Daniel Ashini, one of those arrested, passed the crowd a note: "Good morning, NATO busters!" He explained the prisoners would plead not guilty in the hope of ensuring that Igloliorte maintain jurisdiction over the case.

Tshaukuesh, also among those jailed, looked drawn and tired as she walked towards the courthouse. "Why was I jailed again when the judge already agreed I was doing nothing wrong by going on the runway?" she asked. Resisting efforts by the police to move her inside, she began to speak to reporters. "We will continue our struggle. We know the government is trying to intimidate us but we will never stop fighting to protect our land." She shrugged off the grasp of an R.C.M.P. officer while a translator repeated her words in English.

Another arrested woman, Manimat Hurley, handed me a note when police escorted her inside the courthouse. "We can't understand why Tshaukuesh and I are kept in custody. My sister Clem, and Germaine Rich weren't kept, even though they were in Stephenville [jail] with us recently, and also entered the runway yesterday."

The Crown argued the jailed Innu should not be granted bail as long as they refused to stay off the runway because they posed a threat to public safety. Crown witnesses said a disaster had narrowly been averted when three British fighter pilots and a pilot flying a private Cessna had difficulty landing on the runways occupied by Innu demonstrators.

According to Bart Jack, an Innu witness, however, the schedules of private aircraft companies had been checked to ensure there would be no planes on the runway, and the weather office had said the skies were too overcast that day for much flying.

The Innu remained defiant. They argued through a local legal-aid lawyer that it was unfair to detain just eleven of the thirty-three arrested the previous day. They challenged the court to jail everyone, but police officials pointed out they did not have enough room for that many people. Then Tshaukuesh asked to speak, and Igloliorte, in keeping with his informal courtroom style, allowed her to do so. She stood facing the judge, her thick black hair tied back in a scarf, a translator at her side. Tshaukuesh spoke in a trembling voice that bore witness to her fatigue and frustration.

We are continuing our actions today because of your earlier ruling about our honest belief we own the land. We understood your decision and wonder why DND is still persecuting us when we honestly believe this is our land and our ownership predates European contact. You know yourself the aboriginal people were here first. We are standing firm in our decision to fight the governments who use our land as a military wasteland and we will continue to fight. We are also going to be strong. We are getting stronger every day because of our belief that this is our land.

We really have strong ties to our land. Our interest is our duty to the animals, the land, the environment. Today as I am standing here there are people in the country reporting they are harassed by the aircraft. They can't hunt. As I am standing here in court this is happening.

The minister was here not long ago. He walked out, so you can imagine our difficulty having dialogue with the government. In a snickering manner the minister left, instead of staying to learn something from the Innu. The Innu are always portrayed as irresponsible and ignorant. This is how we are always portrayed. The government probably felt the Innu would always stay quiet and let the government do what it likes with the land. We will not be quiet and let them do what they like.

Now we are jailed for what we are doing. I have been in court and jail five times. My mother and father never ended up in jail. I have to go to jail to fight for my rights. I have not eaten since yesterday. I keep thinking about this.

My husband is in the country right now while my son and I are in jail. When I looked at the cell this morning—a blanket and no bed—I must remember I am doing this for my children. Do the governments have any heart, any remorse? How are they going to proceed? What are they going to do next? I stand here and pledge before you that we will continue to fight for our honest belief that this is our land.

There were few dry eyes in the courtroom when she finished speaking. The judge scribbled furiously in his notebook. An elderly Innu woman beside me wiped her eyes with a shredded tissue and Matshen, Tshaukuesh's son, wept, covering his face with his hands.

After lunch Igloliorte returned. There was the same mood of expectation, the same suspense that had been in the makeshift courtroom at North West River only ten days earlier. This time there was no preface; the judge launched immediately into a statement he seemed to have written especially for Tshaukuesh, whom he referred to by her English name.

Elizabeth Penashue and her people have good reason to feel frustrated and angry since they have not been given a chance to decide how their lives as a distinct people should be directed.

I have no doubt that the strength and determination of the Innu to try and regain self-respect has not been shaken, but rather strengthened in their combined effort to have the authorities pay attention to them. There will be many Elizabeth Penashues that Canadian authorities and administrators are going to have to listen to, because these people believe their concerns are real and long-standing. To expect that one meeting or any number of trials will ever allow Innu grievances to be sufficiently met is unrealistic. Listening to what the people are saying will be the first real test for authorities.

But Igloliorte was under a lot of pressure this time to discourage more Innu protests on the runway. He accepted the Crown's argument that public safety must take precedence over Innu land rights and put conditions on the prisoners' release:

The Innu feel compelled by their beliefs and commitments to maintain their protests. They have expressed a willingness to forfeit their freedoms as individuals in their struggle for self-determination . . . to emphasize their plight to the Canadian public and possibly the larger world community. I have no difficulty with this position. As a judge, however, who routinely deals with all manners of people, I must emphasize safety over individual freedom . . . . Consequently I rule that the Crown succeeds on the basis of public safety and the protection of the public, of whom the Innu are an important part. They can all be released by signing undertakings before a justice with the first two conditions sought by the Crown.

It seemed Igloliorte felt he had gone as far as he could to support the Innu. The prisoners met during a recess to decide what to do. Many of them, anxious to regain their freedom, signed the necessary conditions for their release.

"It's a minor problem, the fact that we have to sign an undertaking to get out," Tshaukuesh explained to reporters outside the courthouse. "The important thing to understand is it is our land and we will continue to fight for it, the way we have been fighting—by going over the fence."

Weeks later Mary Adele Andrew, one of the first Innu to camp on the bombing range, died of cancer. Her death brought the community close together once again, this time in mourning. People paid tribute to her in a distinctively Innu funeral service. When Mass was over, everyone filed past the open coffin and kissed the dead woman on the forehead. In the tiny burial ground beside the church, mourners encircled the grave and tossed wildflowers as the coffin was lowered.

Tshaukuesh stood beside the grave with her rosary beads in hand and said a silent prayer to her dear friend. She vowed that she would keep up the struggle her friend had started and prayed for success on a voyage she was about to make. Tshaukuesh went home after the funeral to pack her bags and bake enough bread to supply her family while she was away.

Help from the Outside

"It is much easier for us to support struggles removed from us—for example, the struggle against apartheid in South Africa. But when the struggle is brought home to ourselves, it is much more difficult."

GORDON HUSK, CHURCH LEADER, ST. JOHN'S

The plight of the Innu was attracting so much attention that the National Action Committee on the Status of Women invited representatives from Sheshatshit to their annual general meeting in Ottawa in May 1989. Tshaukuesh, her sister Rose Gregoire and Kathleen Nuna were chosen to go. Tshaukuesh was forty-four years old and had travelled very little outside her homeland. She had been to Maliotenam, an Innu reserve near Sept-Îles, and to the Catholic shrine at Ste-Anne-de-Beaupré, but never to a large city. The Innu women didn't know what to expect, but they saw the trip as an important opportunity to build public support.

The three women were met at the airport in Ottawa and taken to Carleton University. Three beds were squeezed into a tiny residence room so they could stay together. Tshaukuesh set up her tape recorder and treated the others to music by her favorite country and western singer, Kitty Wells. Rose sat by the window concentrating on writing a speech. Kathleen lounged on the bed, a copy of the Bible in Innu-aimun in front of her; she looked up occasionally to suggest ideas for the speech. Tshaukuesh sewed a pair of moccasins.

At the opening night banquet, the three women sat shyly in the back of the dining room. The six hundred women at the conference were from many different backgrounds and walks of life. The sound of everyone talking at once made Tshaukuesh smile, for it reminded her of large flocks of geese. Soon, though, she became frustrated because she couldn't speak English well enough to join in. Occasionally she nudged Rose to translate, but Rose was too busy talking herself. Kathleen stood shyly against a nearby wall.

On the first day of the conference the three were taken on a tour of the city. The stately buildings on Parliament Hill were a dramatic reminder of how much money and power the Innu were up against. Near the West Block, the women came upon a large group of native people gathered to protest cutbacks to student funding. They wandered closer to hear the energetic Wolf Pack drummers entertain the crowd, and when the music ended they found themselves alongside the drummers on the podium. Konrad Sioui, vice-president of the Assembly of First Nations, who had met the women in Sheshatshit, greeted them enthusiastically and introduced them to the crowd. Embarrassed to find themselves suddenly in the limelight, the Innu women shrank back.

Tshaukuesh was the first to find her voice. She spoke to the crowd in Innu-aimun, perhaps unaware that these native people did not speak her language. "I am happy to be in Ottawa and to see so many other native people defending their rights and their land," she said. "I wish everyone luck and wish to thank you for your support." The drummers dedicated a song to the Innu, and red ribbons were tied around the womens' arms.

The Innu women presented their story at a NAC conference workshop the next day. Tshaukuesh and Kathleen carefully placed framed pictures depicting life in nutshimit along blackboard ledges while Rose reviewed her text. The room was crowded when she began to speak.

Rose began by describing the past thirty years of Innu history in Sheshatshit and the present social conditions of village life. She spoke about the militarization of her homeland and what it is doing to her people. She spoke of the number of "little blond children" appearing each year in Sheshatshit who will never know their British, American or West German fathers. An informal tally had revealed that approximately fifteen children in the village had been fathered by military personnel; "souvenir babies," they are called. Young Innu women from dysfunctional alcoholic families hang around the base, Rose explained, looking for love or a better life in the arms of a handsome pilot, but instead are sexually exploited and left to bear the consequences. Rose told her listeners that a Canadian Air Force employee had recently been tried and convicted for raping a young Innu woman, who subsequently tried to kill herself. Several German soldiers with AIDS had recently been sent back to Europe from Goose Bay, prompting fears that the disease might reach the village, especially if the numbers of transient military men continued to grow. If the proposed NATO base were to be established, more than 65,000 men would pass through Goose Bay each year for training.

"I have watched my people begin to fall apart," she said. "I have seen our children robbed of everything that makes us Innu in a school system which makes them look down on their own people and culture. The government that invaded our country now thinks we are weak enough to bury alive. The one thing that has stopped our complete breakdown as a people has been the months we still live away from the village in our tents in the country."

Rose told her audience that the low-flying jets harass people in nutshimit and endanger wildlife. "For the families who now have houses in Sheshatshit, we find ourselves right alongside what Canada wants to make into a NATO base," she explained. "Even with no base, each year the military grows bigger and bigger. There is now one bombing range and many, many targets, where they do not yet drop anything but use for practice attacks. Most of these are on or near lakes where the Innu go in the spring and fall. Nitassinan is our land. We never gave it to them. What makes them feel they can come in and take it, and treat us as if we are not human beings, as if we are invisible?"

Kathleen and Tshaukuesh next spoke about the photographs, describing the landscape, the importance of hunting and the work women do in the country. Tshaukuesh moved along the blackboard gallery and stopped at a nature scene, a breathtaking vista of snow-covered tundra bathed in the vivid colours of a subarctic sunset. "This is a scene in the country," she said. "This is why we're fighting to keep our land and our culture—because it is so beautiful."

Pointing to a photo of a hunter grinning from ear to ear as he butchers a caribou in the snow, Tshaukuesh explained: "This fellow is very happy. He's very proud that he got a caribou. It's just like gold. It's just like winning a million dollars for him to get a caribou. When he's in the country he's very happy. When he's in the community he's drunk most of the time. This is why we're fighting so hard to keep our land, because if the land is gone, there is no culture."

Next the women spoke of their experiences in jail. "What kind of a people are they? They have no heart," Tshaukuesh said of the politicians.

The Innu women spoke of intimate things they did not normally share with strangers; they felt they could trust these non-Innu women whose faces displayed great sympathy. Tshaukuesh spoke of her greatest sorrow, a son who has tried to kill himself. "I don't quite know how to describe the feelings I have," she said. "When he's in the community he always has trouble, drinking, once he took an overdose of pills. He almost died. But when he's out in the country he lives very well, he doesn't drink alcohol, all he does is work hard and tend to his traps, he is very healthy out there."

Tshaukuesh explained how government wildlife regulations hamper life in nutshimit. She told her audience she had phoned home that morning only to learn that Francis's camp had been raided by wildlife officers and that a group of Innu hunters from St-Augustin had been arrested for hunting on the "wrong" side of the border.

Word of their story rapidly spread beyond the classroom, and the next morning the Innu delegates were invited to speak in front of the whole assembly. "Show us the paper we signed giving away our land," Rose said to the large group of women. "We were not asked if the military could invade our land. The government has stolen our land. We are treated as though we don't exist."

Delegates of the National Action Committee passed a resolution asking the government to immediately demilitarize the Innu homeland, and a collection was taken to help pay Innu legal costs. Strangers came up to Rose, Kathleen and Tshaukuesh to express their concern and ask what they could do to help. This display of support was a big boost to the trio's morale.

From Ottawa, the women travelled to Toronto for public meetings organized by supporters there. Joanna Manning heard them speak, and wrote this for the *Catholic New Times*:

As I walked out of the meeting into the early summer evening, I thought of how, as an immigrant from Europe flying in over Northeastern Canada, I had been so struck by the sheer vastness of the Canadian landscape and the quiet overarching emptiness of the Canadian sky. I remember how, in my first job as a high school history teacher, I had to cover the tragic story of the slaughter of the Beothuk in Newfoundland. And now the survival of another of the world's oldest aboriginal cul-

tures is at stake—not in the rain forests of Brazil, nor in the outback of far-away Australia, but right here in our own country. There is still time to act. Otherwise, what will we teach our children about the Innu?

■

Support grew dramatically for the Innu following their trial. The Inuit Tapirisat and the International Inuit Circumpolar Conference, organizations that represent Inuit from all over the world, condemned the low-level flights. John Amagolick, president of the Tapirisat, explained why his people are against a military buildup in the North: "Our people's experience with the military has always been socially negative. The availability of alcohol, for instance, is very destructive. Military men are very well known to go after young women, and the military activities will have an effect on the traditional lifestyle."

In May, a St. John's Sunday *Express* editorial said: "The manner in which they [the Innu] have become accustomed [to living] is nothing less than a national disgrace. We implore Mr. Wells [the new Newfoundland premier] to treat the requests of the Innu and other aboriginal groups seriously."

Douglas Roche, a former Canadian ambassador, wrote in the *Toronto Star*: "It's a pity at least some of the 9,000 training flights over Labrador this year aren't being flown over the Gatineau hills or Georgian Bay cottage country. Canadians would soon be storming Parliament Hill."

Alarmed by the momentous increase in public support for the Innu, businesspeople in Goose Bay moved to do something about it. On 23 May a parade of cars carrying hundreds of residents drove to the base and then around town, honking horns and carrying pro-NATO banners.

In an effort to generate more good publicity for the base, Lt. Robert Jodoin, Colonel Engstad's second-in-command, leaked a copy of the defence department's Environmental Impact Statement to a Toronto reporter. The plan backfired when the reporter identified Jodoin as the source of the leak. The statement was not officially released until six months later, leading to speculation that it was being rewritten at DND headquarters.

Politicians and the military continued to extol the economic benefits of the NATO base, and they were more interested in impact than in accuracy. The speech from the throne opening Newfoundland's legislature that spring, for example, claimed that military operations in Goose Bay had injected $150 million into the provincial economy in 1988 and created five hundred jobs. In fact, few new jobs were created: four hundred and fifty employees from Newfoundland's Public Works Department were transferred to the military payroll after the defence department was given control of the base.

The Newfoundland government and the Department of National Defence continued to make dire predictions that the Goose Bay economy would be destroyed if the base did not grow. Yet when the Americans drastically reduced their operations at Goose Bay in 1976, the local economy had not died. It diversified, and recovered so well that by 1983 the town's residents were earning more money on average than people in Newfoundland: $19,895 compared with $17,504 on the island. Government services previously headquartered in St. John's and Ottawa were transferred to Goose Bay when the Americans pulled out. In 1989, 80 per cent of Goose Bay's work force was employed in the service sector, and 40 per cent of those people worked for one level of government or another. The town had become a service centre for tourism and outfitter trades, and supported a thriving fishery—activities that might actually suffer with military expansion.

Some independent sources disputed the government's claims. Dr. Michael Bradfield, an economist at Dalhousie University, estimated that 80 per cent of jobs created by military expansion in Goose Bay would go to military personnel and their families. Jobs created outside the base would be low-skill service jobs, including prostitution. "Most of the people of Labrador will lose if the NATO base goes ahead," he predicted, "because of increases in prices, taxes, economic stability, environmental damage and social breakdown."

According to Bradfield, a few residents of Goose Bay would become richer, particularly the Woodward family, whose business supplies jet fuel, while those on the lower end of the social scale would suffer. "The base will put considerable strain on local services and cause severe social problems," he concluded, "particularly for the native communities who will, according to DND's Environmental Impact Statement, bear most of the cost and few benefits if the NATO base is approved."

But the propaganda war continued, and few in the press bothered to dig below the economic rhetoric.

■

Tshaukuesh joined Francis and the children in nutshimit as soon as she returned from her trip. The family was camped with several others at Minai-nipi, a long, narrow lake about forty kilometres south of Goose Bay near the Quebec-Labrador border. The presence of Innu at Minai-nipi that spring made the military very nervous. The camp was close to the bombing range and some Innu men had made trips to the range, forcing it to close for several days.

In June of 1989 the minister of Indian and northern affairs, Pierre Cadieux, visited Sheshatshit. Cadieux too was concerned about growing public support for the Innu. He decided not to repeat Bill McKnight's mistake, assuring everyone at the outset that he had come to listen.

And listen he did, for hours, as speaker after speaker came to the microphone. The meeting went on all morning and part of the afternoon, and the Innu did most of the talking. They poured out their hearts to the government man. Cadieux listened politely, his face rarely exhibiting any emotion.

The chief of Utshimassit, Cajetan Rich, described the legacy of twenty-three years of village life for his people. "Children in our community are now addicted to gas sniffing. We haven't got a decent drop of water to drink."

Peter Penashue returned to the theme he first raised in court with Judge Igloliorte, that the patriarchal attitude of governments makes it difficult for the Innu to be taken seriously. "Could you get the mandate to treat us like adults?" Peter asked. "If you went to cabinet and said that we have to treat the Innu like adults, what would they say? They'd say Cadieux, get the fuck out. We have to find a way for the Canadian government to treat us like adults. I'm very interested in sitting down with the federal government because I know we can't keep fighting. But you'll deal with us as adults only when you're shamed into it."

Old Mary Pasteen, dressed in the fashion popular with women of her generation—a long plaid wool skirt, her hair gathered in two knots at the side and covered with a multicoloured hat—spoke in a whisper that was barely audible. "I remember the day we lost our independence. Now we've become so dependent it has destroyed us. It seems we always need more money because of the institutions that now serve us. Your hunting laws are obstacles to the continuation of our lifestyle."

Simeo Rich told Cadieux that his father is one of the people buried under the Smallwood Reservoir near Churchill Falls. "If I had been told about the planned flooding I would have made arrangements to move my father's body somewhere else."

One of the teenagers who had been on the bombing range, Eric Andrew, gave the minister a lesson in Innu civility. "It is considered very rude to tell someone where they should sit in a tent. You've entered our tent and told us where we should sit . . . Sheshatshit is like a box and people can't get out."

After everyone had spoken, Cadieux made a cold, bureaucratic response. He stuck to a prepared text and did not even address the other issues raised by the speakers. He was ready to offer money for uninsured health benefits and money to enable the Innu to intervene in the environmental review process, he said. He was also ready to discuss land claims negotiations but would not halt military expansion while those talks were underway.

The minister was not heard from again. There were no political developments after his visit; little seemed to have been accomplished except that the government appeared in public to be doing something about Innu concerns. Over the summer the community became divided about what should be done next. A decision on the NATO base was expected in the spring of 1990, and press reports indicated that Goose Bay was favoured over Turkey. Many feared that they had gone as far as they could and that their efforts were futile.

Rose Gregoire refused to accept defeat. She was invited to speak about the Innu problem to groups in Atlantic Canada, and, buoyed by the support she received there, returned home full of fervour and renewed commitment to keep her people "awake" and politically active. "I made up my mind when I got home," Rose says, "that I would plan a demonstration to get my people back together again, and be strong, even if it meant going back to jail."

But getting the people together that fall was not easy. Tshaukuesh and Francis were preparing to leave for the fall hunt, as were many other families. It had been a difficult summer. The protests the year before had sapped people mentally and physically, and they wanted to restore their health in nutshimit. The will to protest was weakened further by the fact that security on the base had been tightened. A heavily guarded checkpoint at the main entrance ensured that any Innu entering the base, whether to take a child to hospital or a relative to the airport, attracted an uninvited police escort. Phones were tapped, and the military encouraged divisions in the community, paying informers to alert them if protests were planned.

Rose Gregoire had a plan, however. She looked for people she could trust. One night she gathered a small group together at her house—Manimat Hurley, Raphael Gregoire, Daniel Ashini's sister Jackie and Joachim Selma. All five decided to go back on the runway, their action to be recorded for European newspapers by a supportive young photographer from Paris who had arrived at the village a few weeks earlier. They hoped this would convince NATO governments that Goose Bay would be a poor site for a jet fighter base because of weak security.

At midnight on 18 September, the five Innu and their photographer crept stealthily over a fence and spent the night hiding in woods near the runway. At 9:30 A.M., when the first military jet began to taxi from its hangar, the Innu ran in front of it holding their flag. The jet had to swerve to avoid hitting the demonstrators. The Innu managed to disrupt base operations for only half an hour, the time it took for them to be arrested and taken away. They were brought before Judge Igloliorte the next day.

An R.C.M.P. witness told the judge that this was the seventeenth time Innu people had violated base security (ten times on the runway) and argued that it was important to make an example of these five to discourage other Innu from doing the same. Manimat could not have realized the risk she was taking when she decided to join the others that night. She had not been on the runway any more often than the rest, but she had been arrested and jailed more frequently, and in April she had signed an undertaking promising to remain off the runway. Police and military officials were eager to make an example of the twenty-nine-year-old mother of three. Judge Igloliorte was being pressured by the justice department to do something to discourage the Innu from ever going back on the runway. He told Manimat she must remain in police custody until her trial several months later. The other four could go free only if they promised to stay off the runway. Manimat's companions, bristling at the unfair treatment of their friend, refused to sign the release papers and were sent to jail with her.

Manimat appealed the decision in provincial Supreme Court, but Judge Seamus O'Regan proved unsympathetic. He humiliated her by asking how a mother could behave so irresponsibly, and was unmoved when she explained tearfully that she was acting to safeguard

Nitassinan for her children and grandchildren. O'Regan called the woman a threat to public safety.

Manimat was sent to join Rose Gregoire and Jackie Ashini at New-foundland's Correctional Centre for Women. Located on the west coast of the island, it was hundreds of kilometres away from their families—the most brutal punishment of all.

"I wish my children won't be at the airport when I leave," Manimat wrote as she waited in the Goose Bay lockup for the flight out. "It will just tear my heart in two. I am suffering enough in here. I will miss them, they will always be in my heart. My little boy Trevor will be three years old October 9. Our wedding anniversary will be on October 8. These are important dates to remember. My birthday is October 15. I will have to remember these dates."

Manimat passed all of these family landmarks in prison. Fortu-nately she had Rose and Jackie to keep her company most of the time. For more than a month they refused to sign bail conditions and stayed with her in a remarkable show of love and respect.

I first got to know Manimat when I visited the Minai-nipi camp a few months prior to her arrest. The Hurley tent was perched high on a hill overlooking the lake, and one day I found Manimat putting the finishing touches on the Innu equivalent of a freshly washed and waxed floor—a soft carpet of new boughs. She had just made a batch of doughnuts, and we sat eating them outside in the sunshine as a family of mergansers floated serenely by on the water below. Manimat confided that she had been keeping a diary. She disappeared inside the tent for a moment, then brought out a stenographer's notebook. The pages were filled with tidy handwriting in English. It was a day-to-day account of life in the camp and she invited me to read what she'd written.

"Here in the country Innu are always telling how people used to suffer in order to survive," I read in one passage. "I listen to their stories and wonder how the Innu were so courageous and brave. They really put strength into what they were doing. Our ancestors cannot be forgotten for their bravery when they continued to pass on tradi-tions from generation to generation. I often ask questions to myself: Is it wrong for us Innu people to walk in the footsteps of our grand-fathers, grandmothers, ancestors? Is it wrong for us to continue prac-tising the Innu traditional way of life?"

Manimat wrote most powerfully about how her involvement in the protests has changed her. "I always used to think that I was a useless Innu. I felt that non-natives always beat the Innu. But now everything has changed since our protest has begun. I feel we are stronger and frustration feelings are being let out . . . It feels like trying to get out of the years and years of being stamped under."

While in prison Manimat continued to write, and her diaries reflect her strong commitment to preserving Innu culture. In a moving letter to her children she wrote: "Don't ever feel that what I did was wrong. I did it mostly for you children. I want to see you grow up and be proud of yourselves and our identity. No one has the right to destroy our culture. . . . I always wonder why people with dark colour skins have to be treated differently, why is it that we have to be put down like we don't even exist?"

During the time that Manimat, Rose and Jackie were in prison the Sheshatshit Innu staged another demonstration. A press release explained that they wanted to show solidarity for those behind bars.

Sparked by the action of five fellow Innu who attempted to stop a military jet at CFB Goose Bay one week ago, approximately fifty Innu today streamed through a gate and under a fence to occupy one of the main runways at the military base. An Innu grandmother picked berries beside the runway, on the very ground where she and her family picked berries before the coming of the military base.

Five F-16 fighter jets waiting to take off were forced back to their hangars. Military police had thought their new security precautions had made the base impenetrable, but they were wrong. While police were arresting one group of protesters, a second lot made their way onto the runway from another entry point. Among those arrested were two European citizens—the Parisian photographer Louise Oligny and a West German critic of low-level flying—and a Montreal member of the Alliance for Non-Violent Action. This time police concentrated on arresting all the non-Innu (among them Father Jim Roche and Lyla Andrew), and only a handful of Innu were charged.

"They arrested us," Oligny complained in Montreal's daily *La Presse*, "because they want to leave the impression the Innu are being manipulated by outsiders."

Like Manimat, Jim Roche had signed an undertaking promising not to go back on the runway. But his commitment to the cause had grown so strong that he was willing to risk a long jail sentence.

"Throughout the world a small people like the Innu have gotten nowhere without a sustained struggle and effort of resistance," Roche told Judge Igloliorte when he appeared in court the next day. "The fact that a small number of Innu have been within the airfield should not overshadow the real danger to public safety posed by the military operations here. The fact is, Canada has offered the homeland of the Innu, Nitassinan, as a place to rehearse and develop more advanced and efficient ways to kill each other. Any discussion of public safety must be seen in that context."

But Roche's words had little effect, and he was jailed until his trial in the spring. Raphael Gregoire, who had been arrested with Rose and Manimat, was happy to have the popular young priest for company at the Goose Bay detention centre. Roche spent more than six months in jail, but he didn't waste his time there. He organized the native prisoners in his cell block into an encounter group.

By the fall of 1989 the Innu in Sheshatshit knew the stakes were higher than ever before. Five of their people were now in prison, and Judge Igloliorte could no longer be counted on as an ally. Their campaign of civil disobedience seemed to have been stretched as far as it could go. In the months ahead their agenda was filled with court dates, the most important of which was the appeal of their historic acquittal.

Victory Is Snatched Away

*"The native peoples have little confidence in the Canadian judicial
system and my personal experiences over twenty years in the area of
native law have provided me adequate reasons to be very sympathetic
to this view."*

JAMES O'REILLY, LAWYER

On 3 October 1989, John Olthuis stood beneath the high, ornate
ceilings of Newfoundland's Court of Appeal facing a group of men
who knew very little about Labrador's aboriginal inhabitants. Newfoundland's five Appeal Court judges had been asked to review
Igloliorte's decision, and Olthuis feared they might overturn it.

The Crown had requested the appeal on the grounds that the trial
had been improperly conducted due to a procedural error. During
the original trial, Tshaukuesh, Daniel Ashini, Ben Michel and Peter
Penashue had been tried together even though they were charged on
separate informations (the piece of paper containing the charge). The
Crown should have tabled a joint information once it was decided
that the four would be tried together. Olthuis told the Appeal Court
judges that the Innu should not be penalized for the Crown's mistake, particularly since the error had violated the rights of the Innu.
He added that the accused had been acquitted on the substantive
ground of colour of right, and this fact should also be taken into
consideration. But the Appeal Court judges seemed unimpressed.

Tshaukuesh, Francis and Maniaten were in St. John's the day of
the hearing, along with Daniel Ashini, his sister Janet, Rose's chil-

dren and Manimat's family. They planned to listen to the decision, then travel to Stephenville to visit the three Innu women in prison there. Supporters had helped to pay their travel expenses.

A rally was planned, and by noon a small crowd had gathered in a park on Duckworth Street next to the Court of Appeal. Sitting on a stone wall beside her nephew Daniel, Maniaten made an impassioned plea for the release of her daughter, sister and niece from prison. Tshaukuesh and Francis slipped away from the crowd to watch what was going on in the courtroom.

The five judges of Newfoundland's Appeal Court represent the cream of the St. John's establishment. Two of them are brothers-in-law, all are members of the same golf club, and all five live in the city's prestigious East End. Most have ties to one political party or another. One is a personal friend of federal cabinet minister John Crosbie's, another is a former justice minister in the Smallwood government, a third is past president of the province's Liberal Party, and the most recent appointment to the bench, Bill Marshall, had been one of Brian Peckford's most trusted cabinet ministers.

The men seated on the bench before Olthuis had much more experience with government and big business than they had with people like the Innu. The sharp and impatient way they directed their questions at Olthuis raised the suspicion that their minds had been made up before they entered the courtroom. "Let's be sensible here," one of the judges interjected when Olthuis tried to outline his argument.

The Crown was hoping the Appeal Court would order a second trial with a different judge, effectively removing Igloliorte from the case to prevent further acquittals. Olthuis argued that subjecting the Innu to another trial would be cruel, particularly since the Innu had been acquitted, and would compound a violation of their rights that began with the Crown's error in the first trial. The Appeal Court judges adjourned for a couple of hours and then returned with their decision.

"The Court derives no satisfaction in having to nullify the trial and the acquittal in this matter on technical grounds. It has no choice. . . . The decision of the Court is that the trial and the acquittal of the respondents are nullities."

The judges, in a pen stroke, sent Innu hopes into a tailspin. When the meaning of the Appeal Court decision was explained to them, Tshaukuesh shook her head in dismay while Francis looked angry and disgusted. Manimat's husband Melvin sat on the grass near the courthouse, cradling his children in his arms, tears unabashedly flowing from his eyes, aware that his wife would take the news hard in prison. Before he left Sheshatshit, Melvin had put up a sign outside his house that read, "My wife shouldn't be in jail, Canada should be."

(It is important to note that the Appeal Court verdict did not strike Igloliorte's decision to acquit the Innu, based on the colour of right argument, from the books. His decision was used as a precedent in November 1990 when Gary Potts, chief of the Temagami Cree, was acquitted of mischief charges. Ontario Provincial Court Judge R. N. Fournier notes in his decision that Igloliorte's ruling was defeated on a legal technicality and not on the merits of the case. John Olthuis has received requests from other lawyers for his legal brief on the colour of right and says that this defence is being put forward in aboriginal rights cases across the country.)

It was not until after the written decisions of the Appeal Court judges were released that it became clear there was a dissenting opinion among them. Judge William Marshall had not agreed with his colleagues that the Igloliorte trial should be overturned on a technicality.

"I have come to the conclusion that acquittals of persons jointly tried on charges laid in separate informations ought not to be set aside on jurisdictional grounds," Marshall wrote. In arguing that the "separate informations" ruling, first used to overturn a trial in 1921, is outdated, he quotes from a recent ruling of the Ontario Court of Appeal: "Obsolete judicial precedents ought not to bind modern society when they are shown to serve no real purpose." Marshall concludes, "This appeal should be dealt with on its merits which centre on Innu ancestral claims and the application of the Colour of Right defence provided in the Code."

But Marshall's opinion was only one in five, not enough to influence the outcome. The Innu felt the historic decision—that they were not guilty of trespassing since they believed themselves to be the rightful owners of the land—had been snatched away.

The Appeal Court did not recommend a new trial; it left that decision up to the Crown. Olthuis warned that if a new trial were held he would appeal to the Supreme Court of Canada on the grounds of Marshall's dissent and the Charter argument that the accused had been acquitted and should not be tried twice for the same offence.

But the Crown found a way around this problem. It ordered a trial for a different group of Innu protesters, to take place in February 1990, at a time when James Igloliorte was not available to hear it.

Manimat, Rose and Jackie wept when they watched the TV news in prison that evening. They caught quick glimpses of their families at the rally outside the courthouse, and then heard the Appeal Court decision. The only consolation the women had was knowing they would be seeing their children the next day.

"My daughter Janet didn't cry, I was very proud of her," Rose wrote to a friend later about the visit. "I felt really bad when she left. I held back my tears even though it broke my heart. I wish I was free to go home with them. My little girl Theresa said she wants to stay in Stephenville so she can visit me every day. I told her she couldn't stay and she said, 'Why? You're my mommy.' I feel so sorry for her."

"It was a sad day for me, inside me, when they left, but I did not show it here, I didn't want to," Rose told someone in another letter. "Sometimes, I wonder what people think of us, leaving our kids behind. Maybe they think that we don't love our kids. . . . We love our children so much—that is why we are in prison."

Rose and Jackie were flown to Goose Bay for a hearing on 16 October, and at that time they signed the undertakings so that they could leave prison. They could not bear the separation from their families any longer. Manimat had no choice but to remain in jail until her trial. When she was finally released from prison on 6 November 1989, she had been jailed for a total of fifty-two days.

Authorities had achieved what they wanted: Manimat's long confinement discouraged other Innu from going onto the runway. The setback in Appeal Court seemed to underscore for many in Sheshatshit that they were fighting an uphill battle. For a while at least, the fire of Innu resistance seemed to have been extinguished. Fortunately, their supporters held the torch in the months that followed.

One cold, drizzly morning in November 1989, activists tied up rush-hour traffic in Ottawa after the Remembrance Day weekend. More than a hundred people sat on the street, blocking the entrance to national defence headquarters and tying up traffic on the busy Mackenzie King bridge. Some, following the Innu example, set up small tents and carried banners calling for the demilitarization of the Innu homeland.

The protesters refused to cooperate with the police who tried to move them. Each person had to be carried off by two officers, and because the police were unprepared for the size of the demonstration, city buses had to be commandeered to take the demonstrators to police headquarters. A seventy-year-old woman from Montreal, Charlotte Debanné, was among those arrested, along with a couple of women from Sheshatshit. In all, 112 people were found guilty of public mischief, and the *Ottawa Citizen* called their trial the largest in Canada. Many refused to pay their $100 fines and said they would give the money to charity instead; a sympathetic judge even agreed that some of this money could go to the Innu defence fund. News of the event cheered people in Sheshatshit and gave them reason to hope, once again, for change. Clearly, they were winning the battle on the public relations front.

Ben Michel and his family were invited by European supporters to tour Great Britain, the Netherlands and West Germany. Ben's mother, an artisan who makes beautiful things from caribou skin, dressed her grandchildren in Innu clothing. On the day the Michels gave a news conference in London, American members of Survival International and a small band of South American Indian leaders marched with placards in front of the Canadian embassy in Washington to support the Innu.

Even public opinion in Newfoundland was changing. In December 1989, an editorial in the St. John's *Evening Telegram* said the economic spinoffs of a NATO base should not be the only consideration. "Moral questions enter into it as well," the editorial stated. The newspaper criticized Liberal MP Bill Rompkey for promoting the base and ignoring his Innu constituents. "It has to be asked whether Newfoundlanders and Labradorians have the moral right to impose upon the aboriginal Innu people a scheme which they find repugnant. These are all matters for us to ponder. And Mr. Rompkey should certainly ponder them before he runs off lobbying for the base as if it were just another project like a post office or government wharf."

∎

The public learned more about the proposed NATO base in the winter of 1989 when the department of defence finally released its impact statement, twenty-two months behind schedule. The document, called an EIS (Environmental Impact Statement) was required as part of the environmental assessment review process ordered by the federal government. It was clear from reading a description of the $555-million project that it was unlike any other make-work project in Canadian history. Not unexpectedly, the impact statement, financed by DND, gave the NATO base a green light, but it made many environmentalists and supporters of the Innu see red. The scale of the project as described in the EIS was so massive it threatened to totally wipe out indigenous cultures in northeastern Quebec and Labrador, turning their homelands into one of the largest simulated battlefields in the world.

Eleven bombing ranges were to be built. The largest, called an air combat manoeuvring range, was to cover 8100 square kilometres. Three bombing ranges were to be used for live weapons training, enabling rockets, bombs and guided missiles to be dropped by the thousands each year, the same kind of artillery that led to a forest fire near CFB Petawawa in the winter of 1990. There was also to be an "academic range," in which aircraft flying 150 metres above ground would release their weapons over targets as observers in nearby towers scored their performance. Bombing practice would not be confined to the land, either. Under the NATO scheme, from June to November each year jet bombers would be allowed to release inert weapons over the ocean.

In all, Canada was offering for NATO's use 120 000 square kilometres of territory—almost a third of the entire Quebec-Labrador peninsula. In one promotional brochure, DND says: "Labrador alone is bigger than all the British Isles; one third larger than Germany; and about the same size as Italy; and twice the size of Greece. Truly, this is the ideal location to carry out productive, realistic tactical flight training!"

Military planners say the area's aboriginal people are unreasonable for wanting to keep the land to themselves. But very little is left for the animals and their aboriginal hunters after subtracting the territory that is most heavily populated (on the Atlantic coast and the Quebec north shore), the land planned for military use, the land that has been developed for mines and hydro projects, and the land that lies underwater or is covered by mountains. It has been estimated that the climate and resources of the Quebec-Labrador peninsula can support only one person per twenty-five square kilometres.

The military claims in the EIS that 40,000 jet bomber flights, flown by fledgling pilots, can avoid both the hunters and the more than half a million migrating caribou. Neither the Innu nor the Inuit believe this is possible.

The fears of indigenous hunters seem to be borne out by the compensation DND has had to award Canadians whenever military aircraft stray from approved routes. In 1989, $145,000 was paid in damages, particularly to farmers. A farmer in Chatham, New Brunswick, was awarded $45,000 because a CF-5 jet flew low over his fox farm, causing the females to eat newborn kits and pregnant foxes to abort. A farmer in Mountain Grove, Ontario, was paid $10,000 because over-passes of military aircraft caused the deaths of his goats and hens. "The [pregnant goat] mothers would lose their kids when the flights went over," Frank Bennett told the *Ottawa Citizen*. "The flights were so low, the ground actually shook." Bennett eventually sold his farm. He says his hens stopped producing eggs and his turkeys had heart attacks, while neighbourhood cows stampeded and broke down fences when startled by aircraft noise. Innu and Inuit hunters say they ex-pect wild animals to respond more dramatically, particularly since what was planned to happen over their heads in northeastern Que-bec and Labrador was on a scale unimaginable to most Canadians.

Realistic air-to-air combat, involving all of the air forces training at Goose Bay, was to take place on a large scale several times a year. The airstrips at Schefferville and Churchill Falls were to be upgraded to serve as alternate airfields. Luftwaffe aircraft, playing the enemy role, would take off from one airport, while the other team left from another. As many as ninety jets were to be involved at any one time. Forty jets, flying at low levels, would be responsible for carrying weapons to assigned targets, while fighter escort aircraft, flying at 300 metres, would engage the opposing air force in combat to en-sure that the bombers reached their targets unmolested. Meeting in the air, the two sides could then practise dogfighting by firing simu-lated ammunition and air-to-air missiles at one another, using after-burners to descend quickly from high altitudes, then darting out of sight at supersonic speeds. This kind of training is incredibly dan-gerous, and it creates sonic booms that can be heard and felt many kilometres away.

Sonic booms are already a problem in the Innu homeland. Shishin Rich told me that people in her camp heard them in the fall of 1988.

We had a lot of trouble with the military jets when we were camping, supersonic booms. You can hear them far away, literally shaking the tent I was in. I was reading some magazines as my sister was sewing away, it shook me up nervously. I went outside to stand and listen. I didn't hear any jets at all except what was supposed to be a practice bombing range, not far from where we camped, "beaver lake." The children were running and crying . . . I was frightened for the children because they were between ten to two years old, plus a newborn baby who was only four months old.

The establishment of a NATO base would result in up to 466 sonic booms a month, although the military have said that most months only 71 would be audible, small comfort to Rich and her family.

The EIS acknowledged that conditions in Labrador aboriginal communities are "third world" and that the people of Sheshatshit were most at risk from base expansion. "Not only is the range of social impacts on the Innu residents of this community expected to be more extensive than the impacts on any other community," the EIS admitted, "but the impacts may involve both the more rapid marginalization of the community and increased racial tension between the residents and those in nearby communities." The defence department's document also confirmed the higher than average suicide rates in Innu communities and concluded that the problem would worsen with military expansion. "These communities are neither stable nor resilient to any further change that may occur in their social, economic or environmental circumstances."

High-profile support for the Innu came at a press conference in Toronto when entertainers like Bruce Cockburn and Gordon Lightfoot joined scientists in condemning the EIS. The Environmental Assessment Review Panel ordered the defence department to rewrite the document.

■

Innu hopes of ever winning recognition of their rights in court faded after the Appeal Court decision. However, the people had little choice but to try again in February, when the second trial had been ordered. On 6 February 1990, more than a hundred Innu from Sheshatshit tried to squeeze themselves into the tiny courtroom in Goose Bay. Those who could not sit on the floor stood by the door, determined to hear what was going on.

Judge Richard LeBlanc was on loan from Labrador City to hear this trial. LeBlanc, like Igloliorte, was a recent appointment to the bench, but, unlike Igloliorte, he was extremely businesslike in court, anxious to do everything by the book. Many Innu felt that the new trial was being held to give the government the verdict it wanted. LeBlanc refused to hold the trial in North West River as his predecessor had done, even though it would have been more convenient for the Innu. "Maybe people in Goose Bay would like to come to this trial," LeBlanc said, turning down the request. None ever did.

There is no public transportation between Sheshatshit and Goose Bay, and it costs $60 to make a round trip by taxi. To attend the trial, the Innu had to make the two-hour journey each day crammed unsafely and uncomfortably into the village's few cars and trucks. Some even rode in the back of open trucks in -20°C temperatures.

During the trial the judge spoke so softly most of the time that no one except the lawyers who faced him could hear him. A translator told the judge what Innu speakers were saying, but there was no translation for the Innu when the judge spoke, except when he asked a particular witness a question. Few Innu could follow what was going on.

The Crown once again argued that the Innu endangered public safety whenever they went on the runway. The Crown's star witness was Capt. John Ravinda, an air traffic control officer. Ravinda spoke in a monotone and called the Innu intruders. He testified that on 26 September 1990 two fighter jets almost ran out of fuel because they could not land while the Innu were on the runway. Olthuis argued that there was plenty of room on other parts of the airfield, but Ravinda insisted this was not the case.

Olthuis planned to present his colour of right defence, but also to argue "defence of necessity," to prove that any threat posed to public safety was insignificant compared with the threat the Innu believe low-level flying poses for the future of their society. The first defence witness was the respected hunter Pien Penashue. Pien used a large map to point out the vast territory over which he has hunted and travelled in his lifetime. R.C.M.P. officers stood up to see where Pien was pointing, amazed at the distances he has covered on foot and by canoe. The Crown lawyer and judge seemed equally captivated as the energetic old man gave them a geography lesson on the Innu homeland. Pien explained that all his travels were "done for survival." "We never used maps," he said, straining to locate a familiar lake or river on the chart in front of him. "All the places I've been to are mapped in my head."

Pien testified that in 1930, when he was a young man, there was no town of Goose Bay. "The place where this courthouse is located used to be good berry-picking grounds. There was no presence of government at that time," he said. "If the government owned the land they'd have had some presence here. It's a new thing, the concept of the government owning the land."

His people never gave Canada, Newfoundland or Quebec permission to take Innu land, Pien said, nor to rule over Innu lives. He cast a powerful spell in court that morning, and it held everyone—until he started to talk about the effects jet bombers have had on the environment. "The difference between the military men and me," he said, "is that they're flying in the air, they don't see what's happening on the ground. They don't see the contamination they cause. But I'm down there, walking around, hunting the animals. I see what is happening and it's not good. There are lots of things happening to the land that nobody knows about. It's in the interest of the military that nobody knows."

Gorman jumped to his feet. He objected, saying that Pien was not a scientist and was not qualified to speak about the effects of low-flying jets on the environment. The judge upheld the Crown's objection. He asked the translator to tell Pien he could continue talking but must leave out references to any harm he may have noticed to the environment because he was not an "expert."

When Peter Penashue translated the judge's instruction, Pien looked deflated; his energy seemed to disappear, and he sat in the witness bench looking for the first time that day like an old man. But he could not be so easily contained. He reverted to a metaphor. "The other day I found a partridge with a dollar bill in its throat," he said, suggesting that money now rules the Innu homeland and is threatening to choke the animal masters.

Pien continued to talk about the changes he has seen on the land until Gorman objected again. Once more the judge favoured the objection and once again he ordered Pien to avoid areas in which he was not an "expert."

"The so-called experts aren't out on the land and don't see the animals every day," Pien explained. "I know a lot about what's going on in the country. The scientists aren't on site like the Innu are. There's lots happening to the caribou," he warned. "There's lots happening out there."

Pien concluded his testimony with a question he directed at his people. "What are we doing here?" he asked, and then left the stand.

Tshaukuesh was called next, but she did not get very far in her testimony. She had been preparing what she would say for weeks and had written important points down on a piece of paper.

"These days, when people go to the country," she said, "they are frightened. . . . Innu people tell of how poor the animals are, they are skinny. . . . Now we are poor because of government interference with our lives. . . .When the federal government tells the Innu people something, it is always lies."

Gorman jumped to his feet. "Your Honour, the witness is referring to notes."

The judge ordered Tshaukuesh to lay down her notes and begin again. She looked crushed and confused, then spoke to the translator, who asked for a recess. Court was adjourned until the following day. As soon as the judge left the room the storm burst and everyone began to talk at once. Olthuis and John Joy, a St. John's lawyer and second counsel, huddled in front with a few of the accused until an anguished voice cried out in English: "There are many people who don't understand what is happening here." It was Louisa Penashue. "Please tell us what is happening."

Olthuis spoke while someone translated his explanation of why the judge had kept interrupting Innu witnesses.

"Why couldn't Tshaukuesh refer to notes?" Mani May Osmond asked. "The R.C.M.P. officers referred to their notes."

"We are wasting our time here," Shimun Michel said. "That judge is like the government, he doesn't want to listen to us."

After more discussion, those assembled decided to pull out of the trial and refuse further cooperation. They planned to announce their decision formally when court resumed.

The next day when the clerk ordered all to rise as LeBlanc entered the courtroom, the Innu remained in their seats.

"Your Honour," Olthuis announced, "I have been asked by my clients to withdraw from this case. I think they have something they'd like to say to you directly."

Olthuis took a seat at the back of the courtroom and one of the six accused, thirty-year-old Nikashan, Maniaten's son, began to speak. He explained that he had decided not to participate further in the trial because he was upset at the way Pien and Tshaukuesh's testimonies had been interrupted.

The elders are the heart and soul of our resistance against foreign laws made by foreign governments. The elders should be given a chance to say their full story. . . . They are the generation that first witnessed the onslaught of exploitation and negative development on our land.

I now find myself, and I'm pretty sure all Innu do, at the final stage of our 9000-year history of hunting and gathering. This is not what we want to see, and I guess that is why we are here today, to defend our 9000-year history from disappearing forever. . . .

Here we have a judge, Crown, defence lawyers, R.C.M.P., all playing perhaps at the very existence of a people who have a nation, a common language, history. . . . We are a people beaten to the ground but are still breathing because we refuse to die. We are adamant in protecting our culture, our land, our history and the future of our people. My people have endured too much pain.

Nikashan's sister-in-law, Lyla Andrew, was the next to speak.

The Innu who have filled this court have sat both patiently and politely and tried to listen to these proceedings, without the court providing any simultaneous translation into the only language most of these people speak. . . .

If Innu abuse their families and drink themselves to death it seems non-Innu would see no loss, but to stand up for themselves and fight for their children's future, this is seen as the greatest sin. When I walked on the runway with my children who are Innu, and with my family, I was privileged to be with them. Innu have taken me with them into the country and over the years have shown me, more than any other non-Innu has had the privilege to witness, the strengths and joys of life which is still being lived in the country by Innu of all ages. When I followed Innu onto the runways I knew why I was there and so did the hundreds of Innu I was following. . . .

You have labelled our conduct as mischief. You are wrong. The Innu have taken actions of collective self-defence. The Innu as one people are defending themselves against ethnocide, as they continue to struggle against the systematic attempts to kill their culture. They are seeking justice, a justice which since the beginning of the occupation of their land has been denied.

Jim Roche, by now sickly pale as a result of his four-and-a half-month confinement in jail, rose to speak. He told the judge that Canadian society's belief that it has somehow been divinely ordained to impose its culture, religion, and economic, political and military power upon the Innu has had dreadful consequences.

"We came first to take, and we have never learned to give," he said. "We came to teach and instruct. We have not learned to listen.

We came to save, and in doing so, have inflicted terrible suffering, even in the name of God. Today we refuse to allow these people to speak—or we refuse to hear them—for fear that *we* now have something to lose."

"Yesterday I heard something very hard to take," said Sebastian Nuna in Innu-aimun, his head obscured by the large hood of his parka. "You told one of our people he was not an expert, not qualified to speak about low-level flying. Pien is very qualified to speak about the issue."

LeBlanc was shaken by the morning's events. Setting legal formality aside, he spoke from his heart:

> *I am thirty-five years old. I have been a judge now for approximately six months. I have practised law for ten years before I became a judge, and little did I realize when I accepted an appointment to the bench that I would be involved in a situation such as this before the court today. If I ignored the amount of compassion, sympathy and in some ways blame that I feel here this morning, I truly would not be expressing what I feel. . . .*
>
> *I can understand what you people are saying, I really understand it. The problem is, though, that no matter how we look at it, somehow, some way, Canada has arrived here. . . . I say earnestly, the only place that you are going to get justice is going to be in a court of law.*

LeBlanc ruled on the Innu case several months later, even though a full defence had not been presented. Any sympathy he may have felt for the people had sharply cooled by then. His ruling casually overturned Olthuis's "colour of right" defence (even though the lawyer had not been able to present it properly) and urged the Innu to look at matters with what he called an "air of reality."

"A claim by the accused that the Innu have sovereignty over the land in question . . . totally ignoring the historic claims and occupation by the British and Canadian governments . . . does not assist the accused in asserting their defence in this case.

"The court has before it no evidence related to the Innu people being members of an organized group or society during early occupation, nor any sufficient evidence of possession of land claimed, or the time period over which the land had been possessed," the judge concluded. Pien's history and geography lesson had fallen on deaf ears.

There were more trials to come. On 19 February, another twenty-eight Innu were summoned to court to face charges laid under the National Defence Act. Neither LeBlanc nor Igloliorte was on the bench. Brought in from St. John's instead was E. J. Langdon, associate chief judge of Provincial Court. The Innu suspected that LeBlanc was not there because he, like Igloliorte, was thought to have "gone soft" on the Innu issue. Judge Langdon, they believed, was going to be the "hanging judge."

Langdon did little at first to calm Innu fears. He cleared the courtroom of Innu who were seated on the floor and ordered that the doors to the hallways be closed, preventing people standing outside from hearing what was going on. The mood in court was sombre; many Innu felt the appearance of yet another judge was further proof that they could never expect justice from a Newfoundland court of law.

The Crown called the first witness, an R.C.M.P. officer who had witnessed the Innu breaking a fence to get onto the runway. Just before the witness was sworn in, Ben Michel whispered something to the person seated next to him and a message began to be passed around the courtroom. Suddenly all of the Innu, including the accused, rose from their seats and abruptly left the room. It was an electrifying moment, an elegant rebuff of the whole process. The only people left in the courtroom were a handful of non-Innu—a couple of reporters and R.C.M.P. officers, the judge and the Crown prosecutor.

After a short recess, the judge announced that the trial would go ahead even in the absence of the accused. "It's a summary offence. If they don't want to participate that's their right," Crown prosecutor Ed Hearn explained.

"It should come as no surprise to anyone," the Innu said in a press release, "that we should finally cry 'enough is enough,' and refuse to supply this kangaroo court with the appearance of legitimacy by continuing to cooperate with it."

When it came time to present a defence, however, the Innu re-entered the courtroom. Apetet Andrew was the first to speak. He rose, cleared his throat and began speaking in his own language.

"Could I have a translator, please?" the judge inquired.

The Innu sat mute. I was next to Raphael Gregoire, who has often translated for the courts in the past. The police pointed at him and asked him to come forward. Raphael's legs and hands were shaking, but his face did not reflect his fear. He stayed in his seat without saying a word. Judge Langdon adjourned court until the next day, in the hope that a translator could be found.

An Innu prisoner, happy to have a day out of his cell, walked innocently into the courtroom the next morning, fully prepared to translate. However, once the spectators, many of them relatives, asked him not to, he refused to say anything in court. Langdon adjourned court and gave the Crown several months to find a translator.

For five months the R.C.M.P. searched high and low throughout the Innu homeland. They engaged the services of police forces in Quebec to scour Innu communities there, but without success. Large sums of money were offered. One woman I know was offered $1800 to translate, but she refused, even though she lives in great poverty. Tshaukuesh appealed for solidarity in broadcasts over the Innu radio network, and she got it. An Innu resident of Montreal was getting ready to go until she heard from friends why she should not. No Innu anywhere would help, and no one who has been close enough to the Innu to learn their language would turn against them. The state was now being paid back for its arrogance. There was not a single person employed by Newfoundland's justice system who could speak Innu-aimun.

Critics of the legal system took the opportunity to point out that the Innu had not been well served by the translation services offered them in the courts. In the St. John's Sunday *Express*, former Innu translator Matthew Rich explained that police typically pick someone up on the road in Sheshatshit when they are stuck for a translator. "It's a nightmare from beginning to end," he said in an interview. "These instant translators don't know the law and can never guide a native person adequately through a trial; many are overwhelmed by confusion and fear when they face a judge."

Finally, in the fall of 1990, Judge Langdon was forced to drop charges against the Innu because a translator could not be found. In a landmark decision, he ruled that the Innu people had the right to be tried in their own language, a right that had so far been universally extended only to the French minority in this country. He refused Crown attempts to have Innu testimony tape-recorded to be translated by someone later in private. Later that winter Daniel Ashini, Ben Michel and Peter Penashue, who were known to speak English, were found guilty in yet another trial presided over by LeBlanc and given suspended sentences.

Lawyer John Olthuis does not think harassment of the Innu by the police and the Crown will stop here. He is convinced that the Newfoundland government will continue to push hard to help secure land for jet bomber training. "They figure they can outlast the Innu who don't have much money. That's the justice department's strategy. It's probably coming from a political direction, not only in St. John's but from Ottawa too. The Crown is being told to put these people in jail and subject them to trial after trial, in the name of restoring law and order, but I think it's primarily to avoid embarrassment. It's enormously embarrassing to the military that the Innu keep finding ways onto the runway, with all their military police. They've been telling the allies that this is a good and secure place, yet any time they want to, the Innu can get on the runway. The only way the government can think to stop them is to keep arresting them, and I don't think they'll back off, even if there is acquittal after acquittal."

Refusing to speak English in court had been a clever way to outwit the akaneshau, but it could only carry the Innu struggle forward a few more steps. It would take events in other parts of the world to give the Innu cause a greater push, and perhaps no people outside Germany cheered more loudly than the Innu when the Berlin Wall came tumbling down.

Innu Nation

"The Innu represent, not just a political problem for the country, but a moral problem for our society. It seems to be a part of human nature to want to lord it over other races, and the harm that has sprung from this tendency throughout history has been enormous."

EDITORIAL, ST. JOHN'S *EVENING TELEGRAM*, 26 APRIL 1990

I had been with Innu families at Minai-nipi in the spring of 1989 when Chinese students were massacred at Tiananmen Square. We had all gathered in Maniaten's tent to listen to the radio. News that unarmed demonstrators had been run over by tanks and shot down in cold blood shook the Innu in our camp as though it had happened to their own people. Subsequent international events, such as the release of Nelson Mandela from prison, were followed with equal interest. More than ever before, what happens in other parts of the world now affects the Innu. The people of Sheshatshit in particular have become well informed and highly politicized as a result of their protests, and they now keenly follow stories of other oppressed peoples around the world. Perhaps no international event has influenced Innu lives as significantly as the dismantling of the Berlin Wall. It gave the Innu a reprieve, some precious time to rebuild their society.

The people watched on television as, brick by brick, the greatest symbol of the Cold War for which jet bombers in Nitassinan were training was torn down. After twenty-eight years of virtual imprisonment, the citizens of East Germany were told early in the winter of 1989 that they could go to the West. Mikhail Gorbachev's glasnost policy had begun it all; then came free elections in Poland and Hungary's decision to dismantle barbed-wire fences along its border with Austria. Thousands of Czechs gathered in the streets of Prague to demand freedom from Soviet rule, and by Christmas Rumania's Communist dictator Nicolae Ceausescu had been executed. It all happened at a dizzying pace, and each newscast increased hopes in Sheshatshit that talk of a NATO base might end.

But even after the collapse of the Warsaw Pact, Canadian politicians continued to insist that the gigantic NATO base was needed. "It would not be prudent," wrote Defence Minister Bill McKnight to a base opponent in Beaconsfield, Quebec, "to dismantle the structures of Western Defence, including low-level flying exercises, until the overall impact of this process is more clearly known." In truth, however, Canadian politicians saw the NATO base more as a quick fix for Newfoundland's economic stagnation than as a requirement for western defence. "It's as important to the economy of this province as the Hibernia oil development," declared Newfoundland's new premier Clyde Wells.

Nevertheless, public opinion was changing. A poll taken early in 1990 indicated that 71 per cent of Canadians wanted cuts in defence spending and preferred to see more money channelled into foreign aid. Another poll revealed that a majority of Canadians were against low-level flights over Quebec and Labrador. Columnist William Gold, writing in the *Calgary Herald*, said: "In stubborn rejection of events worldwide, the government of Canada is still doggedly pursuing its plan to establish a major NATO base at Goose Bay. To lease one's land for the perpetual war games of other nations . . . is degrading."

Southam News' Christopher Young, in a column suggesting ways for the government to save money, asked, "What about telling the defence department to drop its campaign to put a NATO low-level air training base at Goose Bay?"

John Cruickshank, associate editor of the *Globe and Mail*, found Canada's continued enthusiasm for the base "strange and sad." "Canada should not waste its precious defence dollars on a military theme park at Goose Bay," he wrote, "especially while the needs and desires of the vulnerable Innu people go unanswered. The Goose Bay NATO proposal is the wrong initiative for the wrong time."

Canadians in the peace and environmental movements had stepped up protests, hoping to influence the NATO decision. In January 1990, members of the Toronto Disarmament Network, Pax Christi, Ontario Greens and Innu Rights Now! posed as university students to get into a luncheon banquet at Toronto's prestigious Empire Club, where Manfred Woerner, NATO's secretary-general and a former Luftwaffe pilot, was to give a speech entitled "The Enduring Atlantic Alliance." The activists interrupted Woerner's speech with questions about the NATO base until they were thrown out. "Certainly the threat has receded," Woerner acknowledged to reporters afterwards, "but the risks have not disappeared. There is still unrest. Look to the headlines . . . without NATO, who would coordinate Western forces?"

Hope glimmered when the United States announced it would postpone B-52 bomber flights over northern Alberta and the Northwest Territories, to the great relief of aboriginal people there.

In the months leading up to the anticipated NATO decision, the Department of National Defence launched a major public relations campaign. Armed with a document called "Facts and Fallacies," DND officials met with the editorial boards of several major newspapers to discredit Innu opposition. One newspaper editor was told that the Innu simply refused to sit down and negotiate, and that they had set up camp at the end of the runway to produce "photographic evidence of camps overflown by low-flying jets." At considerable expense, DND flew reporters and external affairs employees to the base in the hope that they would write favourably about the facility. Needless to say, no visits to Innu villages were on the itinerary.

Each week was filled with speculation. In March the *Toronto Star* reported that the base would go to Turkey because there was no opposition to it there. John Crosbie stated that the Innu would be to blame if Goose Bay lost out, and many in Sheshatshit feared a violent backlash. Tension between the Innu and their neighbours grew. Peter Penashue received a call at home telling him that Innu leaders would be "shot in the head" if they went into Goose Bay bars; police arrested a Goose Bay man after Penashue received a second death threat. Vehicles from Goose Bay were seen cruising the village late at night, prompting more fear.

Prime Minister Brian Mulroney told law students at Dalhousie University in March that he felt changes in Eastern Europe might cause NATO to shelve its plans for the multimillion-dollar training centre. Mulroney assured reporters that he was just expressing an opinion and had no inside knowledge, but his comments sent Defence Minister McKnight scrambling to control the damage. McKnight told reporters emphatically that Canada still wanted the base. Community leaders in Goose Bay began gearing up for the worst, and the rhetoric surrounding their efforts to get the NATO base softened considerably as hopes faded. Sadie Popovitch-Penny, vice-president of the local Chamber of Commerce, was quoted in the *Toronto Star* as saying that she felt the community would be better off without base. "We don't want development at any cost; we want orderly development," she said.

The waiting was nerve-racking. People in Sheshatshit wanted to let the decision-makers in Europe know how they felt but were at a loss to know what more to do. Few wanted to go back on the runway and risk jail, especially after Manimat's experience, so they decided to play their last card—a court injunction to stop the flights. It was a risky move because the outcome of an injunction depends very much on the judge, and the Innu had not been having much luck with judges. However, as the NATO decision loomed nearer, they felt they had little choice but to once again take their chances in the courts.

John Olthuis advised the Innu to choose the Federal Court in Toronto to hear their injunction application, since it was geographically removed from the controversy. The hearing was held in April, before Madame Justice Barbara Reed. Judge Reed, in her midfifties, had been appointed to the bench after a long career as a lawyer in the federal justice department. Since evidence for an injunction application in Federal Court is presented in written affidavits and legal arguments, Judge Reed did not hear first-hand testimony from Innu witnesses. The hearing lasted only three days.

Olthuis presented evidence that low-level flying from CFB Goose Bay contravened the country's Environmental Review Guidelines, and he argued that the flights should be halted until the environmental assessment review panel had finished studying the defence department's impact statement and completed its own work. He was hopeful of success, since another Federal Court judge had recently ruled that the proposed Rafferty-Alameda dam project in Saskatchewan could not proceed until it had undergone an environmental assessment. "It was my position," he says, "that the next logical step for the courts was to order a project stopped until the environmental assessment is completed." Olthuis asked Judge Reed to order DND to stop authorizing further low-level flights and to withdraw the NATO bid until after the environmental review. The DND lawyers replied that any such action would ruin the economy in Goose Bay, threaten Canada's chance to get the base and breach international contracts.

"When I raised the argument that the Innu wish no ill on the people of Goose Bay but that Nitassinan is the Innu homeland and they have no other place to go," Olthuis said later, "the judge lashed out and said, 'That's an emotional argument. I'm not going to listen any more to your emotional arguments.' I was trying to keep it very low-key and stick to a legal argument, but that was very difficult when you know that there's a whole mind-set, not of a particular judge, but the mind-set of a legal system that is geared to protect the status quo."

Reed soon announced her decision. "The orders sought will not be granted," she said tersely. "Any order of this nature would result in extensive prejudice and harm to the civilian communities of Happy Valley and Goose Bay, as well as to the military personnel and their families."

Reed accepted DND arguments that a temporary curtailment of low-level flying would harm Goose Bay but not Innu arguments that the activity was harming them. "They will lose no rights which they presently have," she said.

The judge criticized the Innu for not cooperating with military authorities by telling them where Innu camps were located. "They take the position that such cooperation would amount to condoning the low-flying activity," the judge wrote in her decision. "This is not valid reasoning. . . . The refusal to cooperate does, of course, raise the question in a person's mind as to whether or not much use is being made of the territory in question by the individuals presently before the Court." She called Innu evidence about environmental damage "speculative and hypothetical" and was content to accept assurances from DND that the environment would be protected.

DND had also provided affidavits from doctors in Goose Bay testifying that no Innu patients have ever complained about health problems associated with low-level flights. "It was as though she wanted us to produce dead bodies to prove the flights are harmful," John Olthuis commented afterwards. According to Olthuis, the Innu do not take their complaints about the flights to doctors, since the doctors work on the base and do not speak Innu-aimun. He says health problems associated with low-level flying show up psychosomatically and in diseases related to increased alcohol abuse and poor nutrition.

Just days before the court hearing, an angry exchange of letters had been made public by the chairman of the environmental assessment review panel, Dr. David Barnes. Barnes had written Canada's deputy minister of defence, Robert Fowler, warning him to stop the escalation in the number of low-level flights, which had gone from 6000 in 1986 to 9000 in 1990, an increase of 50 per cent. Fowler replied that his department had no intention of capping the number of flights. "For Canada to impose an arbitrary limit on sorties such as you suggest would likely cause the allies to withdraw from the international agreements, and perhaps seek compensation from Canada," he wrote back.

Some Innu were afraid that Reed's judgement and DND's blatant refusal to respect the environmental review process meant they had lost everything. The legal judgement was bad news for environmentalists as well. Reed said she found nothing in law to require a developer to obey directives from a federally appointed environmental assessment review panel, whose guidelines are supposed to be the toughest in Canada. "Any obligation not to proceed while the project is under review depends for 'enforcement' on the pressure of public opinion," she wrote, "and the adverse publicity which will attach to a contrary course of action."

As expected, Reed's judgement was a great boost to morale in Goose Bay. But the euphoria was short-lived; other things were happening that threw cold water on prospects for a NATO base. That spring the federal government had cut off funding to the Mokami Project Group, which had been founded to promote the base, putting Goose Bay's leading military proponent, Ian Strachan, out of work. Over half a million dollars had been provided to the group since 1986, largely through the intervention of John Crosbie. Strachan mounted a last-minute public relations campaign, but his speeches attracted little attention outside Labrador.

The months of speculation finally came to an end on 22 May, when NATO defence ministers meeting in Brussels decided to can the $555-million Tactical Fighter Weapons Training Centre.

"In light of the evolution of the international security environment, and of pressures on defence budgets, ministers decided not to proceed with plans . . . at this time," their statement said.

Bill McKnight expressed his government's disappointment with the decision but said current and future training operations at Goose Bay would continue.

"It's the best thing that could have happened," enthused Bill

Rompkey, Goose Bay's member of Parliament, in a perplexing about-face. Only two months earlier he had told the St. John's *Evening Telegram* that the loss of the base would be "a major blow to the area."

Even Ian Strachan recanted. "Most people in Goose Bay were am-bivalent about the NATO base because this community is relatively well off," he told reporters. "Unemployment is under 4 per cent, so there wasn't a lot of screaming for jobs. Now that we've got this behind us, and the tumult is dying down, we can get on with diversi-fying this economy."

At any other time these quick flips might have made people in Sheshatshit laugh, but not after all they had been put through. The Innu got very little satisfaction from watching the shallowness and deceit surrounding public debate about the NATO base rise to the surface. The truth—that the base would have been more trouble than it was worth—came out only as politicians tried to save face. There had always been a current of opinion in Labrador that did not favour the base, but it had rarely been reflected in the media. Voices like this one, from Fred Andersen, a Metis student who wrote a letter to the editor of the *Labradorian*, were heard only after the base decision was announced: "The proposed NATO military training base for Goose Bay would have gone directly into the heart of Labrador. The native people of Labrador realize that the Innu struggle is in the best inter-est of Labrador. All of us who silently admire their courage and reso-lution recognize the fact."

■

Many Sheshatshit Innu were in nutshimit when the news broke. Raphael Gregoire told reporters that his community was pleased but cautious, because it meant only partial victory. Jet bombers contin-ued to fly over nutshimit, and there was little to stop Canada from signing more agreements with foreign air forces. Current agreements permitted 18,000 flights annually until 1996. Innu families still lived with the terror of jet bombers, a terror that intensified that spring as three of them crashed near Innu camps.

The first, a British Tornado, had crashed not far from Sheshatshit on 30 April 1990, only twelve kilometres from a bush camp. Fortu-nately no one was hurt; the pilot and navigator managed to eject safely. Eleven days later, Germaine Pokue was preparing supper in her tent when she and her two small children heard a terrifying ex-plosion. Two Dutch F-16 jet fighters had collided in midair less than eighteen kilometres from her camp, killing one pilot and injuring another. It was the last straw for Pokue and her family. Earlier that day they had seen two jets flying at low level near their camp, outside the area designated for this activity, just as the Tornado had been when it crashed. They packed their belongings and headed back to the village. Pokue says life in nutshimit is no longer a safe refuge for her family, especially since the land is tinder-dry in springtime and she fears jet crashes could start forest fires.

The Innu asked the House of Commons Standing Committee on Defence to investigate these crashes at the same time it was investigating the loss of two Canadian Hornets (CF-18s) that had crashed in West Germany earlier that spring, killing one pilot and bringing to four the number of CF-18 crashes since the beginning of the year. Defence officials refused to connect the crash of European jets in Nitassinan with the crash of Canadian jets abroad, and only the latter warranted a full-scale Canadian inquiry.

Seven Canadian pilots have been killed during their training since CF-18s came into use in 1982, and twelve of the multimillion-dollar machines have been seriously damaged or destroyed. In the spring of 1990 Canadian defence officials restricted CF-18 pilots from flying below 75 metres, yet did not apply the same restrictions to foreign pilots flying over Nitassinan, even though the British Tornado has the same high crash rate as the CF-18.

Many countries have begun to raise flight altitudes in an attempt to improve safety. West Germany took the dramatic step of banning all low-level flights in its airspace in the fall of 1990, sending the U.S. and British air forces scrambling to find new places to practise. Belgium soon followed West Germany's lead and prohibited low-flying exercises within its borders. Philippa Helme, a U.K. House of Commons defence committee clerk, told the St. John's Sunday *Express*: "The committee accepts that the lower you fly, the more dangerous it obviously is." Her committee recommended that Britain restrict flights below 75 metres, leading the London *Daily Telegraph's* John Harlow to speculate that "the [British] ministry of defence may have to find extra funds for Tornado training in Turkey and Canada."

A year earlier the government of the Netherlands had announced plans to reduce low-level flights in that country, cutting them by a quarter over the next ten years to prevent further damage to the environment, according to Dutch defence minister Jan Van Houwelingen. Van Houwelingen said at the time he wanted to shift more Dutch military ground manoeuvres to Canada.

Of serious environmental concern are the many dangerous chemical substances associated with the low-level flights. The two Dutch jets that crashed in Nitassinan were part of an exercise in which ten F-16 and six F-4 fighter bombers were practising air-to-air combat 5000 metres above the ground. The Dutch F-16s were carrying an extremely toxic and explosive fuel called hydrazine. A Canadian base commander assured reporters that the hydrazine released by the crash had dissipated in the air and was harmless, but the Innu fear local lakes or rivers may have been polluted by the substance. "Could hydrazine canisters have reached the ground intact, ruptured there, contaminating the local area?" their press release asks. (After the 1988 crash of a U.S. F-16 in Forst, West Germany, the inhabitants of more than forty homes had to be evacuated because the wreckage was emitting hydrazine.) Since the foreign armed forces operating in Canada are not required to publicize the results of their inquiries, the Innu may never learn more about the mishaps in their homeland.

■

Politicians continue to promote military expansion as a means of regional development for Labrador, even after the NATO base fiasco. Ralph Surette, a Nova Scotia columnist, writes that Atlantic Canada is particularly vulnerable to what he calls "the warped logic of economic stimulation." "As in the U.S., where defence installations are usually set up in poorer parts of the country whenever possible, so it is here," Surette notes. "The Mulroney government has been trying, with some success, to militarize the civilian economy. It's what the [1987] Defence White Paper openly called for."

The Mulroney government has already provided close to $100 million to upgrade facilities at the base in Goose Bay, yet communities all along the Labrador coast lack roads, good housing, running water and sewage facilities. "It hurts people here . . . to see the millions of dollars that are being proposed for the base, the money that's going into the military," says a Labrador woman in a 1988 Status of Women's Council report. "You see all this wonder and glory up there, and yet social services is hurting, they don't have the money to do things; the schools are hurting; all the other social agencies are hurting."

Many experts say that far fewer jobs are created when money is spent on the military than would be created by the establishment of other industries, and subsequent events at Goose Bay have borne out the contention that military economies are inherently unstable because they depend on the international political climate and on foreign military strategies.

A few months after the NATO decision, the United States announced plans to withdraw its air force detachment from Goose Bay. The decision stunned town officials. News reports from St. John's a year later indicated that Canada had gambled, and lost, when it raised American user fees at the base. The Americans had pulled out because they felt the new fees were too high.

The U.S. decision did not herald the diminishing of military activity in Nitassinan, however. In the spring of 1991 there were five bomber overflights of a camp at Utshishku-nipi in a seven-day period, and people there experienced a frightening sonic boom. At Shipiskan, several jets flew directly over Innu tents. The West Germans have built a $40-million hangar in Goose Bay to house twenty jets, and there is talk that they will extend their flying season by several months. The Dutch began construction of a new facility, and in 1991 increased the number of their jets stationed at Goose Bay from twelve to sixteen. (Great Britain's air force did not fly from Goose Bay in the spring and summer of 1991 only due to the fact that six RAF bombers crashed while on low-flying missions in the first ten days of the war in the Persian Gulf.)

The Innu and their supporters continue to resist the military activity in Nitassinan. In August 1990 there was another impromptu incursion on the runway at CFB Goose Bay. A dozen young people between the ages of sixteen and twenty broke through a fence near a wooded area and wandered about as a U.S. transport plane was being refuelled for a flight to Saudi Arabia. The youths were arrested and charged. A Freedom for Nitassinan Walk was held by central Canadian supporters in the fall of 1990 and Innu from various villages participated as the walkers made their way through several Canadian centres to Ottawa. The walk culminated in yet another demonstration outside DND headquarters after the Remembrance Day weekend.

■

As the result of a landmark Supreme Court of Canada ruling, the Innu won a small victory on a different front in 1990—a greater measure of control over their hunting and fishing activities. In the Sparrow decision on 31 May 1990, the court made the first constitutional interpretation of aboriginal rights. The decision states that judges must give native rights a generous and liberal interpretation, and that these rights cannot arbitrarily be restricted or abolished by governments. The court acquitted a B.C. Musqueam Indian man charged with a fishing violation, finding that it was his aboriginal right to fish in the Fraser River without interference from government authorities. The ruling was a very important one for the native peoples of Canada. "The fisheries dimension of the case is significant enough," said Lewis Harvey, a lawyer for the Musqueam. "But the implications of the case for unresolved aboriginal titles across the country are very significant."

Shortly after the Sparrow decision, the head of the R.C.M.P. in Newfoundland sent out a directive telling officers not to prosecute native people for subsistence hunting and fishing. And when a group of Innu hunters from Schefferville went to trial in Wabush a few weeks later on charges of illegally hunting across the border, the federal government issued a "stay of proceedings."

But it remains to be seen whether or not the Newfoundland government will honour the spirit of the Supreme Court ruling. On 11 May 1991, one year after the Sparrow decision, Jerome Pone and Andrew Penashue had their boat, shotguns, ammunition and five ducks confiscated by provincial wildlife officers; even though duck hunting is under federal jurisdiction, two other Innu hunters received the same treatment the next day. Following the Supreme Court decision, Ottawa instructed the province to drop the charges, and wildlife officers were told to return the food and equipment. However, one Newfoundland wildlife official has warned the Innu that it will be "business as usual" if they are caught violating provincial statutes in the bush, such as the killing of caribou out of season or the killing of porcupine at any time.

■

Although progress has been slow in the Innu people's struggle to defend their homeland, an important change has taken place within Sheshatshit: the Innu have once again begun to take pride in who they are. In one conversation, Tshaukuesh told me about a man her son Peter had spoken of. In halting English, she described him as "a black man, maybe a priest," who had led his people to freedom. Peter had been telling his mother about Martin Luther King. He had translated for her something King had written during the civil rights movement of the 1960s. This is how Peter remembered it: "I think the greatness of this period was something internal. The real victory was what this provided to the psyche. We armed ourselves with dignity and self-respect. We straightened up our backs, and a man can't ride your back unless it's bent."

King's words are strikingly apt for the Innu. As Peter Penashue says,

I think history will tell us that people who don't fight back for what they believe in just become a lost cause. Here, people used to fight amongst themselves, with their families, with their children, and that's where all the social collapse comes from. Now I think they are putting their anger in the right place. More and more people are finding that they are proud, part of their dignity is starting to come back. A lot of people have said to me they will never again sit back and watch developments, and other negative things, go on. Never will they sit down and watch those things happen again.

In the fall of 1990 Peter checked into an alcohol detoxification program in Windsor, Ontario, and started the process of healing himself. He began to forgive his father and learned the importance of getting on with his own life. Peter was so changed by the experience that he managed to convince his father to give it a try, and neither Francis nor Peter has had a drink since. Daniel Ashini has also stopped drinking, and a number of other Sheshatshit residents have checked into alcohol rehabilitation programs in the past year. The programs have not worked for everyone and alcoholism remains the village's greatest problem, but there is now hope for change. Rose Gregoire spoke of this hope at the ceremony that heralded the formal opening of Innu land rights negotiations with the governments of Canada and Newfoundland in July 1991.

"In gaining control over our lives, we have started to heal the hurt in our community," Rose said. "When we, as a people, were able to work together in a common fight, when our grandparents, parents and children were willing to face jail together to protect our ways, we were greatly strengthened. People who had been drunk for weeks became sober. People who felt they were nothing saw that they had the ability to stop NATO. Parents who had neglected their children now walked with them."

Tshaukuesh and Francis Penashue, with two young sons at home and a grandson to care for, remain politically active in their community. In July 1991 Francis was re-elected chief of the band council. Tshaukuesh is one of fourteen Innu from Sheshatshit and Utshimassit who will represent their people at the land rights talks. (Innu on the Quebec side of the border, united under the umbrella of the Conseil-Attikamek Montagnais, have been at the bargaining table with Quebec and Ottawa for several years.)

The Sheshatshit Innu position has not changed substantially since they filed their original statement of claim with the federal government in 1977: "We want our property rights to our land recognized and preserved, not extinguished. Such recognition of aboriginal land has happened elsewhere in the world and can happen here. However, our rights are more than property rights, we have important human rights recognized in international laws such as the right to self-determination as a people."

The Innu people will not exchange their rights to Nitassinan for money, although they expect to be compensated for the damage that has been done to their traditional economy. They want formal recognition of their land rights and a land base that is large enough to ensure self-sufficiency for future generations. They must be in control of the airspace as well, to ensure a healthy, peaceful environment for families who continue to go to nutshimit each year. "We want to keep the door open to our children, our grandchildren, for them to be able to pursue the traditions of our ancestors in the interior of Nitassinan," says Daniel Ashini.

Although they are still awaiting a response, the Innu made several requests of the provincial and federal governments at the outset of negotiations. They want low-level flight training curtailed and all government and private development stopped during the negotiation process. They also want all outstanding hunting charges to be dropped.

There are a number of developments currently underway that concern the Innu, but the people have not been consulted as part of the planning process. In the fall of 1990 businesspeople in Goose Bay plotted a groomed snowmobile trail across the Mealy Mountains to link the town with another community; they see the trail as the progenitor of a paved road. A discussion paper on the project discusses the problem of encroachment on private property but makes no mention of Innu land rights. A sawmill that will harvest 62,500 cords of wood per year is proposed for the Goose Bay area, and there are plans by some scientists to set off explosives on a popular Innu salmon river for research purposes. "The Innu must oppose projects that will take their land before an agreement with governments," Peter Penashue told a meeting of the Labrador Friendship Centre in June 1991. "We are willing to sit down and talk out difficulties that arise from this situation but we will not compromise on basic principles where Innu interests are being severely affected."

The Innu in Sheshatshit are working on a blueprint for a new economy, based on a model they call sustainable cooperation. A "made in Nitassinan" economy, they say, would use revenues earned from resource development to establish cooperatives. Four fundamental principles will guide resource development: projects must be environmentally safe, politically just for aboriginal people, economically sustainable and geared to the employment needs of people in the region. "In the past, the resources of Labrador have been seen as an economic motor to solve the unemployment problems of island Newfoundland and everywhere else in Canada," says Peter Armitage, a consultant working with the Innu on this plan. "We can't keep looking to native lands as resource larders for our cities."

"What the frontier vision of development and newfound wealth ignores is the great importance of the land to aboriginal peoples such as the Innu," Daniel Ashini told the Newfoundland Teachers Association in 1990. "The frontier vision is, for us, a vision of death. It says that we have no place in Labrador and eastern Quebec, except as a rotting heap of humanity clustered in rural ghettos."

The Innu also want self-government, something they have already begun to put into practice. In 1990 they locked the doors to the school in Sheshatshit (sometimes referred to as the assimilation centre), and they are studying ways to run it for themselves. The Sheshatshit Innu have not been happy with their treatment at the hands of the Grenfell Regional Health Service, which presently administers more than half a million dollars of federal money for native health care in Newfoundland and Labrador, and they plan to spend the $20,000 they received from the Danish Peace Foundation in 1991 on a village health clinic that they would run themselves.

Rose Gregoire feels these measures of local control are important steps on the road to rebuilding her people's self-confidence, worn down by years of racial discrimination. "It's just like talking to a youngster," she explains. "If you say to him or her, 'You're no good,' he'll always think that he's no good. It's the same thing white people are saying to an Innu, something like, 'You're lazy, you're a drunk.' I think when God made Innu he did not make junk, he made people, and this is very important to understand. I wish more of my people would understand this."

The Innu are confident that once they regain control of their resources, their treatment at the hands of non-natives will begin to change. "As long as the traders were dependent on our people for food and fur," the Innu say in their 1977 statement of claim, "we were treated with respect and recognition."

Jim Roche is no longer a Roman Catholic priest, but he still lives in Sheshatshit where he writes, helps build and renovate houses, and carves wood. He waits with the Innu to see if government attitudes, and Canadian attitudes, have really changed towards native people.

Chapter Notes

CHAPTER 1: NUTSHIMIT

Portions of the diaries of Paul Le Jeune, translated by scholars Eleanor Leacock and Richard Lee, appear in "Seventeenth-Century Montagnais Social Relations and Values," *Handbook of North American Indians (Subarctic)* (Washington: The Smithsonian Institution, 1981); "The Montagnais-Nascaupi of the Labrador Peninsula," in *Native Peoples: The Canadian Experience*, edited by R. Bruce Morrison and C. Roderick Wilson (Toronto: McClelland and Stewart, 1986); and "The Montagnais' Hunting Territory and the Fur Trade," *American Anthropological Association*, Vol. 56, no. 5. Accounts of life in Cree bush camps appear in Adrian Tanner's *Bringing Home Animals* (St. John's: The Institute of Social and Economic Research (ISER), Memorial University, 1979) and Boyce Richardson's *Strangers Devour the Land* (Vancouver: Douglas & McIntyre, 1991).

CHAPTER 2: AN INDEPENDENT PEOPLE

As there is no written history of the Innu before European contact, important clues are contained in Innu legends. Arthur Lamothe's films contain rare accounts of Innu beliefs, and they are available from Les Ateliers Audio-Visuels du Quebec. Remi Savard explores Innu legends in *Le Rire Precolumbien dans le Quebec et aujourd'hui* (Quebec: L'Hexagone, 1977) and in *Carcajou et le Sens du Monde* (Quebec: Série Cultures Amérindiennes, 1972). *What They Used to Tell About* is a book of Innu legends edited by Peter Desbarats (Toronto: McClelland and Stewart, 1969).

The archaeologists who have worked most extensively in the Innu homeland are William Fitzhugh, Moira T. McGaffrey, Gilles Samson, James Tuck and Stephen Loring. Some of their research has been published by Newfoundland's Historic Resources Division in a series called *Archaeology in Newfoundland and Labrador*. I found William Fitzhugh's article in *Our Foot-*

prints Are Everywhere, edited by Carol Bryce-Bennet (Nain: Labrador Inuit Association, 1977) to be a useful summary. Stephen Loring has been most generous in keeping me up to date on his research. He has published, among other things, "Keeping things whole: Nearly two thousand years of Indian (Innu) occupation in northern Labrador" in *Boreal Forest and Sub-Arctic Archaeology* (Occasional Publications of the London Chapter of the Ontario Archaeological Society, #6, 1989). Loring has just completed a Ph.D. thesis entitled "Princes and Princesses of Ragged Fame: Innu Archaeology and Ethnohistory in Labrador" (University of Massachusetts, 1991).

Selma Barkham has written about the early period of European contact in "A Note on the Strait of Belle-Isle During the Period of Basque Contact with the Indians and Inuit," published in *Etudes/Inuit Studies,* 1980, 4 (1–2). Francis Jennings's *The Invasion of America* was published in New York by W. W. Norton and Company in 1975. Bruce Trigger's *Native and Newcomers: Canada's "Heroic" Age Reconsidered* (Montreal: McGill-Queen's University Press, 1985) is indispensable. Harold Horwood's book *Newfoundland* was published by Macmillan of Canada in 1969. Sylvie Vincent presents the benefits and costs of European contact from the Innu point of view in "La Tradition orale Montagnaise—Comment L'Interroger?," in *Cahiers de Clio,* 19, (2). Innu elder An Antane Kapesh writes somewhat angrily on European contact from an Innu point of view in *Qu'as-tu Fait de Mon Pays?* (Ottawa: Les Editions Impossibles Inc., 1979). She has also written *Je Suis une Maudite Sauvagasse* (1975), and her books are also available in Innu-aimun.

My information on the impact of the fur trade comes largely from Alan Cooke's "A History of the Naskapis of Schefferville" (Montreal: McGill University, 1976) and *The Ungava Venture of the Hudson's Bay Company, 1830-1843* (Montreal: McGill University Press, 1969). Frank Speck's best-known book about Innu life in the early part of the twentieth century is *Naskapi, the Savage Hunters of the Barrens,* published by the University of Oklahoma Press in 1935. William Brooks Cabot's account of his travels to Nitassinan is called *Labrador* (Boston: Small, Maynard and Co., 1920). There are a number of other books in the same genre, including W. G. Gosling's *Labrador: Its Discovery, Exploration, and Development* (London: Alston Rivers Ltd., 1910); Wilfred Grenfell's *Labrador: The Country and the People* (New York: MacMillan Company, 1909); R. Hammond's *The Naskapis of Northern Labrador, from a Trader's Viewpoint* (American Philosophical Society Library, APS No. 2293, 1935), and John McLean's *Notes of Twenty-five Years' Service in the Hudson's Bay Territory,* 1849, republished by the Champlain Society in 1932. José Mailhot explores the origin of the term "Naskapi" in an article entitled "Beyond Everyone's Horizon Stand the Naskapi" in *Ethnohistory,* Vol. 33, no. 4, Fall 1986.

Georg Henricksen, a Norwegian scholar, was in Utshimassit in the 1960s when Innu families first settled into houses there. His book *Hunters in the Barrens* (St. John's: ISER, 1973) is a poignant account of this experience, and I look forward to reading the results of Henricksen's 1991 field work.

Anthropologist Peter Armitage has written a history of the people in *Innu*, part of Chelsea House's *Indians of North America* series (New York, 1990).

CHAPTER 3: JETS OVER NITASSINAN

An account of my overflight at Penipuapishku-nipi appears in the September/October issue of *Harrowsmith* and in that article I also discuss other aspects of the environmental debate about low-level flight training. On this same topic see: "Effects of Aircraft Noise and Sonic Booms on Fish and Wildlife" by Douglas Gladwin, Duane Asherin and Karen Manci (Colorado: Fort Collins, U.S. Fish and Wildlife Service, February 1988). Innu comments on low-level flying and the NATO base proposal are contained in eight volumes of transcripts—the result of public hearings that were conducted by the Environmental Assessment Review Panel (EARP) in 1986—entitled "Review of Military Flying Activities in Labrador and Quebec." The Canadian Public Health Association (CPHA) investigated the startle effect and other problems associated with low-level flying and produced a report in May 1987 entitled "CPHA Task Force on the Health Effects of Increased Flying Activity in the Labrador Area." Dr. Richard Bargen, an American physician, has documented the problems experienced by civilians living near the Nellis Airforce base, Nevada, in two works: *Airspace Blues* and *Sonic Booms versus the American Way: Rural America Under Assault*. These can be obtained by writing to Airspace, Box 117, Gabbs, Nevada 89409, U.S.A.

Canadian physician Dr. Jeannie Rosenberg surveyed international medical research on the effects of low-level flying, and her conclusions are published in "Jets over Labrador and Quebec: Noise Effects on Human Health" in *The Canadian Medical Association Journal*, Vol. 144, no. 7, 1 April 1991. Thomas Berger's *Northern Frontier, Northern Homeland: The Report of the Mackenzie Valley Pipeline Inquiry* was published by Supply and Services Canada, 1977; a revised edition was issued by Douglas & McIntyre in 1988.

CHAPTER 4: CHURCHILL FALLS AND OTHER "IMPROVEMENTS"

Hugh Grant's research is contained in "The Exploitation of Natural Resources in Nitassinan: Estimates of Past and Future Rents 1975–1990," a document prepared for the Naskapi-Montagnais Innu Association, November 1981. Jacqueline Driscoll writes of how the Innu were pushed around by the Iron Ore Company of Canada in her paper "Development of a Labrador Mining Community: Industry in the Bush" (Ann Arbor: University

Microfilms International, 1984). For an account of the IOC mine closures, read Boyce Richardson's *A Time To Change* (Toronto: Summerhill Press, 1990). Paul Charest documents the losses suffered by the Innu as a result of military activity and hydroelectric developments in "Les vols de basse altitude et le renouveau culturel des Innus Montagnais-Naskapis," published in *Option Paix*, Vol. 5, no. 2, Summer 1987; and in "Hydroelectric Dam Construction and the Foraging Activities of Eastern Quebec Montagnais," in *Politics and History in Band Societies*, edited by Eleanor Leacock and Richard Lee (Cambridge: Cambridge University Press, 1982). Read also Phil Smith's *Brinco, the Story of Churchill Falls* (Toronto: McClelland and Stewart, 1975).

The trip to Churchill Falls with Maniaten and Tshaukuesh was not included in the final version of *Hunters and Bombers*. The film transcripts are available with permission from the Innu Resource Centre in Sheshatshit.

CHAPTER 5: SHESHATSHIT

A report of José Mailhot and Andrée Michaud's field work in Sheshatshit is contained in their "Etude Ethnographique North West River" (Quebec: Centre d'Etudes Nordiques, 1965). José Mailhot went on to learn the Innu language and has become the foremost scholar of modern Innu society. Publication in both French and English of her book *Les Gens de Sheshatshit* is pending. Mailhot's colleague, linguist Marguerite MacKenzie, has written "The Language of the Montagnais and Naskapi in Labrador," in *Languages in Newfoundland and Labrador*, edited by Harold Paddock (St. John's: Memorial University, 1982). John T. McGhee's M.A. thesis, "Cultural Mobility and Change among the Montagnais of the Lake Melville Region of Labrador," was published by the Catholic University of America Press in 1961. See also James Ryan's "Economic Development and Innu Settlement: The Establishment of Sheshatshit," published in *Canadian Journal of Native Studies*, Vol. VIII, 1988.

David Zimmerley has written about the construction of the Goose Bay air base in *Cain's Land Revisited: Culture Change in Central Labrador, 1775–1972* (St. John's: ISER, 1973). Adrian Tanner used transcripts from the Labrador Boundary Dispute inquiry and interviews with Innu hunters to compile his "Indian Land Use and Land Tenure in Southern Labrador" (St. John's: ISER, March 1977). *Woman of Labrador*, the autobiography of a Metisse woman, Elizabeth Goudie (Agincourt: The Book Society of Canada, 1982), contains accounts of conflict between settlers and the Innu over trapping grounds. Lydia Campbell's *Sketches of Labrador Life* (Happy Valley, Goose Bay: Them Days, 1980) and Margaret Baikie's *Labrador Memories* (also published by Them Days, 1983) reveal early settler attitudes towards the Innu. Ben W. Powell's *Labrador by Choice* (St. John's: Jesperson Press, 1984) is also revealing. Powell, who moved to Labrador from Newfoundland in the 1930s, writes that the Innu were a remarkable people "who never destroyed any-thing more than was needed." Despite his admiration, however, Powell had no compunction about appropriating Innu trapping grounds. "Right in this very spot was my choice place," he writes, "and the Indians' choice place until I took it over." Evelyn Plaice has done a valuable study of mod-ern settler attitudes towards the Innu in *The Native Game* (St. John's: ISER, 1990).

Richard Budgel's article "Canada, Newfoundland and the Labrador In-dians, 1949–1969" was published in "The Innut of Labrador-Quebec: Con-temporary Concerns," *Native Issues*, Vol. IV, no. 1, October 1984. Budgel has also written, with Dr. Michael Staveley, "The Labrador Boundary" (St. John's: Labrador Institute for Northern Studies, Memorial University, 1987). Walter Rockwood's papers are available from the Provincial Archives of Newfoundland and Labrador. Principal among them is his "General Policy in Respect to Indians and Eskimos of Northern Labrador" (St. John's: Gov-ernment of Newfoundland, 1957).

The contemporary Innu quotes used in this chapter come from the tran-scripts of interviews done for the film *Hunters and Bombers* (available on video cassette, 60 min.; distributed by the National Film Board). The tran-scripts were translated from Innu-aimun into English by Nikashan Antane of Sheshatshit. Ed Tompkins prepared a report entitled "Pencilled Out: New-foundland and Labrador's Native People and Canadian Confederation, 1947–1954," for Jack Harris, M.P. for St. John's East, in 1988.

Constance Farrington's translation of Franz Fanon's *The Wretched of the Earth* was published by Grove-Weidenfeld of New York in 1988.

CHAPTER 6: "NOT THE GOVERNMENT'S CHILDREN"

An account of Tshaukuesh and Francis's wedding is contained in Mailhot's and Michaud's *Etude Ethnographique North West River*. James Ryan's paper "Economic Development and Innu Settlement" was also helpful in recon-structing life in Sheshatshit in the 1960s. The Innu tell the painful story of these years in interviews conducted for the film *Hunters and Bombers*. The chapter "Bridge Apart" in Evelyn Plaice's book *The Native Game* talks about the relationship between the communities of North West River and Sheshat-shit. Remi Savard writes of the first years of settlement at Pakuat-shipit (St-Augustin) in his book *Le Rire Precolumbien dans le Quebec et aujourd'hui*. I wrote an account of the Malec trial for the *Globe and Mail* on 25 April 1990, entitled "How Canada drives its native people to drink." Kay Wotten's research is contained in a report entitled "Mental Health of the Native People of Labrador," presented to the Canadian Mental Health Associa-tion's annual meeting on 24 October 1983.

Magistrate J. Woodrow's "Judgement on a charge against seven Innu

hunters under Newfoundland wildlife regulations" (Provincial Court of
Newfoundland and Labrador, 6 May 1977) is typical of legal responses to
Innu challenges of the province's Wildlife Act.

CHAPTER 7: ONE FAMILY'S STORY

In *Unholy Orders* (Markham: Viking Press, 1990), Michael Harris has written an account of the sexual and physical abuse of boys at Mount Cashel
Orphanage in St. John's. Children of Sheshatshit and Utshimassit were not
spared sexual abuse by Roman Catholic clergy. José Mailhot was present
(as a translator) when an Innu mother told the bishop in Schefferville that
her son was being sexually abused by the resident priest. The priest was
simply reassigned to another Innu parish.

CHAPTER 8: THE TURNING POINT

I was present at many of the events described in this chapter, and I also used
newspaper accounts, interviews with participants and court transcripts to
help reconstruct this period. In 1986, the International Federation of Human Rights sent a delegation to investigate the low-level flight controversy
in Nitassinan, and it produced a report entitled "Report of the Mission on
low-altitude jet overflights of Labrador and North-Eastern Quebec, Canada"
(May 1986).

   Judy Rowell, an environmental advisor to the Labrador Inuit Association, told me in a personal communication that she has spoken with people
who saw American aircraft mow down caribou from the Mealy Mountains.
William A. Anderson's report to the Newfoundland Wildlife Service is entitled "The Nascopi Indians of Davis Inlet" (1975).

   There is a detailed description of the NATO base proposal in "An Environmental Impact Statement on Military Flying Activities in Labrador and
Quebec," *The Goose Bay EIS*, prepared for the Department of National Defence by Lavalin Inc., Montreal, 1989; the report is available from national
defence department headquarters in Ottawa. Lindsay Peacock's article "Then
and Now at Goose Bay" in *Aviation News*, March 3–16, 1989, is a good
short history of the military in Goose Bay.

CHAPTER 9: OUTWITTING THE AKANESHAU

The EARP transcripts of hearings held in Goose Bay, Hull and Montreal
contain the views of Goose Bay town officials quoted in this chapter. They
are available from the Environmental Assessment Review Panel, Fontaine
Building, Hull, Quebec K1A 0H3. Press accounts of this period from the
St. John's Sunday *Express* and the *Labradorian* were also helpful. I relied as
well on interviews and correspondence provided by Bob and Dorothy Bartel,
particularly their written reports to the Mennonite Central Committee.

An account of the problems journalists had covering the low-level flight controversy appears in the Fall 1989 issue of the *Bulletin*, published by the Centre for Investigative Journalism. Another good media analysis appears in John Crump's article "The Innut and the Struggle against Militarization in Nitassinan," *Borderline*, Summer 1988. The article I wrote that raised the ire of defence department officials is entitled "Fear of Flying," and it appeared in the Montreal *Gazette*, 16 June 1988. DND officials failed to block publication of a second article entitled "This Labrador Business" in *Peace and Security*, Autumn 1988. David Murrell's study of media response to the Innu protests was published by the Mackenzie Institute for the Study of Terrorism, Revolution and Propaganda (Toronto: The Mackenzie Institute, 1990). For more on the work done by this institute, read *The Terrorism Industry: The Experts and Institutions That Shape Our View of Terror* by Edward S. Herman and Gerry O'Sullivan (New York: Pantheon Books, 1990). These authors suggest the Mackenzie Institute, registered with Revenue Canada as a charitable organization, is nothing more than a "private company operating as an idiosyncratic kind of university protectorate." The institute's founder, Maurice Tugwell, is, according to the authors, a former director of the Canadian-South African Society, an apartheid-government support group funded by South African businessmen. In Herman and O'Sullivan's words, "Tugwell has also lent his services to corporations bothered by environmentalists, regularly speaking on the best ways of coping with their 'irrational challenges.'" Among the Mackenzie Institute papers is Tugwell's "A Mythology of Peace" and Jack Rosenblatt's "Soviet Propaganda and the Physicians' Peace Movement."

The *Toronto Star* published "Innu were barred for not wearing jackets, ties, as Crosbie woos NATO over big air base" on 1 June 1986. For more about the struggle the Labrador Inuit are having with their land claims negotiations, read Veryan Haysom's "Labrador Inuit Land Claims: Aboriginal Rights and Interests v. Federal and Provincial Responsibilities and Authorities" and Judy Rowell's "Life on the Edge: The Inuit of Labrador," both in *Northern Perspective*, Vol. 18, no. 2, March-April 1990.

Anthropologist Peter Armitage was on the front lines during the Innu confrontation with the military and helped document their case in *Homeland or Wasteland? Contemporary Land Use and Occupancy Among the Innu of Utshimassit and Sheshatshit and the Impact of Military Expansion*, submitted to the Federal Environmental Assessment Review Panel in 1989. His 1990 "Land Use and Occupancy Among the Innu of Utshimassit and Sheshatshit" is available with permission from the Innu Nation office in Sheshatshit.

CHAPTER 10: WHO'S TRAINING THE INNU?

Bob Bartel wrote a detailed account of his meeting with CSIS and kindly provided me with a copy. For more on CSIS's activities in Canada, particularly with regard to native people, see Richard Cleroux's book *Official Se-crets* (Toronto: McClelland and Stewart, 1991). The *Mennonite Reporter*, 12 June 1989, contains an account of the Mennonite delegation's treatment in Goose Bay. The Canadian Press report on Peter Penashue's treatment by customs officials was carried in the Montreal *Gazette* on 14 August 1989 and an update appeared in the *Sherbrooke Record* on 18 August 1989. Thomas Perry's letter was published in the *Globe and Mail*, 5 November 1988.

CHAPTER 11: A HISTORIC TRIAL

Many international newspapers have files on the issue of low-level flight training. Some of the articles cited in this chapter were first published in the *Washington Post*, the *New York Times*, the *Los Angeles Times*, the London *Independent*, the *Guardian* and Germany's *Stern*. Malcolm Spaven is a Brit-ish defence analyst, and his article "RAF low-fliers raise public ire" was published in the 2 August 1989 edition of the *Guardian*.

I reconstructed the trial using court transcripts and interviews with par-ticipants. Press accounts, particularly those written by Penny MacRae of Canadian Press, were also very helpful.

CHAPTER 12: THE JUDGE UNDERSTANDS

I was present during many of the events described in this chapter, and I also consulted trial transcripts and press reports.

CHAPTER 13: HELP FROM THE OUTSIDE

Although the footage does not appear in *Hunters and Bombers*, we filmed the Innu women at the National Action Committee meeting in Ottawa, and some of the speeches referred to are available in the transcripts.

Maria Fidalgo, a Filipino woman, spoke about the sexual exploitation of women by American military personnel stationed in her country at a con-ference called "Military Bases—In Whose Interest?" held in New York City in April 1989. Daniel Schirmer, a U.S. historian, intervened on behalf of the Innu during the environmental review process with a paper entitled "The impact of U.S. military bases on the Philippines and an indigenous people of that country." Another connection with the experience of Fili-pino women was made at a conference held in North West River in May 1989. The report from that conference, "The Effects of Militarization Con-ference Report," is available from Oxfam in St. John's. Camille Fouillard, one of the organizers, submitted a paper entitled "Identification of major deficiencies with regard to women in the environmental impact statement on military flying activities in Labrador and Quebec" to the EARP on 12 February 1990.

Dr. Michael Bradfield's report is included in a "Compendium of Critiques" compiled by Peter Armitage for the Innu at Sheshatshit and submitted to the EARP on 12 February 1990. For another point of view, see "A comparison of the base employment multiplier and the input/output model in economic forecasting," prepared by the Mokami Project Group and submitted to the EARP in October 1988. Some of the information I use on the Goose Bay economy comes from the defence department's environmental impact statement. Lt. Col. Jodoin leaked the EIS to Toronto physician and journalist Dr. Brian Goldman, who did a radio documentary for CBC's "Sunday Morning" in the spring of 1989.

I was present at the meeting with Cadieux, and there are excerpts from this meeting in *Hunters and Bombers*. The events of 18 September 1989 were put together from interviews with participants, press accounts, court transcripts and the diaries of Rose Gregoire and Manimat Hurley. On 17 October 1989, following *La Presse*'s story on Louise Oligny's arrest, the Federation Professionelle des Journalistes du Québec demanded that charges against her be dropped, and the Fall 1989 *Bulletin* article also contains an account of the incident.

CHAPTER 14: VICTORY IS SNATCHED AWAY

James O'Reilly comments on judicial prejudice towards native people in "The Courts and Community Values," published in *Alternatives*, Vol. 15, no. 2, 1988. My account of the appeal court hearing is first-hand. Judge William Marshall's dissent was dated 3 October 1989. The "colour of right" argument was used again in "Her Majesty the Queen v. Gary Potts," 28 November 1990 (Temagami: Temagami Ontario Court, Provincial Division). The St. John's Sunday *Express* carried a series of articles profiling the Appeal Court judges in November 1989.

I wrote an account of the Innu trials for *This Magazine* in the Spring and Fall 1990 issues. CBC Radio in Ottawa and the CBC national news service provided live coverage of the November 1989 demonstration outside national defence department headquarters. The trial following this protest was also covered by the *Ottawa Citizen*. I was present at the trials presided over by Judges LeBlanc and Langdon and have also made use of court transcripts. Copies of the statements made by the accused during these trials are available from the Innu Resource Centre in Sheshatshit. The *Ottawa Citizen* ran a story on compensation paid to farmers for low-level flight noise on 9 June 1989. The scientists' critique of the EIS is contained in the "Compendium of Critiques" submitted to the EARP in February 1990. The *Toronto Star* carried coverage of the news conference attended by Bruce Cockburn on 15 February 1990. Cockburn called the EIS a "$6-million farce," while Valerius Geist, a wildlife expert based at the University of Calgary, is quoted as saying, "One cannot escape the impression of some sort of cover-up." Matthew Rich's comments on the problems facing Innu translators are contained in a 4 February 1990 St. John's Sunday *Express* story entitled "Newfoundland natives echo concerns tagged in [Donald] Marshall report."

CHAPTER 15: INNU NATION

A great deal of the information in this chapter is taken from press reports, speeches by Sheshatshit Innu and personal communications. Bill McKnight made his comments about the continued need for a NATO base despite changes in eastern Europe in a letter to Mary Rowan of Beaconsfield, Quebec, dated 9 January 1990. John Gray's story "NATO [was] thrown into confusion by sudden prospect of peace" was published in the *Globe and Mail*, 19 January 1990. The 15 March 1990 edition of the *Toronto Star* reported that the air force section of the Euro-NATO Training Group recommended Konya over Goose Bay at a special meeting in Essen, West Germany. Brian Mulroney's speech to Dalhousie University students was made on 7 March 1990. On 13 March 1990, the *Labradorian* ran a story entitled "German air force social club, hangar unveiled at last." On 16 March 1990 the *Toronto Star* carried a story from Goose Bay entitled "Residents fear economic 'disaster' if Labrador fails to get NATO base." Canadian Press reported on the injunction hearing on 4 April 1990 with a story entitled "Limits on flights would shut base, top official warns." After the NATO base decision the dramatic change of heart in Goose Bay was best exemplified in a story carried by the *Labradorian* on 28 May 1990, headlined "NATO decision met with little remorse."

For more on the CF-18 crash rate, see the *Ottawa Citizen* for 18 April 1990—"CF-18 jet crashes spur review of flight training"—and the 1 May 1990 issue of the *Toronto Star*—"CF-18 fighter pilots tell of stress, grind."

The two polls cited in this chapter were conducted for the Canadian Imperial Bank of Commerce in 1989 and the Canadian Institute for International Peace and Security in 1990. William Gold's column appeared in the 12 January 1990 edition of the *Calgary Herald*. Christopher Young's column was carried by Southam News on 22 February 1990. John Cruickshank's editorial appeared in the *Globe and Mail* on 9 March 1990. Fred Cleverley reported on DND's "Facts and Fallacies" campaign in the *Winnipeg Free Press*. Fred Anderson's letter appeared in the *Labradorian* on 6 May 1990.

A press release from Sheshatshit in July 1990 refers to the NATO decision not to build a base: "Many of us here feel that had we not resisted the training centre from the beginning, a decision may have been made sooner, at a time when the reduced tensions in Europe were not yet a reality. In that climate, perhaps NATO defence planners would have decided differently."

The Sheshatshit Innu indicated their willingness to begin land rights discussions in a letter to Indian and Northern Affairs Minister Tom Siddon and Newfoundland's premier Clyde Wells on 14 August 1990. Formal talks did not begin until almost a year later. The "Economic Blueprint for Nitassinan" was first outlined in a speech made by Daniel Ashini to the Newfoundland Teachers Association in the fall of 1990. His article "David and Goliath: The Innu vs. the Nato Alliance" in *Drumbeat*, edited by Boyce Richardson (Toronto: Summerhill Press, 1989) is also helpful for an understanding of the Innu position.

A good historical review of the evolution of Canada's land claims policy is presented by Geoffrey Lester in *Our Footprints Are Everywhere*. John Olthuis outlined the Innu land rights argument in the St. John's *Evening Telegram* on 16 November 1988 in an article called "Land claims is based in domestic, international law." See also the report of the Coolican Task Force set up to review Canada's comprehensive claims policy and the reply from the Assembly of First Nations entitled "From a draft analysis of Canada's Comprehensive Claims Policy," both available from the Assembly of First Nations, 47 Clarence Street, Ottawa, Ontario K1N 9K1.

Press releases from Sheshatshit on 30 April and 10 May 1990 describe the jet crashes in Nitassinan, and the *Ottawa Citizen* provided coverage on 11 May 1990. Garfield Warren, the Newfoundland House of Assembly representative for Torngat [Labrador], called in the House for all military flight training out of CFB Goose Bay to be halted until a full investigation was made of the accidents, but his request was ignored. An account of the young people arrested for going onto the runway in the fall of 1990 was carried in the *Labradorian* on 4 September 1990. Rose Gregoire's comments were made at a public meeting in St. John's on 13 October 1990.

Index